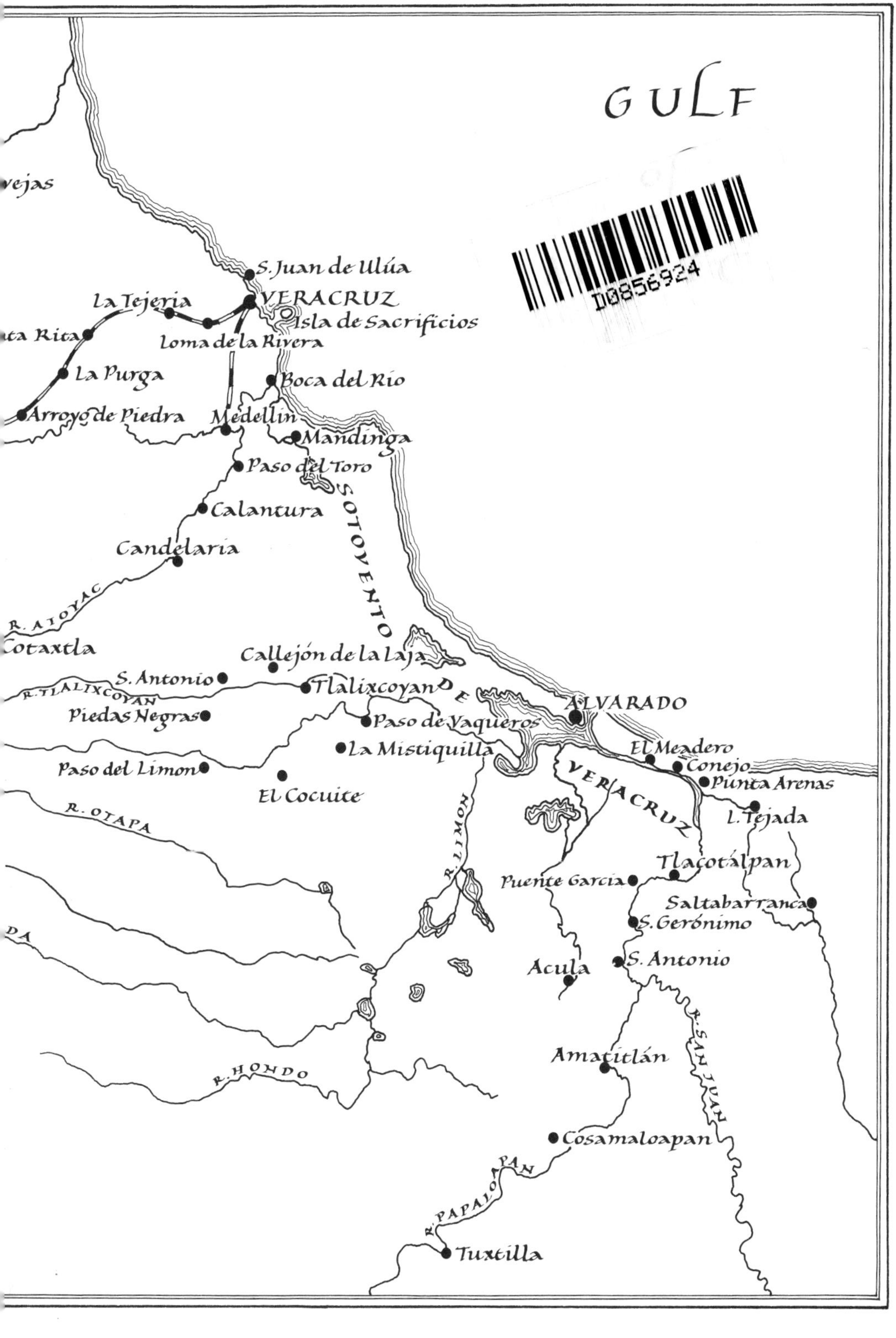
GULF
vejas
S. Juan de Ulúa
VERACRUZ
La Tejeria
Isla de Sacrificios
ta Rita
Loma de la Rivera
La Purga
Boca del Rio
Arroyo de Piedra
Medellin
Mandinga
Paso del Toro
Calantura
Candelaria
SOTOVENTO DE VERACRUZ
R. ATOYAC
Cotaxtla
Callejón de la Laja
S. Antonio
R. TLALIXCOYAN
Tlalixcoyan
Piedas Negras
ALVARADO
Paso de Vaqueros
La Mistiquilla
El Meadero
Conejo
Paso del Limon
El Cocuite
Punta Arenas
R. OTAPA
L. Tejada
R. LIMON
Tlacotálpan
Puente Garcia
Saltabarranca
S. Gerónimo
DA
Acula
S. Antonio
R. SAN JUAN
Amatitlán
R. HONDO
Cosamaloapan
R. PAPALOAPAN
Tuxtilla

A Black Corps d'Élite

A Black Corps d'Élite

An Egyptian Sudanese Conscript Battalion with the French Army in Mexico, 1863-1867, and its survivors in Subsequent African History

Richard Hill and Peter Hogg

Michigan State University Press
East Lansing
1995

Copyright © 1995 Richard L. Hill and Peter C. Hogg

All Michigan State University Press books are produced on paper which meets the requirements of American National Standard of Information Sciences—Permanence of paper for printed materials ANSI Z39.48-1984.

Michigan State University Press
East Lansing, Michigan 48823-5202

02 01 00 99 98 97 96 95 1 2 3 4 5 6 7 8 9

Library of Congress Cataloging-in-Publication Data

Hill, Richard Leslie.
A Black corps d'élite : an Egyptian Sudanese conscript battalion with the French Army in Mexico, 1863-1867, and in subsequent African history / Richard Hill and Peter Hogg.
p. cm.
Includes bibliographical references and index.
ISBN 0-87013-339-X
1. Mexico—History—European intervention, 1861-1867—Participation, Sudanese. 2. France. Armée. Bataillon nègre égyptien—History. 3. Sudanese—Mexico—History—19th century. I. Hogg, Peter C. II. Title.
F1233.H65 1994
972'.07—dc20

94-28244
CIP

Contents

Illustrations, Maps, Plans

1. Officers taking the oath of allegiance, from a copy in ‘Umar Ṭūsūn, *A Military History of the epoch of Muḥammad ‘Ali al-Kabir* (Arabic), Cairo, Dar al-Ma‘arif Press, 1950, 290. Source not stated.

2. Troopship *La Seine* (Photo copyright Musée de la Marine, Paris).

3. The Egyptian Sudanese Battalion disembarking at Veracruz, from a sketch by J.A. Beaucé (*L'Illustration*, Paris, XVI, 1863, 244).

4-7. Four tailor's designs of a uniform and equipment for the Egyptian Sudanese Battalion made by the Intendance branch, (this copy from Archives historiques, Service de Santé des Armées). (Photo copyright, Musée du Val de Grâce, Paris).

8. Tierra Caliente: land and river operations involving Sudanese units. Topographical additions for the Sotavento de Veracruz supplied by Architect Humberto Aguirre Tinoco.

9. Railway Bridge, constructed by French military engineers at La Soledad, 1863. The slightly anachronistic locomotive, a British Fairlie double engine, was introduced to Mexico shortly after the French evacuation (from A. García Cubas, Album del Ferrocarril Mexicano, view by Casimiro Castro, Mexico City, 1877). (Copyright, if any, unknown).

10. Mexican Railway timetable from the *Eco del Comercio*, Veracruz, 16 July 1863 (courtesy Public Record Office, London).

11. Ambushed train defended by Sudanese and French West Indian escort, 2 Oct. 1863 (*L'Illustration*, Paris, XLII, 1863, 340).

12. Gunboat *Ste Barbe* (photo copyright, Musée de la Marine, Paris).

Preface and Acknowledgements

This is the story, recorded in detail for the first time, of an exotic incident in African American relations in the mid-nineteenth century.

Secretly, on the night of January 7-8, 1863, an under-strength battalion of 446 officers and men with one civilian interpreter, sailed from Alexandria in a French troopship for service with the French expeditionary force in Mexico. They were being dispatched by the ruler of Egypt at the urgent request of Emperor Napoleon III to replace French troops who were dying in unacceptable numbers of yellow fever while guarding the line of communications across the low-lying fever belt between the Gulf of Mexico and the healthy plateau, where the bulk of the French army was deployed. Most of these troops had been forcibly acquired by the Egyptian government which, by emancipating them at enlistment, avoided the stigma of slavery and held them as military conscripts for the rest of their working lives. They did not act like slaves; they lacked the servile attitudes and manners of address portrayed in anti-slavery literature circulating at this time in the United States and Europe. They were in effect the victims of misclassification. For the Sudanese conscripts regarded themselves as members of the ruling institution which they, simple men, called *al-hukuma*, the Government.

They were also Muslims. Their French allies were quick to notice their unanimous observance of the Fast of Ramaḍan during their voyage from Alexandria to Veracruz. The French medical officers in the military hospital at Veracruz reported that the Sudanese patients would eat only meat prepared by their Muslim comrades in strict accordance with religious slaughtering requirements. What made them unique was that they were members of the last Mamluk mission founded by Muḥammed Ali Pāshā, himself founder of the dynasty which ruled Egypt until 1952.

With the best intentions, the French Command at Veracruz was ill-equipped to receive this utterly "un-French" battalion. The initial hindrance lay possibly in the restricted European culture of the times—a culture which made little provision for understanding the ways of people outside the European norm, a deficiency which left them politically disadvantaged. In the end, a sense of common humanity prevailed; after four years of patrolling and campaigning together, the Sudanese were never goaded into mutiny, and the French developed a permanent admiration for their African allies.

Almost inevitably a military unit that pursued so unprecedented a course was bound, somewhere along the way, to encounter controversy and even to challenge the canons of received history.

The biographical and ethnic core of our work is the Appendix for which our main source was the French nominal roll of the battalion. To the uninitiated, this document presents a medley of duplicated names, nicknames, and additional names owned by men who each answered to several aliases. The late Professor Rowland Stevenson, formerly of the Institute of African and Asian Studies, University of Khartoum, explained the rationale behind this apparent disorder, which has parallels in other parts of Africa.

The ethnic origin of many names on the roll can be traced only by those familiar with the languages of the men concerned. A number of names were inter-tribal. As we are incompetent in this field, we invited a band of volunteers to guide us. They ranged from university undergraduate students to eminent public figures such as Abel Alier, a veteran statesman, Francis M. Deng, ex-ambassador, now litterateur and satirist, and Bona Malwal, editor and political activist. Among our younger helpers were Damazo Dut Majak, then a student, Dr. Gabriel Gíet Jal and Lazarus Leek Mawut, to name only six from those volunteers to whom we owe a considerable debt. We invite readers to report names incorrectly identified.

The Mexican part of our book is almost wholly of Mexican, Sudanese, Egyptian, French and North American concern. Our narrative must therefore accommodate this multi-national situation. We have tried to emulate the Chinese example in topographical politeness by avoiding spellings in roman characters that reflect and perpetuate those survivals of European arrogance and narrow nationalism—elements which have occasionally cheapened the quality of European studies of Northeast Africa in the past.

We have used an internationally recognized transliteration for rendering Arabic characters into roman, and we have limited diacritical marking to the more technical sections of the work except where their absence would have led to ambiguity.

The Sudanese were brought to Mexico because of their hoped for (and later happily confirmed) resistance to yellow fever. But they were not immune to other fevers or to the effects on their health of rapid climatic and dietary change. In this field, we resorted to Professor P. Foëx of Worcester College, Oxford, who modernized our French Second Empire medical and hygienic terminology and to Miss M. E. Gibson of the London School of Hygiene and Tropical Medicine who eased our way through the health problems posed by frequent climatic and dietary changes on the welfare of the troops.

In Mexico City, Mtra. Virginia Guedea of the Institute of Historical Research in the Universidad Nacional Autonoma was unfailing in her introductions to the printed literature published in Mexico on various aspects of the French Intervention. In Veracruz, Lic. F. Vela Lopez and his colleagues at the Instituto Veracruzano de la cultura instructed us on the fortress of San Juan d'Ulua where some Sudanese attended the military hospital or endured the prison. He also explained the stages by which the small, overcrowded, walled town and Sudanese base was absorbed into the modern urban complex.

In the southeast, the Sotavento de Veracruz, lies the navigable river Papaloapan and the small riverain city of Tlacotalpan, which the Sudanese occupied by landing from gunboats in 1864. Accurate maps for locating sites of small engagements are not always easy to find. French military maps were drawn hastily, under the stress of war, while modern Mexican maps published by I.N.E.G.I., a state institute with its necessary dependence on air photography, can make river sites problematical.

Arq. Humberto Aguirre Tinoco, Director of the Casa de la Cultura "Agustin Lara" of Tlacotalpan, himself a Tlacotalpeño born and bred, liberally compensated us for our deficiency with copies of his own maps for plotting land and river operations in the campaign of 1864. Our benefactor went further: he produced from the little-known genre of popular propaganda a polemic aimed in general at the French and, in particular, at the *Egipcios*. Architect Humberto was so enthralled by its appeal that he composed a ballad on the theme of the heroism of the Mexican defense against French aggression made worse by Egyptian brutality. This may have been the only occasion on which the sins of the Sudanese have been immortalized in literature.

The cartographical ingenuity of Erich Korger of the Austrian National Library, Vienna, has made this Franco-Austrian-Sudanese disaster strategically understandable.

The Summary Concordance of Military Ranks obtaining in 1863-1867 is a result of international cooperation. It does not presume to be more than approximate equivalents in the French, British, and United States armies to the Turkish and Arabic ranks shown in the first column. For parallels in the U.S. army recorded at the first convenient date after the end of the American Civil War in 1865, we profited from the expertise of a Civil War historian, Professor A. R. Millett of The Mershon Center, Ohio State University.

The Danish Royal Army Library, København, made us an important gift of copies of printed military and biographical documents, and an original photograph, of the officer, Søren Adolf Arendrup, who was killed and half his army massacred, in an attempt to invade Ethiopia in 1875. The circumstances which led this skilled technical officer with no combat experience to accept the command of an Egyptian army in the field (including veterans from the Sudanese Battalion), remain unexplained.

Finally, we express our deep obligation to those friends who shared with us the laborious stages of editing the manuscript, whose criticisms and corrections of fact, inference, or translation, or whose suggested clues have led to unexpected discoveries, or whose advice has brought some discipline into a naturally untidy theme: Professors R. O. Collins, M. W. Daly, and J. J. Ewald, Robin and Elizabeth Hodgkin, Professor P. M. Holt, Dr. D. H. Johnson, Thirza Küpper, Dr. Yoshiko Kurita, Professors G. N. Sanderson and G. R. Warburg, and Mag. Dr. M. H. Zach.

But the ultimate responsibility for what we have written is ours.

Richard Hill and Peter Hogg

Abbreviations

Fuller titles of printed works noticed here in brief may be found in Appendix 2.

adj.	adjudant, adjutant
A.H.	Anno Hegirae (Latin) = in the year of the emigration (Arab. al-hijra) of Muhammad from Mecca to al-Madina, marking the beginning of the Muslim lunar calendar
ʻAlī Jifūn	ʻAli Jifun, *Memoirs of a Sudanese Soldier*, 1896
A.M.A.E.	Archives du Ministère des Affaires Étrangères, Paris
Arab.	Arab, Arabic
ʻAwn al-Sharif	ʻAwn al-Sharif Qāsim, *Qamus al-lahjat al-ʻamiyya fi'l-Sudan* (Dictionary of rustic Arabic in the Sudan), 2nd ed., Cairo, 1985
BA	Bazaine Archive, Latin American Library, University of Texas, Austin
Baker	Baker Pasha, Sir S. V., *Ismailïa*, 1874
Blanchot	Blanchot, C., *L'Intervention française au Mexique*
BD	*A Biographical Dictionary of the Sudan*, comp. R. Hill, ed. 1967
bn.	battalion, bataillon
brig.-gen.	brigadier-general
Campos	Campos, S.I., *Recuerdos historicos* II

capt.	captain, capitaine
Chenu	Chenu, J. C., *Aperçu sur les expéditions. . . du Mexique. . . Bataillon égyptien*, 1877
cl.	class, classe
cn.	contrôle nominatif, battalion nominal roll
col.	colonel
coy, Coy	company, compagnie
cpl.	corporal, caporal
DAB	*Dictionary of American Biography*
Dabbs	Dabbs, J. A., *The French Army in Mexico*
DBF	*Dictionnaire de Biographie Française*
Douin	Douin, G., *Histoire du règne du Khédive Ismaïl*
Du Barail	Du Barail, F. C., *Mes Souvenirs*
fl.	flourished, was active
For. Regt.	Foreign Regiment. See Régiment Étranger
gen, gén	general, général
Génie	Section du Génie, expédition du Mexique, See S.H.A.T.
Gov	Governor
Historique	Raveret et Dellard, *Historique du Bataillon Nègre Égyptien*
hsp.	hospital
lt.	lieutenant
maj.	major, commandant
M.M.	Military Medal, Médaille Militaire
n.d.	no date, undated
Nuṣḥi	Muhammad Nuṣḥi Pasha, Report on the siege and fall of Khartoum, SNR, XIII, pt. 1, 1-81, 1930
o.c.	officer commanding
pte	private, soldat
q.m.c	quartermaster-corporal
q.m.s	quartermaster-sergeant
Régt. Étr.	Régiment Étranger, later renamed Légion Étrangère

SAD	Sudan Archive, University Library, Durham, England
St-Cyr	École spéciale militaire de Saint-Cyr, the French counterpart of the British Sandhurst and the American West Point
sgt	sergeant, sergent
S.H.A.T.	Service historique de l'armée de terre, Château de Vincennes, Paris
S.H.M.T.	Service historique de la marine, Toulon
s.m.	company sergeant major
SNR	*Sudan Notes and Records*, Khartoum, 1918 -
S.S.A.	Service de santé des armées, archives, bibliothèque, Hôpital du Val de Grâce, Paris
Taqwim	Amīn Sāmī Pasha, ed. *Taqwīm al-Nīl*, vol. III, pt. 2, Cairo, 1936
Ta'rikh	'Umar Ṭūsūn, Prince, *Ta'rīkh mudīriyyat khaṭṭ al-istiwā 'al-miṣriyya*
Toral	Jesus de León Toral, Gen., *Historia documental militar de la intervención francesa en Mexico*
tr.	translator, translation, traducteur, traduction
Turk.	Turk., Ṭurkish
Tusun	'Umar Ṭūsūn, (French Omar Toussoun) Prince, *Buṭūlat al-orṭa al-sūdāniyya al-miṣriyya fī'l-ḥārb al-Maksik*
w.o.	warrant officer, rank between commissioned and non-commissioned officer
Willing	Willing, Col. P., *L'expédition du Mexique (1861 - 1867)*
X	Name recorded in this form only in the Contrôle nominatif, battalion nominal roll
Zaki	'Abd al-Raḥmān Zakī *I'lām al-jaysh wa'l-baḥriyya fī Miṣr*, Cairo, 1947

Summary Concordance of Military Ranks Obtaining in 1863-1867

Arabic/Turkish	French	British States	United (1867)
farīq (Arab.), ferik (Turk.) divisional general; birinjī farīq (Turco-Arab.), senior divisional general	général de division	major-general	major general
liwā', short for amīr al-liwā' (Arab.) from Turkish liva	général de brigade	brigadier see note 1	brigadier general
mīrālāī, from Persian mir + Turk. alay ultimately from Byzantine Greek αλλαγιον (alayion),name of a Byzantine military unit	colonel	colonel	colonel
qā'im maqām (Arab.) kaymakam (Turk.)	lieutenant-colonel, chef d'escadron (artillerie)	lieutenant-colonel	lieutenant-colonel
binbashi, bimbashi (Arab.) colloquial forms of Turk biñbāşı, written in Arab. bikbāşı (the letter k here representing the old Turk. letter saghir kef pronounced ñ as in word canyon)	commandant chef de bataillon	major	major

Arabic/Turkish	French	British States	United (1867)
ṣāgh qōl aghāsī (Arab.) from Turk. sağ kol ağası	adjudant-major	no British equivalent	no U.S. equivalent
yūzbāshī/yūzbāshā (Arab.) from Turk. yüzbaşı	capitaine	captain	captain
mulazim awwal (Arab)	lieutenant	lieutenant	1st lieutenant
mulāzim sani/tani for mulāzim thānī (Arab.)	sous-lieutenant	ensign (infantry) cornet (cavalry)	2nd lieutenant
musā'id (Arab.), ṣōl, for Turk. sol kōl ağası	adjudant	warrant officer nearest British equivalent	regimental sergeant major nearest U.S. equivalent
bāshjāwīsh/bāshshāwīsh (Arab.) from Turk. başçavuş	sergent-major	company sergeant major	company sergeant major
bulūk amīn (Turco-Arab.)	sergent-fourrier	quartermaster sergeant	For U.S. senior enlisted ranks see Note 2
jāwīsh/shāwīsh (Arab.) from Turk. çavuş see Note 3	sergent	sergeant	
onbāshī/ombāsha (Arab.) from Turk. onbaşı	caporal	corporal	corporal
onbāshī/ombāsha bulūk amīn (Turco-Arab.)	caporal-fourrier	no British equivalent	no U.S. equivalent
birinji nafar (Arabo-Turk.), nafar awwal daraja (Arab.)	soldat première classe	lance corporal	no U.S. equivalent

Arabic/Turkish	French	British States	United (1867)
nafar	soldat	private	private
burūjī (Arabicized Turk.) Turk. borucu	clairon	bugler	cavalry company bugler, usually corporal or private
trampetçi (Turk.), Arab. form used in Egyptian army trumbāṭjī for drummer or bandsman	tambour	drummer	infantry company drummer, usually private

Notes

1. The British brigadier/brigadier-general had a record of interchangeability, usually held by a colonel appointed to a special responsibility. Not then a substantive rank.
2. The U.S. Senior enlisted cadre included in each regiment a regimental sergeant major, a drum major, quartermaster sergeant, commissary sergeant and two color sergeants. In addition each company had its own quartermaster sergeant, commissary sergeant, ordnance sergeant and orderly sergeant. The designation of the orderly sergeant was later merged with role of first (senior) sergeant though the holder was not necessarily orderly sergeant.
3. The simple cadre of senior n.c.o.'s in the Egyptian regular infantry (for example there were no sergeants above company rank) was in sharp contrast with U.S., British and general European practice. On the other hand the Sudanese ignorance of the French language required the secondment of officers, n.c.o.'s and senior privates for administrative and interpreting/translating duties.

Some Contemporary Ottoman Honorifics

Pasha and bey were distinctions of Turkish origin conferred on soldiers, sailors and civilians by the Ottoman sultan and, in increasing measure, by his representative, the governor-general (wālī), who from 1867 was designated khedive (Persian khidev, rendered in Arabic/khidiw/khidiwi) of Egypt. In the Egyptian army distinctions were usually, but not automatically, associated with specific ranks, that is, brigadier-generals and above were usually pashas while most colonels and some lieutenant-colonels were beys. Officers of the regular army who were neither pashas nor beys were addressed, if they were literate in Turkish or Arabic and had graduated from the military schools or were assimilated to the Egyptian educated classes, as efendi, a title of Greek origin, afthentis, (compare English authentic) adopted by the Turks of Anatolia in the 12th century A.D., and one of the titles of Ottoman sultans from Mehmed the Conqueror to the abolition of the sultanate in 1923. Illiterate or near-illiterate officers and senior non-commissioned officers were customarily addressed by the Turkish honorific *agha*, a term from the Mamluk family vocabulary, literally eldest paternal uncle. The term has many other applications.

Background to the Egyptian Sudanese Presence in Mexico

1. The Sudanese Battalion

2. Slavery

3. Muhammad 'Ali: Creation of a New-Model Army, *al-Nizam al-Jadid*

4. The French Intervention: Napoleon III

5. The Military and Medical Crisis in Mexico

6. The Emperor's Request for Sudanese Troops

Chapter 1

Background to the Egyptian Sudanese Presence in Mexico

1. The Sudanese Battalion

The African soldiers who fought so gallantly in Mexico were, in one sense, pawns in a Euro-American imperial conflict. But they were not demeaned by it. Their story not only highlights some of the differing perceptions that prevailed about the institution of slavery—Egyptian, French, American—it also shows how the men themselves transcended their narrow lot. In Mexico, and in their later service in Africa, they took pride in all they did. They had been converted to and shared the faith of Islam, but their origins were African.

In the 1860s, what is now called the Sudan was a loosely administered colony of the Ottoman province of Egypt. From its grassy plains and forests, licensed agents, whether foreign, Egyptian, or Northern Sudanese, collected ivory and ostrich plumes for fashionable Europeans and slaves for comfortable Ottoman households. Many of the slaves eventually became soldiers and subsequently formed the crack battalion whose epic we here relate. They were "lent" to Emperor Napoleon III and sent to support the establishment of a French influence in troubled Mexico.

The soldiers became disciplined and tempered as they fought the Republican Mexicans in the congenial company of French officers. The Republicans accused them of brutality. Their adventures and exploits were recalled and embroidered many years later by a Shilluk veteran. He told his tales in Arabic to a young English officer who wrote them down in English translation. Both men were active officers in the new Egyptian army during the campaigns which made possible the foundation of the Anglo-Egyptian Sudan.

2. Slavery

Centuries of confusion have resulted from the misuse of the term slavery as an omnibus word to denote two disparate forms of it; the first, plantation and domestic slavery, the second, life-long military conscription.

Slavery in the first sense was taken for granted in the ancient Middle East and was accepted as a social and economic institution by Christianity and Islam, inheritors of the wisdom of the preceding civilizations of Mesopotamia. It was recognized that, if slavery were suddenly abolished, civilized society would collapse. Christian thinkers sought to improve the conditions of slaves rather than abolish the institution itself. Islam likewise neither condemned nor approved of slavery but recognized it as a category of labor. In both Christianity and Islam the voluntary manumission of slaves was considered a pious act.

The expansion of Christianity from the Mediterranean basin into the European hinterland, combined with changes in land tenure, eroded the advantages of slave-based economies in Europe. Not long afterward, the discovery and subsequent occupation of the Americas by European immigrants resulted, in the warmer regions, in a revival of plantation slavery but of a type different from its European predecessor. The new slave-owners, born of the European Renaissance and Reformation and their energetic commercialism, brushed aside any religious restraints imposed by the medieval Church and converted slavery into an impersonal machine of repression in the interest of profit. Apologists sought scriptural justification for the system.

Toward the middle of the eighteenth century, the formal, elegant, aristocratic European culture began to question the relevance of some of its own cherished values in a world being brusquely assaulted by technical and industrial revolutions which produced problems beyond the wit of the existing wisdom to solve. Some called the Romantic movement a spontaneous release of human emotions—enthusiasm, imagination, and questioning—which influenced the main fields of human endeavor: religion, morals, literature, and the arts. Slavery and the slave trade did not escape scrutiny, first among the Quakers and Methodists in England closely followed by the Evangelical wing of the Church of England concerned with British involvement in the African slave trade.

It was the anti-slavery movement in the United States that reflected the strengths and the weaknesses of the Romantic approach to social wrongs. The abolitionists were deeply religious, but they also partook of the prevailing strict social inhibitions of their day. In 1863, under President Lincoln's judicious tutoring, Congress concentrated on a politically possible and emotionally satisfying legal emancipation of the slaves. This form of emancipation not only satisfied the consciences of the great majority of abolitionists in the United States but was welcomed abroad. In Britain, *Uncle Tom's Cabin* had been widely read; in France, the educated liberal classes had also been moved by *La Case de l'oncle Tom.*[1] In February 1863, Emperor Napoleon III and Empress Eugénie attended a public performance based on the book. Lincoln could rest assured that, with this timely gift of international good will, there would be no armed interference from Britain or France to bolster the Confederacy notwithstanding some internal commercial interests in both nations not averse to a Southern victory.

The year 1865 marked the zenith of active public interest in the end of slavery in the United States. The Union was victorious, and the slaves were freed. The matter was closed. Whether in North America or in Europe, the public feeling was the same: benevolent support of Negro emancipation coupled with a reluctance to even consider the idea of completing emancipation by preparing for an eventual partnership of white and black citizens in a free, equal, integrated society. It was not so much a matter of white opposition to the principle as utter disbelief in its possibility.

3. Muhammad 'Ali: Creation of a New-Model Army, *al-Nizam al-Jadid*

The black Muslim battalion of lifelong conscripts, combined with a few volunteers who had joined the French army in Mexico in 1863, represented a type of slave altogether unlike those emancipated by the American Civil War.

As a category of bonded men this Muslim force had a long history. The first recognizable prototypes of Muhammad 'Ali Pasha's conscript regular army of the early nineteenth century were the Mamluks of Egypt. The Mamluks had governed the province for almost three centuries as independent rulers and then, from 1516 to 1798, as agents of the Ottoman sultans. They were originally slaves procured in their native homelands in Central Asia or from Circassia north of the Caucasus, and sent to Egypt for sale to the reigning sultan and his high officials. They were given a rigorous military training and an Islamic education. Upon "graduation," they would be manumitted by their owners—to whom they remained bound by ties of patronage and a quasi-family relationship with continuing family loyalty, as between father and son.

Their descendants were superb horsemen and swordsmen in the traditional heroic cavalry combat. But in 1798, a portentous event occurred. The Mamluks clashed in two battles at the gates of Cairo with a French army commanded by General Napoleon Bonaparte and were routed. For the first time in over a thousand years *al-Qahira al-Mahrusa*, the God-Protected Cairo, had fallen to an infidel commander who introduced the Muslim enemy to a revolutionary way of fighting.

Napoleon's triumph in 1798 made a deep impression on the Ottoman Captain Muhammad 'Ali when he arrived in Egypt in 1801. He brought a draft of Macedonian reinforcements to campaign against the Mamluks who were reasserting their anarchic strength in the military vacuum caused by the French withdrawal from Egypt. By cunning as much as soldiering, Muhammad 'Ali survived until 1805 when the Ottoman sultan appointed him governor-general of Egypt. This gave him access to the Cairo citadel, but it did not lessen the constant threat of Mamluk rebellion in the provinces. By 1811, he felt strong enough to eliminate the last Mamluk opposition with a general massacre in Cairo and the provinces. Only then could he turn to planning an Egyptian version of military reform, which in Istanbul had fomented so serious an opposition from the traditional forces that an attempt at reform had cost Sultan Selim III his throne and his life in 1807.

The nation chosen by Muhammad 'Ali to transform the Egyptian army was a foregone conclusion: the French. Although the military might of the Emperor Napoleon had been broken at Waterloo in 1815, there was a prevailing opinion in Europe that French military organization and quality of arms and armament were superior to any other. It had taken almost all Europe to beat Napoleon.

Muhammad 'Ali appointed a junior officer from the debris of Napoleon's *Grande Armée*, J. A. Sève, who had joined his service in 1816, to command the infantry officers' school. The first intake of cadets contained many youths from Muhammad 'Ali's own family and those of leading Mamluks unused to the drudgery of marching like automata and drilling *à la française*.

For the rank and file of the new infantry, Muhammad 'Ali had no choice but to follow the ancient Islamic tradition of enlisting African blacks; they could be had for the taking. In the course of 1820-1821, he dispatched two pre-reform armies into the Sudan. The first, advancing up the left bank of the Nile and crossing the White Nile to the Blue Nile Valley, occupied the region of Sinnar. The second, ascending the Nile Valley as far al-Dabba, crossed the steppe into central Kordofan. Both forces encountered and crushed opposition on the way. Within a few months, a stream of captured blacks was being dispatched to Upper Egypt where training camps had been set up for their reception.

A grand passing-out parade of the first six regiments of the Nizam infantry was held near Asyut in December 1823. Muhammed 'Ali Pasha himself was present; his son, Ibrahim, the general in command; and Colonel Sève, director of the officers' corps, along with a few invited guests including the English and French consuls-general, H. Salt and B. Drovetti. After the inspection each regiment formed square, facing inwards with the officers inside. The imams then intoned prayers for the triumph of the Ottoman dynasty and every officer took the oath of loyalty. A standard was presented to each battalion standard bearer who thrust his hand into the blood of a slaughtered ram and with a finger made a small blood stain on the banner ribbon. A salvo of artillery completed the solemnity.[2]

On 5 January 1824 the First Regiment of the Line, commanded by Colonel 'Uthman Jarkas, appropriately named al-Birinji (the First), perhaps after his regimental Number One,[3] set out on its long march to Sinnar and Kordofan.

The officer cadre of the regiment in its early days included the sons of many former Mamluks who had made their peace with Muhammad 'Ali and who took the European novelty with resignation. While their elders called their battalion by the Turkish word *al-orta*, the young preferred the more expressive Arabic *al-tabur,* conveying the meaning of a file of troops marching in step, one behind the other, at its best "The Drill," at its worst "The Grind."

As the years passed, a few Europeans serving the Egyptian government reported incidents between the Nizam and the Sudanese public which gave some inkling of the relations between them. In 1839 Louis Lefèvre, a French mineralogist in Egyptian government employ, was prospecting for gold near the Ethiopian border. A corporal in charge of a working gang of local men threatened them with his loaded musket. The gun accidentally fired killing two of them. The gang wanted to kill the corporal there and then but their makk (here the local head of the tribe) dissuaded them; so the men brought the corporal to his colonel, Farhad Bey, in command of the 8th Nizam regiment protecting the gold workings, and demanded justice. A court martial condemned the corporal to death but added an extenuating plea. The other shaykh of the place explained that it was impossible to save him; blood must be paid for by blood. The *lex talionis* (the law of suchness) as the lawyers in Europe called it, a life for a life, was the universally accepted punishment in the Sudan. The corporal was executed the next day.[4]

Upon enlistment, the slave-recruit would be provided with uniform, rifle and bayonet, rations, and a capricious issue of low pay. As a conscript, he would be fed and sheltered for life in a world where life was hard and his needs were simple, and as a symbol of his new standing, he would be initiated into the official religion of Islam.

With the mounting expenses of the Syrian wars and occupation, the black army of the Sudan carried out more and more responsibilities as expensive Ottoman units were disbanded or withdrawn. In 1835, 'Ali Khurshid Pasha, governor-general of the Sudan, proposed to Cairo to admit Sudanese to the junior commissioned ranks. Muhammad 'Ali overruled objections from the

Egyptian War Office and permitted his governor-general to accept a few outstanding youths who had a grounding in reading and writing Arabic for training and selection as officers. The financial inducements were modest. After 20 years of its existence, the pay differentials between the highest and the lowest in a Nizam regiment bore little comparison with relative pay rates in contemporary American and European armies.[5]

Rank	Pay per lunar month in Egyptian piastres	Rations in piastres
colonel	8000	726
lieutenant-colonel	3000	271
major	2500	164
adjutant-major	1250	140
private	15	20

The sterling exchange rate was then $97\frac{1}{2}$ Egyptian piastres. 100 piastres = £1 Egyptian.

The misgivings of the Egyptian War Office over commissioning illiterate blacks were justified, to some extent, on rational grounds. Unlike packs of wolves, human troops at war are dependent on planning and written orders for their movements and operations; they cannot fight a battle by instinct alone.

But black illiteracy was not the only obstacle. The Ottoman disliked service in the Sudan, but deeper in his breast was his dislike of the European military system. It made him, a warrior, subject to military discipline like a slave. In the early years of the Nizam formations, some Ottoman officers had already served in the old, unreformed army as Mamluks in the retinue of some Mamluk bey. As a Man of the Sword, a Mamluk saw nothing but dishonor from the efforts of the European military reformers to force him to become also a Man of the Pen, like some despised Christian clerk. The prejudice ran so deep that the so-called "headquarters" of Ibrahim Pasha during the great Syrian campaigns was still little more than a secretariat with the commander-in-chief making all the decisions. Youthful French drill instructors could scarcely have presumed to give orders to senior officers of the New Model army.

The entry of junior Sudanese officers into the Ottoman officer cadre introduced no serious linguistic complication as a result of their ignorance of Turkish—still the first language of the higher échelons of Ottoman Egyptian military society. The use of Turkish in the Nile Valley was in decline; the Khedive Isma'il encouraged the use of Arabic in the fighting services for his own dynastic reasons. He authorized a change in the language of military commands from Turkish to Arabic. While the Turkish spelling of military ranks and other terms was retained, they were increasingly pronounced in Sudanese or Lower Egyptian colloquial Arabic. The Turkish names of ranks, some in quaint Arabic, French, and English deviations, persisted until the end of the Egyptian Monarchy in 1952.

The proportion of Turco-Egyptians to Sudanese in the career structure was another matter; "Turco-Egyptian" was an ethnic, no longer a linguistic, description of an amalgam of "foreigners" whose common language was Turkish. With the growth of Egyptian national identity, Arabic had taken over. In 1863, however, the transition to equality of opportunity in the commissioned grades was still denied to black officers. There had been a significant improvement among the other ranks as shown by the following table of the career structure in 1866 of the 1st Regiment of the Line, which had served continuously in the Sudan since 1826.[6]

Ranks	Turco-Egyptians	Sudanese
majors	3	1
adjutant-majors	4	—
captains	17	17
1st lieutenants	21	10
2nd lieutenants	40	11
Total officers	85	39
warrant officers	7	—
sgt. majors	17	22
sergeants	48	87
corporals	78	197
privates	238	1443
Total Other Ranks	388	1749
Grand Total	473	1788

If life in the Nizam regiments was bearable for the general run of Sudanese conscripts, lifelong conscription could be difficult on exceptional men of a different origin. Such was Sergeant-Major Ahmad of No. 1 Company, 4th battalion, of the 1st Sudanese Regiment, who in 1853 appeared before the Austrian vice-consul at Khartoum with an unusual story. He announced himself as Constantine Bilo, a Greek, captured as a child about 27 years before in Chios by Egyptian troops of Ibrahim Pasha's army in the war of Greek independence. He was sold to one Sulayman Kashif, who in turn sold him to Ahmad Menikli Pasha (then governor-general of the Sudan), who gave him a certificate of manumission and in 1844 enrolled him in the army of the

Sudan. Nine years later he asked his colonel, Hasan Bey, for discharge from the army owing to sickness. Hasan Bey beat him full sore. So, manumission certificate in hand, he approached Vice-Consul Reitz for Austrian protection. Reitz formally accorded him Austrian protection and wrote a stiff letter to Colonel Hasan warning him to cease maltreating the Chiote company sergeant-major, an Austrian protected subject.[7]

The records from many quarters leave no doubt that the Sudanese got on well with their French allies in Mexico. Yet, the military experience of each was altogether different from that of the other. The Sudanese could not look back to memories of *la grande guerre* like the French troops whom they met at Veracruz and on patrol in the Tierra Caliente—men with memories of Sebastopol, Magenta, Solferino, great battles, much heroism, much pain.

All the Sudanese had in the way of fighting memories would have been those of fierce inter-tribal raids before they became government troops, entering a lifetime of dozens of small forays, raids for slaves, and violent arrests of tax-evaders.[8] Only rarely did they enter a combat at more than company strength. They were too young to have been engaged in the great battles of the two civil wars between Muhammad 'Ali Pasha and his Ottoman sultan in 1831-1839, and there would be nothing like it again until the Mahdist revolution over 40 years later.

The Sudanese were to develop an *esprit de corps* different from that of their French allies. The European regimental rituals of the officers' and sergeants' messes; the toasts, the wines, the regimental plate from the home depot, had no counterpart in a Sudanese force. In general, the Ottoman military and naval establishment regarded itself as unconcerned with the dietary prohibitions observed by the more rigorous-minded Muslim civilians. In the Sudan many of the officers drank arrack and brandy to their hearts' content. But generalization has its pitfalls. A local French newspaper reported on a public banquet offered to Ibrahim Pasha, the commander-in-chief of the Egyptian forces, and his staff, at Angoulême during his visit to France in 1845. Ibrahim Pasha ate no meat and drank nothing but water while his officers "sampled with gusto all the wines of France." As for Ibrahim's French chief-of-staff, Sulayman Pasha, a convert to Islam, the newspaper commented "his new religion does not hinder him from drinking like a Frenchman."[9] The beverage of most Sudanese in the Sudan was *marisa*, a mild brew made usually from fermented millet. It is not surprising to find only one recorded case of alcohol abuse among the Sudanese troops in Mexico.

Promotion in the ranks of the Nizam regiments was normally by seniority. With all its shortcomings, it was a reasonable safeguard against favoritism, reputedly the curse of Egyptian military and civil institutions at this time. For a European it was a novelty to meet aged lieutenants and venerable sergeant-majors. In the black regiments the Sudanese officers were commissioned from the ranks and, consequently, there was no social gap, as was common between officers and other ranks in European armed forces. On the other hand, promotion by seniority did nothing to encourage the able juniors by giving them earlier regimental responsibility, which in a European army would be regarded as essential.

We do not know the extent of tribal feeling within any given unit and to what extent men of the same tribe tended to congregate in a particular company, to patrol, mess, and talk together. The nominal rolls with their overlapping of Islamic and native names and nicknames prove to be unreliable indicators. Nor do we know whether any effort was made by the battalion commanders to try to secure roughly equal opportunities for Dinka, Shilluk, Nuer, Jur, Bari, and Nuba candidates for promotion. The battalion records do not reveal any instances of inter-tribal brawling; was this due to the unifying influence of Islam, to the military *esprit de corps,* or to fear of punishment?

There is no clear answer. These men, whatever their tribal roots, seem to have felt a greater loyalty to the army of which they were now full members, not just come-and-go auxiliaries, irregulars, *bāshī būzuq,* but regulars on the permanent establishment, there for life. That they grew proud of their status as "slave soldiers" is evident in the nomenclature. Many troops from the Nilotic language group adopted the name Kuma, in this context short for Hukuma, an Arabic word for government, to signify that the owner of the name was a member of the ruling body. There was a fashion among others to accept the name Sa'id in honor of their ruler, Muhammad Sa'id Pasha, the friend of Ferdinand de Lesseps. By older men who enlisted before 1854, 'Abbas Hilmi Pasha, a ruler remote from their world, was not widely honored—there was only one 'Abbas on the battalion roll—they were born too early to be named Isma'il. Here and there on the roll, names recall pride in military service; one soldier, Private Sa'id al-Jaysh of No. 1 Company: "Sa'id of the Army," made it doubly clear where he stood.

The conviction of the social superiority of the military vocation still persists even though military conscription formally disappeared in the Sudan nearly a century ago. During a recent stay among the people of Jabal Taqali in the Nuba Mountains (a community with a long military tradition), Janet Ewald of Duke University, asked a Taqalawi officer's wife about her family connections. The lady smilingly cut her short with a proud retort: "I am a daughter of the Army" (*anā bint al-jaysh*). Her father's and husband's military ranks counted in her own eyes far more than her own ancestry.

Many of the troops on the battalion roll bore or, more often, were given, Arabic names indicating their association with slavery—usually names of good augury such as Bakhit (Lucky Gift), Baraka (Blessing), Marjan (Coral), and Almas (Diamond) as in Muhammad Almas, the battalion commander. Several names on the roll contain the word for slave, al-'Abd, and one, al-

Riqq, a collective synonym, proclaiming their former status. Adjutant-Major 'Abdallah al-'Abd (No. 4 coy) was one of Sir Samuel Baker Pasha's most competent officers in the Egyptian Equatorial province. The possessors of these and other slave-associated names had no cause to be ashamed; they did not share the European and American horror of an institution which in no way dehumanized them but offered them an honorable career in the government service. The battalion roll was enlivened by a few nicknames such as Elephant Hide, Father of the Lizard, and, more gallant, Slave of the Girls, which the military clerks dutifully entered on the roll.

By 1863, the *lingua franca* of the Sudanese Battalion would have evolved into rustic Sudanese Arabic. Recruits who had recently arrived from their tribal homelands might at first have almost no Arabic, not even the bare bones of trade Arabic picked up from pedlars plying among their villages. Their first step would be to seek out others from their own tribe. Those from the Nuba Mountains, having closer contact with Arabic-speaking neighbors, might have a somewhat larger vocabulary of basic Arabic words than those, for example, from the Western Nile tributaries. A few, brought up in domestic slavery in the larger towns of Egypt and the Sudan, may well have acquired some modest ability not only to read but also to write.

Military slavery, lifelong conscription in the Egyptian Sudanese regular army, offered greater opportunities for promotion and social advancement than were usually possible in agricultural and domestic slavery. Not that advancement was closed even in the "civilian" world. Studious, emancipated, civilian slaves, for example, could enter the *riwāq al-Sinnāriyya* (the hostel for students from Sinnar, i.e. the Sudan) in the university-mosque of al-Azhar in Cairo and who in the fullness of time, would find minor posts in the service of mosques and in elementary education in Sudanese villages. And there was the altogether exceptional case of Michele Amatore, a slave boy from the Sudan, who began his career as the *marmittone* to the cook with an Italian family in Cairo. Michele enlisted in the Piedmontese Bersagliere Corps in 1848, fought in the battles of the Italian Risorgimento, and retired a captain. Admittedly the Sudanese Battalion offered an exceptional range of military employment for black Sudanese whether, like Brig-Gen. Muhammad 'Ali Husayn (No. 3 Coy), they enlisted as volunteers or, like Maj-Gen. Faraj Pasha al-Zayni (No. 3 Coy), General Gordon's chief-of-staff in the siege of Khartoum, and Major 'Ali Efendi Jifun (No. 2 Coy), our battalion chronicler, they were conscripted as slaves. All joined as privates.

What most restricted career mobility among blacks in the Egyptian dominions was color prejudice which, curious to reflect, exists even among the Sudanese, a people already impregnated with "black blood." In the Northern Sudan, feeling against miscegenation is still strong though it tends to be selective. It is less embarrassing, for instance, for a Northern Muslim father to give his daughter in marriage to an otherwise eligible, presentable, and financially acceptable black Muslim suitor than to permit his son to marry a black girl.[10]

This prejudice was mitigated however by a signal advantage which the Sudanese slave possessed over antebellum blacks in the U.S. Whatever his condition as a slave, once he had accepted Islam, he was not excluded from membership of the Muslim community, the *umma*, any more than a Christian slave in Apostolic times was rejected by the Christian community. Slaves in the Sudan enjoyed another advantage which made their transition to freedom less unsettling than in the United States. The communities in which they were released were not only Muslim but were often ethnically akin to themselves, they spoke the same language and frequented the same mosques and markets as those who were free.

We have failed to find any official reference to the domestic arrangements of the black regiments in the eventuality of the men serving long periods away from the home depot; all we have is 'Ali Jifun's bare, translated statement that it was the custom in his early years, when troop transfers occurred, for the outgoing unit to hand over its women and children to the care of the incoming unit.

Finally, there is that heroic quality, loyalty. In return for board and lodging and a life of adventure with the prestige of being a soldier and a member of the government apparatus, the recruit developed a loyalty to the rulers of Egypt. Only in the most flagrant cases of government dereliction would that loyalty evaporate, as in the military mutiny at Kasala in 1865, when the relief battalion intended for Mexico revolted in the face of intolerable injustice, the result of a stupid failure in communication. In the Mexican campaign, which is our immediate concern, their loyalty to their officers, Sudanese and French, was absolute.

It was their patient, dogged loyalty to the Egyptian government that delayed, for four violent years, the destruction of the Egyptian army in the Sudan by the victorious power of the Mahdists. But their loyalty was not the spiritualized, romantic, European concept of loyalty recognized in the medieval courts of chivalry. It was rather a conditional, contractual concept which the *condottiere* of Renaissance Italy would have understood. In brief, you faithfully serve the master or the government who employs, pays, and feeds you, so long as he is capable of doing so. When he is seen to be no longer capable, you transfer, along with your brothers-in-arms, to another master, another government. In Mexico there was never any doubt who was master and, as we shall see, the French looked after them well. In the years ahead, when their master, the Egyptian government, was fighting a losing campaign against the Mahdists and was unable to help them in their desperate straits, the decision of the survivors whether to join the Mahdist Jihadiyya riflemen or make the appalling effort to get to Muṣawwa' and from there take ship to Egypt, their covenanted master, cannot have been easy.

4. The French Intervention: Napoleon III

Napoleon III was the architect of the French intervention in Mexico; the Sudanese Battalion owed its existence to the Emperor's policy. Charles-Louis-Napoleon Bonaparte, nephew of the Great Napoleon, could have been a character out of melodrama but for the absence of a happy ending. After an early manhood of varied conspiratorial activities including banishment from France, imprisonment in a French fortress for treason, and, on his escape, a short stint as a special constable protecting London from the Chartists, Louis-Napoleon returned to Paris in 1848. After the fall of the Orleans Monarchy, he engaged in three years of political maneuvering that led to a *coup d'état* in December 1852 when Prince-Président Louis Napoleon Bonaparte became Emperor Napoleon III.

His very ancestry as the nephew of the Great Napoleon was a constant embarrassment. Louis-Napoleon's faithful following of simple, uneducated believers, especially old soldiers with memories sharpened by the emergence of a Bonapartist legend, saw him as the inheritor of his uncle's military success. Sadly he believed them.

The Great Napoleon would have been an impossible example to follow. Unlike the Prussian General Helmuth von Moltke, a theoretical, calculating, long-term strategist, a *doctrinaire*, Napoleon Bonaparte was not only a great civil organizer, he was a military genius who won victory after victory by lightning-quick perceptions often in the midst of battle. But he left no formulated doctrine of his military genius.

His nephew proved an indifferent commander of armies. Habitual impatience and a lack of decisiveness caused him to waste the resources of France in a series of shoddily planned European campaigns without careful consideration of their ultimate political value. A botched military action was the double battle of Solferino-San Martino, the bloody climax of the war of 1859 by the allied French and Piedmontese armies against the Austrians.[11] Napoleon, joint Commander-in-Chief, cancelled the result of a hard-won victory by making a unilateral truce with the Austrian enemy without the consent of his co-victor, King Vittorio Emanuele. The Emperor had a sudden doubt whether, if Austria were to be deprived of Venetia as well as Lombardy, the victor would not be the French but the Prussians. Seven years later the Prussians, with the now disillusioned Italians as their allies, secured Venetia for Italy and assured a weakened Austria behind them when they marched against Napoleon in 1870.

Napoleon's greatest folly was his last: to risk war with wholly inadequate resources against the Prussians in 1870. It has been said in his defense that since 1867 he had been increasingly a sick man—more and more irresolute in mind and now in agony on horseback. With von Moltke as chief of the

Prussian general staff, the issue of the war was decided in the first month of fighting.[12] The Second Empire collapsed, and Emperor Napoleon died in England.

Napoleon's eccentric transit to power created for him many enemies from those who had hoped to gain some reward for services rendered—real or invented—during his climb to the Imperial throne. They were disappointed and viciously vented their spite on him. Even Victor Hugo may have been one of the disappointed—we do not know—but his rhetorical indictment of the Emperor, *Napoléon le Petit*, a lampoon written in Belgium and published in the safety of London in 1852, does nothing to remove the suspicion.

Napoleon's ideas for America found strange support in France, stemming from a tenacious folk memory among the uneducated of the ghost of Perfidious Albion, the malign influence behind the Anglo-Saxon greed for land which reared its ugly head in Canada with the Seven Years War. Folk memory, which makes fun of history, dismissed the birth of the United States—the perfidious English must have had a hand in it. The alienation of Louisiana in 1803, against the express wish of the First Napoleon, was another blow to France. By 1848, the "Anglo-Saxons" had swallowed up two-thirds of the total area of Mexico; a future President Polk could well devour the rest in the relentless "Anglo-Saxon" drive into the heart of Latin America.

From this perspective Napoleon's political thoughts are logical. France was a Latin empire with a moral duty to stand by her natural allies against further "Anglo-Saxon" aggression. An enlightened Mexican empire inspired by the engineering philosophy of the French Saint-Simoniens and the political liberalism of the Latin American, Simon Bolivar, would be the first link in a chain of cultured, well-governed, liberal, independent states, under the civilizing influence of France.

So much for the ideology. The material prospects for an intervention were speculative—the mythical gold of Sonora and the less speculative cotton of Mexico. Investment was a necessary element in commercial development, and here, a Swiss financier, Jecker, and Napoleon's half-brother, the Duc de Morny, had funds to invest. From 1858, the prospect of some form of European-centered solution seemed likely. All that was needed was a pretext for action.

5. The Military and Medical Crisis in Mexico

The immediate pretext for the French presence in Mexico in 1862 was the failure of the Mexican government to honor its international debts.

The withdrawal of Spanish colonial rule during the first quarter of the nineteenth century, in the face of national movements that gripped Latin

America's politically articulate classes, resulted in the creation of a number of unstable political groupings in a continuous state of ferment. Over the years in Mexico, the endless political wrangling between conservatives (mainly higher clergy, landowners, and their following) and liberals (mainly urban lower middle class) failed to give birth to a ruling institution that commanded general respect.

A financial crisis arose on 17 July 1861 when the government of President Benito Juarez announced a two-year moratorium on loan repayment of its foreign debts. The creditor nations were Spain, Britain, and France. On 29 February 1862, an international convention was held at La Soledad, a small town in the fever-infested Tierra Caliente, inland of the port of Veracruz. The Spanish and British delegates made a speedy accommodation with Mexico's representatives, which their governments ratified, and their token forces sailed away.

The French naval and military contingent stayed. Napoleon III decided to take advantage of the situation in Mexico, effecting a military occupation of the country. This view was to provide a stable form of government in which France would have a friendly influence. As the United States was diverted by civil war, no opposition from the north was expected for some time. Napoleon's orders were short and incisive: the Emperor's government rejected the treaty with the Mexican delegate, concluded at La Soledad, because the convention seemed not to be in keeping with the dignity of France.

On 6 March 1862, a French expeditionary force, commanded by General C. F. L. Comte de Lorencez, landed at Veracruz and advanced on Puebla (then the second most populous city of Mexico) and immediately assaulted the defenses. The forces at Lorencez's command were fewer than 3,000 in the field, inadequate for conducting a siege against a lengthy, defended perimeter. He had no siege artillery. It was a political gesture rather than a military operation. The French were decisively beaten and withdrew to Orizaba to await instructions from Paris. The Mexicans, not without cause, were cock-a-hoop with their easy triumph and never forgot it.[13]

The line of communication between Orizaba and Veracruz lay across the Tierra Caliente, a hot, flat land broken by *barrancas*, gullies ideal for ambushes, swamps during the rains, and fever-stricken quagmires for weeks after. This region was deadly to the French. At the outset of the French intervention, Admiral Jurien de la Gravière had urged the minister of the navy to raise a force of colonial "colored" battalions from Senegal and the French West Indies immediately. The Admiral's suggestion was not weakened by the obvious fact that, at the time, there was no scientific evidence of ethnic or other immunity from, or resistance to, yellow fever. But laboratory tests were not needed to prove that blacks, in general, were more resistant to the disease than whites. It was true in Latin America, and it was true in the United States. At Veracruz another phenomenon had been noticed; natives of the city, whatever their origin, were resistant, while Mexican visitors from the plateau were not.

6. The Emperor's Request for Sudanese Troops

At this point, the Emperor Napoleon took the practical step of applying to the ruler of Egypt, Muhammad Sa'id Pasha, for the loan of a black regiment of 1,200 to 1,500 men in the hope that they would be more resistant to the diseases of the Tierra Caliente than the European troops. The Pasha replied that he could not at that moment spare more than 500, and in the end only 446 embarked for Mexico.

On 3 December 1862, the French foreign minister sent a ciphered cable to his consul-general in Alexandria announcing that 500 blacks were being made available immediately to the French government. The remainder, who would be called forward "from the extremity of Upper Egypt," would take five months to arrive at Alexandria, as Muhammad Sa'id Pasha explained to the Emperor. A second cable informed the consul-general that the battalion was provided with its commander, officers, and other ranks. The minister warned the consul-general to keep the operation secret, even during the actual embarkation, in order to avoid arousing suspicions in Constantinople and London. He did not need to remind the consul-general that Lord Palmerston, the English prime minister, a notorious pryer into other nations' business, might have given trouble had he known what was going on. A ministerial dispatch from Paris dated 28 December 1862 notified the commander-in-chief in Mexico that a black battalion had been placed at his disposal.

Notes

1. Barbara Karsky, "Les Libéraux français et l'émancipation des esclaves aux Étas-Unis, 1852-1870," See Appendix 2 (2), plate 8.
2. Weygand, M. *Histoire militaire*, I, 167.
3. *cf.* the President of Uganda, Yoweri K. Museveni, an echo of the former 7th Bn. Kings African Rifles.
4. Paul Santi and Richard Hill, editors, *The Europeans in the Sudan, 1834 - 1878* (Oxford: Oxford University Press, 1980), 61.
5. Situation générale de l'armée égyptienne au 1 janvier 1846; Sennaar, Barrot to Foreign Minister, Paris, 1 Jan. 1846 (A.M.A.E., corr. pol. 16, fo. 19).

6. Douin, III, pt. 1, 181, citing ma'iyya al-saniyya, proceedings, box (old number) 37, fo. 385 prepared by Shahin Pasha Genc, beginning of 1866.
7. Austrian Consul, Khartoum to Governeur du Soudan, 22 dhu'l-hijja 1269 (26 Sept. 1853) Cairo, Qaṣr al-Jumhūriyya, box 17, misfiled 'Aṣr Isma'il.
8. 'Ali Jifūn, passim.
9. M.A. Borthwick to Consul-General C.A. Murray, 1 August 1851 (Cairo, Dar al-Wuthā'i'q, 'aṣr 'Abbās, box 2, old number).
10. A word of mild caution here. The Egyptian Sudan was a political unit which formed only part of the Bilād al-Sūdān, the immense geographical region extending from the Red Sea to the Atlantic. The Sudan was the savannah border or 'coast' between the desert in the north and the tropical forest in the south and it was known by the Arabic word *al-Sāhil* from the plural of which comes the Arabic name of an inhabitant of the eastern, coastal, section of the region as well as the language, *Sawāhilī*. In the present century the adjectival form *Sūdānī* (sing.), Sudanese, embraces all the inhabitants of the Bilād al-Sūdān, yet it can still be taken in the political Sudan to mean "black Southerner" with the derogatory connotation in the Sudan of "slave," so the use of the word in conversation has still to be tempered with discretion.
11. The battle was not without its Sudanese association. It was here in the action at San Martino under King Vittorio Emanuele's command that the Sudanese Sergeant Michele Amatore of the Bersagliere Corps was commissioned for his outstanding bravery.
12. Thirty-one years before the crowning triumph to his strategic career, Lt. von Moltke was at the end of four years' service in a Prussian advisory mission with the Ottoman version of the New Model Army. On 24 June 1839, he was present, on the losing side, at the battle of Nazib in Syria, Ibrahim Pasha's final Egyptian victory over the Ottoman Sultan. No Sudan regiments were involved.
13. See Dabbs, 28-30, for the battle of Cinco de Mayo.

The Voyage to Veracruz

Chapter 2

The Voyage to Veracruz

1. Embarkation at Alexandria

The French provided one of their smaller troopships, the frigate *La Seine* (plate 2) commanded by Frigate Captain Jaurès.[1] The Sudanese force, detached from the 19th Regiment of the Line, were embarked on the night of 7-8 January 1863 at Dar al-Maks, the old customs house, in a secluded spot just outside the Alexandria harbor entrance. They had come by the new railway from Sa'id Pasha's Barrage fortress, the Qal'a al-Sa'īdiyya, on the Nile 24 kilometers downstream of Cairo. Private 'Ali Jifun, the Sudanese chronicler, was serving there with a mountain gun (howitzer) battery when, "one day, an order arrived for all Sudanese to hand over the guns and proceed to the port."

The total strength embarked was 447 men. There were three officers, Major Jabaratallah Muhammad, the battalion commander, a white, possibly Syrian, veteran of Ibrahim Pasha's campaigns against the Ottoman Sultan, and two blacks, Captain Muhammad Almas and 1st lieutenant Husayn Ahmad. A civilian translator-interpreter, an Egyptian named Ahmad Efendi 'Ibayd, accompanied them. Among the other ranks were at least two men regarded as Lower Egyptians by domicile; three or four possibly came from outside the Egyptian Sudan, including one Somali from the Horn of Africa and one Burnawi from the Chad Basin. The rest, the great majority, were ex-slave conscripts from the black peoples of Southern Dar Fur, the Nuba Mountains, the Ethiopian borderlands, and White Nile Basin: Shilluk, Dinka, Nuer, Jur, and Bari, the whole ethnic mixture typical of the Nizam infantry.

The Sudanese troops went aboard wearing their Egyptian uniforms with equipment pretty well complete in all items. They carried their firearms; their ammunition was stored in cases in the hold. We have no description of these muzzle-loading weapons; the troops called them *shishkhana*,[2] an indication that their barrels were rifled, but they were not of the same calibre as the French. It would have been over-complicated and uneconomical for the French ordnance to have procured nonstandard ammunition for a single battalion, so, on their arrival at Veracruz, their Egyptian rifles, and presumably, bayonets, were put into store and returned to the battalion at the end of the campaign. In their place the standard, muzzle-landing, French rifle was issued to them.[3]

Commandant Jaurès's favorable report on the state of the regular troops contrasts with his brief comment on the squalor of the "recruits" conscripted *ad hoc* off the streets of Alexandria by the police just before sailing: "nearly all of whom had no other clothes but pieces of blue cotton material or some other torn covering."[4]

In Egypt secrecy is always relative. For the first four days after the battalion sailed nobody beyond the dockside and the city markets was aware that anything rumor-worthy had occurred. Five days after *La Seine* had left, the Alexandria correspondent of *The Times* cabled his editor a misleading report: "The Viceroy has placed at the disposal of France 800 negro slaves. They are to be embarked in a French war steamer and dispatched to Mexico."[5] The consul-general of the United States waxed indignant over servants' rumors. He told his secretary of state that no black doorkeeper in Alexandria would open a door during the embarkation for fear of being crimped by the press gangs, and that many black servants had run away to spend a week in the desert for fear of impressment.[6]

2. The Transport La Seine

La Seine steamed out of Alexandria harbor early on 8 January 1863. Such was the official secrecy of their departure that the Egyptian War Office did not tell the men where they were going, and they suspected the worst. 'Ali Jifun admitted that he shared the perplexity on board but was not unduly alarmed. "Although I had by this time been accustomed to variety of every kind, still, this French troopship, crowded with almost 500 Sudanese, many of whom had never seen the sea before, afforded quite a new experience, and the first few days we suffered very much."[7] Officially the ship had accommodation for 15 officers and 350 other ranks. On this voyage therefore, she was overcrowded.

La Seine was launched in 1856 and scrapped in 1884. Her displacement was 2,153 tonnes, her length at waterline 72.70 meters, beam 11.60 meters, and mean draught 4.50 meters. Following the naval practice of her day, she relied on both sail and steam for propulsion. She was three-masted and carried the frigate sail rig. Her steampower came from a single 2-cylinder reciprocating engine of 160 horse power.

The ship's slow speed is easily explained. Marine furnaces were then greedy consumers of coal, which occupied valuable space and cost money. The Ministry of the Navy, urged by the Ministry of Finance, had ordered ships' captains to shut down their engines and hoist their sails whenever the wind was favorable. So *La Seine* crossed the Atlantic mainly under sail.

3. Hygiene and Morale

The first official report on the voyage stated that the troops had been despondent, listless, and inclined to take offence at nothing. The report admitted that their contacts with the French ship's crew proved unhappy despite instructions given to the crew to treat the Sudanese with great gentleness. Some Sudanese insulted French officers whose ranks they were well aware. A serious feature was the contempt Muslims entertain for Christians; there were cases where troops slapped Frenchmen with their sandals and spat in their faces which the report explains, "is a sign of contempt with them as it is with us."[8]

The decks were filthy. The troops left most of the cleaning and swabbing down to the crew. But, the report continued, "these things must not be exaggerated. Most of the trouble was due to the difference of language and lack of understanding between peoples so different as the Negroes and the French."

Discipline among the Sudanese themselves appeared to the French officers to be extremely lax. Officers and sergeants were badly obeyed, a weakness due, they thought, to the Egyptian army's method of "promoting men en masse as required to fill vacancies instead of relying on the results of training and experience." The battalion commander, the report stated, is an honorable exception to weaknesses in the method of promotion. Binbashi Jabaratallah Efendi was well-trained, intelligent, and full of excellent intentions; but "he has shown weakness of character."[9]

The ship cleared the Mediterranean and, heaving-to off Algeciras to report, sailed out into the Atlantic. Once the Mediterranean was left behind and *La Seine* entered the warmer zone, the men's spirits began to revive; and, with the hot weather, the troops would come on deck and be their merry selves again. 'Ali Jifun, our only Sudanese voice from the ship, thought that soldiers ordered on service did not generally trouble their minds much about who their enemy was or why there was a war on. The men had gathered vaguely that their Khedive had arranged to lend their battalion to the French government for duty in Mexico, and that was that.

Late, on 25 January 1863, *La Seine* put into Funchal, Madeira, the first port of call. The vessel's coal reserves were insufficient for the Atlantic crossing even with reliance on sail. So Commandant Jaurès proceeded to top-up his bunkers. As there was no labor available in the harbor on a Sunday, he had to make a special arrangement to ship 120 tonnes.

In his tactful report to the Minister of the Navy, Jaurès wrote that the conduct of the troops since leaving Alexandria had been perfect but regretted that three soldiers had died on the way.

4. Preliminary Organization

Meanwhile, two French warrant officers, Adjudants Mangin and Charpplain of the Intendance (supply branch) who had joined *La Seine* at Toulon on her way to Alexandria, began organizing this amorphous Sudanese unit as a small battalion of four companies. This was a work beyond the knowledge and experience of the three Egyptian officers on board. However, the basic similarity in command structure between the French and Egyptian armies bridged the gulf.

The two French warrant officers summarily filled vacant posts by on-the-spot provisional promotions. By French military tradition this was not the way to promote, but the appointed officers and non-commissioned officers were old campaigners in the Egyptian army; thus each carried a reasonable guarantee that he would be capable of carrying increased responsibility.

According to Commandant Jaurès's report: "this battalion which was composed exclusively of Negroes from the Sudan, consisted of 447 men, as follows":

1 battalion commander	15	corporals
1 captain	359	regular troops
1 lieutenant	39	recruits
8 sergeants	22	boys
	446	
	1	civilian interpreter
	447	

This was the first roll-call of numbers and ranks. Later rolls taken in Mexico were to reveal discrepancies, which are explained in Appendix 1.[10]

By an *arrêté* of 11 March 1863, the provisional scheme of promotion made during the voyage was confirmed—subject to ultimate approval by the Khedive of Egypt which was duly given. The only captain, Muhammad Almas, was promoted adjutant-major and Lieutenant Husayn Ahmad was promoted captain in his place. Provisional promotions of senior, non-commissioned officers to lieutenants and 2nd lieutenants were also confirmed. One 2nd lieutenant, two sergeant majors, and a sergeant became 1st lieutenants, four 2nd lieutenants were created from one quartermaster sergeant and three sergeants. The revised establishment was therefore:

Old Rank	Name	New Rank
capt.	Muhammad Almas	Adj.-Maj.
1st lt.	Husayn Ahmad	Capt.
2nd lt.	Faraj 'Azazi	1st Lt.
sgt.-maj.	Muhammad Sulayman	1st Lt.
sgt.	Faraj Muhammad al-Zayni	1st Lt.
sgt.-maj.	Salih Hijazi	1st Lt.
q.m.s.	Khalil Fanni	2nd Lt.
sgt.	Al-Fawd [sic] Muhammad	2nd Lt.
sgt.	Muhammad 'Ali	2nd Lt.
sgt.	'Abd al-Rahman Musa	2nd Lt.

5. The Mishap at Fort-de-France

The second port of call, the last before reaching Veracruz, was Fort-de-France, capital of the French West Indies, on the island of Martinique. *La Seine* anchored for a day on 11 February. Commandant Jaurès reported to the acting governor of the island: ". . . *La Seine* left Madeira in the evening of 26 January. . .carrying to Mexico a battalion of Egyptian blacks whose conduct on board ever since our departure from Alexandria has been perfect. We have lost two soldiers during the voyage between Egypt and Madeira and three between Madeira and here. Of these five men four contracted pneumonia and one dropsy."[11] The men were not allowed ashore, but a fatal mistake was made. Fresh fruit and cooked messes had been allowed to be brought on board by local traders. Men weary of the sight of food from the ship's galley were sure to eat such delights with double relish and minimal discrimination. Worse, an epidemic diagnosed as typhus was raging on the island, while ashore the Martiniquaises were reported singing in their r-less Creole:

On dit Mexique vous qu'a aller
la gue-e là-bas, mourir beaucoup
et la fièv-jaune, ici tout doux
en-bas méchante, l'Bon-Dieu ga-de vous.

No sooner was the ship clear of the port than men, both troops and crew, began to come down with illnesses, chiefly dysentery and an undiagnosed fever. The Muslim month of Ramaḍan began on 18 February. The fast itself, the commandant reported, was scrupulously observed by the whole battalion, but the medical officers at Veracruz military hospital afterwards remarked that the friendly gatherings after the statutory daylight fasting hours had passed, brought the men together, adding to the risk of contagion. The upshot of that luckless day at Fort-de-France was that five more Sudanese soldiers and two sailors died during the crossing.

La Seine anchored at Veracruz on 24 February. As there was no quay to accommodate vessels of her draught she anchored in the roadstead in the shelter of the Castle of San Juan de Ulua and the men were ferried ashore. J. A. Beaucé, the French official war artist, drew the scene for *L'Illustration* (plate 3).

Notes

1. Constant-Louis-Jean-Benjamin Jaurès (1823-1889), the future Vice-Admiral and Minister of the Navy.
2. *Shishkhāna* (Persian), originally a firearm having six-grooved rifling in the barrel. With the passage of time, it became the common word for any muzzle-loading firearm with rifled barrel.
3. Fusil d'infanterie modèle 1853 and 1853 T. Both French and Egyptian infantry rifles were then muzzle-loading.
4. Jaurès to Minister of the Navy, 25 January 1863 (Paris, Archives Nationales, Marine BB4, 822, *Seine* fo. 515).
5. *The Times*, 15 January 1863.
6. Consul-General W. Thayer to Secretary of State, 27 January 1863, (T.45, rol 4).
7. 'Ali Jifūn, 184.
8. Corps expéditionnaire du Mexique, bataillon nègre égyptien, rapport sur l'organisation, l'état physique, moral et sanitaire du dit bataillon, Vera Cruz, 24 feb. 1863 (S.H.A.T., G7, 224).
9. In the report, these critical remarks have been crossed out and kindlier comments substituted in another hand.
10. *Historique,* 47. As these events occurred before the use of rational transcription by Europeans, the reader must be prepared for variations in the spelling of proper names from and to Arabic.
11. Paris, Archives Nationales, Marine, BB4, 806, Direction movements.

Acclimatization, 1863

1. The Terrain
2. Health
3. Organization and Logistics
4. Military Operations
5. The Railway
6. What Others Thought of the Negro Egyptians
7. A Conflict of Laws
8. Did the Sudanese Serve Outside the Tierra Caliente?
9. Liaison with Egypt: Isma'il Pasha

Chapter 3

Acclimatization, 1863

1. The Terrain

Veracruz in 1863 was a city of about 13,000 inhabitants cramped behind an already obsolete defensive wall—barely 2,000 meters long on the sea side and 700 meters at its greatest width. Travelers remarked that the place looked much like a small city of Andalusia, more Spanish than colonial Spanish. The war had introduced a lively scene of military activity everywhere. The streets were alive with soldiers and sailors of many countries whose tented camps outside the wall received overflow from the city barracks. But the town had a dried-up appearance; the public square was devoid of vegetation, something abhorrent to the French concept of a town square as a place of beauty and repose with shrubs and lawns and, of course, a band playing on Sunday afternoons. For the sensitive, the dust stirred up by the winds made the streets a torture for the eyes. The place to stay, according to the unanimous verdict of Europeans and Americans, was the Hotel de las Diligencias in the main square, if only the guests would refrain from spitting on the floor and loudly gambling all night.

Capriciously protecting the harbor from the north wind was the coral island on which stood the fortress of San Juan de Ulua, "a massive, sombre, forbidding citadel," General du Barail noted in his diary. The castle was built early in the sixteenth century and, by 1863, it housed the military hospital and military prison. Under the floors, rainwater storage cisterns had been built. The majority of householders in Veracruz made do with shallow wells—yielding bitter, tainted water—while the poor drew it in buckets from the public Persian wheel, the noria,[1] installed at the southeast wall to lift water from an underground stream on its way to the sea.

Today, the little walled town is totally absorbed into the modern city and port that now surrounds its traces. The former seafront has been eliminated by dredging, filling, and building of deep-sea quays. The surrounding coral town wall and all the forts but one have been demolished. The survivor, Baluarte Santiago, at the extreme south-eastern extremity of the wall, has been converted into a historical museum.

Of all the rivers that meander over the great plain of the Sotavento de Veracruz to the sea at Alvarado, only the Papaloapan was reliably navigable by French gunboats. These boats irregularly patrolled the lower reaches of the river and, on occasion, carried out combined operations with small detachments of Sudanese, Creole, Austrian, and French troops. The unnavigable streams were usually fordable by infantry, however; two Sudanese were drowned in fording accidents.

The region is fertile and abounds in tropical products. The roads were little more than unmetaled tracks, hard on wheeled vehicles at all times and impassable during and shortly after the rains, when even the main high road between Veracruz and Mexico City was unusable for several days at a time.

2. Health

On landing at Veracruz, no fewer than 71 Sudanese, ill from an undiagnosed fever, were immediately taken to the military hospital of San Juan de Ulúa nearby. Fifty eight of them were too weak to walk and were carried in military wagons; one man died in the act of landing. Within a few days, five more patients died. On the day of landing, nine white sailors from *La Seine* were admitted to the naval hospital. In all, 52 soldiers and sailors died in the hospital during their first fortnight ashore. The military used the nearby island of Sacrificios as a cemetery, which the troops sardonically renamed *le jardin d'acclimatation.*

Prince 'Umar Tusun considered that the Sudanese deaths were due mainly to poor food and neglect. If, by "poor food," he inferred that their diet was nutritionally inadequate, he was probably right as they were issued the same food as the French. The Sudanese diet generally consisted of a millet bread made from pounded millet flour as leavened bread (*'aysh*) or unleavened flat bread (*kisra*) or in the form of millet porridge (*'asida, luqma*). The bread in Mexico was made of maize flour, which has fewer vitamins and proteins than millet. Sorghum (Spanish Sorgo) was, however, grown in Mexico. The Sudnaese may have suffered from pellagra, a niacin deficiency disease. Undernourishment as well as indulgence in tainted foods in humble Mexican eating places could well have undermined their resistance to disease.

A change may also have taken place in the drinking habits of the Sudanese. Their customary *marisa*, beer, was unobtainable in Mexico, though light wine was used by the French doctors as a tonic for hospital cases—which Sudanese patients took with relish.

As a matter of paramount importance, patients suffering from fever were, as much as possible, isolated from other patients and distributed in the large rooms where great attention was paid to ventilation.

The greatest obstacle in the way of the military medical staff was the total lack of communication between them and their Sudanese patients. The doctors could not find out the first things that they wanted to know: ". . . their tastes, habits, needs, dislikes, and religious susceptibilities, to remove misunderstandings and to respect the legitimate wishes of the troops."

The mortality in the battalion raised doubts as to whether the Sudanese could stand the climate and diseases of the Tierra Caliente after all. Médecin-Major Fuzier and his medical colleagues at the hospital attributed the typhus that had developed aboard *La Seine* to a combination of homesickness, complete change of life, habits, and diet—e.g., the consumption of tainted foods from bum-boats at Fort-de-France during the voyage— but chiefly to the vitiated air in the ship's lower deck which was not provided with port holes and had been infected by horses and mules transported on the previous voyage.

Médecin-Major Fuzier explained in his report that, except for some of the officers and non-commissioned officers, the battalion consisted of

> blacks from Dar Fur and south Egypt, men tall and quite robust though some have rather slim limbs. . . .What is most striking about all these hospital cases is the state of extreme dejection into which almost all of them are plunged. . . .The majority are in a state of stupor; the patients respond languidly to the interpreter. . . .The good hygienic conditions in which the patients have been placed, the assiduous care bestowed upon them, and the efforts to raise their morale, have proved their efficacy; in the case of many patients. . .their appetites have responded in proportion, their vitality has returned and, perhaps a little prematurely [for the doctor had not been brought up in an African hut] it was considered best to give way to their vociferous desire to return to their tents.[2]

For most of them, tents were the next best thing to their African huts; all that was lacking were their women to cook food. The joy shown by patients at the prospect of leaving the dry, stone-built hospital for life under tents in brisk March weather surprised the French medical men, who could not fathom the reason for their choice.

It was not long before the battalion commander paid the penalty of vulnerability to yellow fever. Major Jabaratallah Muhammad died at Veracruz on 29

May. The battalion *Historique* predictably wrote a eulogy describing him as a good soldier and a man devoted to his duty. With no official axe to grind, 'Ali Jifun repeated that he was a good man. He left 5,667 French francs which, with compensation of 5,000 francs, were sent from Veracruz to the Egyptian government to forward to his heirs.

During that pestilent spring, Veracruz felt the full force of the plague. Eleven French officers and half the town garrison died of yellow fever. Of four French officers successively attached to the Sudanese battalion, only one, Lieutenant Baron, recovered. Captain Grandin of the Contre-Guérilla, who was at Veracruz at the time, wrote that, without the Sudanese and the Negro engineers from Martinique and Guadeloupe, Veracruz would have been defenseless.[3]

General Forey notified the war minister of the major's death. Until the Governor-General of Egypt provided a replacement, the battalion, he suggested, could operate as self-supporting companies under their French area commander, without a battalion head.[4] The officer chosen to fill the post, Adjutant-Major Muhammad Almas, was no member of the Ottoman ruling institution like his predecessor but a Sudanese black from the Ottoman borderland.

In reporting to Paris the death of the Egyptian battalion commander, the commander-in-chief told the war minister that he himself doubted the contention of the medical officers that the Sudanese battalion was resistant to yellow fever. True, the doctors had assured him that the other Sudanese were not afflicted by yellow fever but by typhus. The fact remained that 20 of them had already died of marsh fevers (*fièvres paludéennes*), and there were many fever patients still in the hospital.[5] The general had never met the major and did not realize that he was the only non-African in the battalion.

For another 30 years, the epidemiological establishment continued to associate yellow fever—like the disease they attributed to mal'aria—with miasmata. The French military medial officers in Mexico were using this basic assumption in their diagnoses and treatments. General du Barail, himself a cavalry officer, advanced a truly comprehensive theory of distribution of diseases originating in miasmata from vegetable decomposition that caused cholera at the mouths of the Ganges, plague in the Nile delta, and yellow fever at the mouth of the Mississippi whence it spread along the Gulf of Mexico to infect Veracruz.[6]

In 1898, a general practitioner in Havana, Carlos Juan Finlay, suggested that yellow fever was carried by the mosquito *Culex fasciatus*, later renamed *Aedes aegypti*. Finlay's hypothesis, politely ridiculed by orthodox colleagues, was found to be correct not only in identifying a mosquito as the vector but also in identifying its species. The hypothesis was firmly established in 1900 by Major Walter Reed of the Yellow Fever Commission of the United States

Army.

Yellow fever has now been virtually eliminated from tropical towns by the destruction of *Aedes aegypti* and related mosquitoes. In rural tropical zones in Central Africa and Latin America, where it has been impossible to eradicate vectors in jungles and freshwater reservoirs, yellow fever remains endemic.

Medellín was a bad place for nervous disorders. An unnamed Sudanese soldier suffered an attack of hallucination during the night, went out of the fort with his rifle, and, for no known reason, wounded an innocent Mexican. Roused by the sound of the shot, the small garrison ran out of the fort and began chasing the demented man, who fled into the bush with his rifle. Turning around, he fired on his comrades; who shot and killed him in self-defense. Another anonymous soldier of the battalion committed suicide by shooting himself in the chest, lingering for several days.[7]

By the end of 1863, the general health of the Sudanese had improved though cases diagnosed as typhus and tuberculosis persisted in progressively declining numbers and virulence. Several men complained of tapeworm. One tragic case occurred on 3 December when a soldier was admitted to the hospital at San Juan de Ulua suffering from acute diarrhea and complaining of worm. During the day a dose of 20 grams of *kousso*[8] was given, but the patient died shortly after. The autopsy revealed a tapeworm 10 meters long.[9]

3. Organization and Logistics

On 25 February, only a day after the Sudanese had disembarked, J. H. Maréchal, officer commanding troops in the Tierra Caliente and headquartered at Veracruz, wrote urgently to general headquarters that the organization of the Sudanese was already giving great difficulty: "Not a single officer or soldier speaks any European language. It is essential to obtain some non-commissioned officers and men from the Tirailleurs Algériens. Each company should have an Arabic-speaking officer attached to it." Interpreters were essential for maintaining communications with the train escorts, as he was expecting railway engineering materials urgently required.

General Forey responded to part of this plea by issuing the following *arrêté*, signed at his battle headquarters in Acatzingo on 11 March 1863:

Arrêté for the Organization of the Egyptian Negro Battalion [precis: full text in *Historique*, 274-79]

With the object of administering the Egyptian Negro battalion in such a way as to compromise as little as possible our own administrative regula-

tions while at the same time providing for the particular needs of this unit, the Commander-in-Chief orders the following arrangements to be made:

Article 1

As no officer or other rank can speak or write French the paperwork of the battalion will be confided to an officer from the Commissariat branch who will discharge the double function of treasurer and clothing officer.

Article 2

Issues in cash or kind and the supply of stores and weapons to officers and men will be regulated according to a scale of charges annexed to this arrêté.

The Chief Commissariat Officer will give instructions which he considers appropriate to ensure the proper functioning of the organization of this unit and a proper authorization for all expenses incurred therewith.

Administrative Instructions

In view of the fact that none of the officers or other ranks know how to read, write or speak French and it is therefore impossible to apply our administrative regulations, the administration and accounts of the battalion will be entrusted to a French officer serving with the unit.

Another two and half months passed before the commander-in-chief could spare time from the gruelling preoccupation of reducing the fortress of Puebla to attend to the language troubles on the line of communication. On 30 May, he approached the war minister, for he still doubted whether these Sudanese could bear the heavy demands that were to be made on them—responsibility for the defense of the railway and the escorting of trains. They might well be resistant to yellow fever, but that did not shield them from liability to other fevers as the hospital admissions records showed. Word had come from the Veracruz command that there had been a breakdown of discipline in Medellín.[10] To crown their difficulties, the Sudanese could not speak any European language. He asked the war minister for permission to add to the Sudanese strength Arabic interpreters from other units.[11]

Consequently, four sergeants, six corporals, and one or two riflemen-interpreters—all bi-lingual—were seconded from III company, Tirailleurs Algérians to the Sudanese battalion headquarters and the four companies.

The name of the supplying regiment, Tirailleurs Algériens, is deceptive. Though based in Algeria, their ranks included not only Arabic and Berber-speaking troops from the Maghrib (North-West Africa), but some who came from sub-Saharan Africa. These men understood the Arabic spoken as a "lingua franca" in Dar Fur and further west and who, by our definition, were Sudanese. A ministerial dispatch of 4 July 1862 ordered the formation of a battalion of Tirailleurs Algériens as a "bataillon de marche" of six self-contained companies. They landed at Veracruz on 29 October 1862 and were given the defense of the line of communication between La Soledad and Orizaba. To this extent, they were the precursors of the Sudanese. They fought well but suffered heavily from fevers in the Tierra Caliente.[12]

The apparent success of the Sudanese in resisting yellow fever was soon forgotten by the non-medical soldiery as soon as it was seen that they were not immune to all other fevers plaguing Latin America. General Forey began to lose faith in the stamina of the Sudanese troops. "The Egyptians," he wrote to the war minister "have no value, and they will never acquire any until they have been properly encadred, and I apologize for my insistence, until the requirements of my dispatch No. 360 of 30 May have been fulfilled."[13]

They were duly encadred, but the language difficulty and the death of their battalion commander seem to have dispirited Forey who, a few months later, would be praising with equal forcefulness their bravery in battle.

The language of administration and correspondence was necessarily French, although there was provision for the use of Arabic, essential in the case of letters and any money orders that the men might send home. The ministry was anxious that the men's mail be handled with the greatest expedition and efficiency because, Paris explained, this was a natural and legitimate preoccupation of soldiers. As it was reported that the men were worrying about their families in the Sudan, provision was made for them to remit money orders to their dependents.[14]

The Turkish-Arabic mixture that comprised the military vocabulary of the Sudanese was a total mystery to the French. So, for the instruction of the French army, the chief interpreter, Ahmad 'Ibayd Efendi, compiled a short glossary of officer's ranks as pronounced by the Sudanese.[15] Colonel L. E. Mangin commanding the 3rd Regiment of Zouaves was charged with the instruction of the battalion in the basic theory and practice of French infantry drill, movements, musketry, and discipline. His success as an instructor over the years was brilliantly evident in the remarkable number of his own young officers who attained the rank of divisional general.

The Sudanese battalion was brigaded with the Foreign Regiment and the Contre-Guérilla. The former was officered primarily by French nationals. A succession of sub-lieutenants: Maupin, Borghella, Brincourt, Patin, and, conspicuously, Baron, were seconded to the battalion for administrative duties but in several operations took command in the field. At this time, the Contre-Guérilla force of Mexican and French volunteers was commanded by Colonel

C. Dupin. A Buffalo Bill in appearance, Du Barrail, then a staff officer, described him as "king of the Tierra Caliente, straight out of Dumas' novel, who wielded his sword and drew his pistol like the late d'Artignan." His corps was trained to fight the *guerrilleros* with their own methods. Unfortunately, the Contre-Guérilla did so only too literally, eliminating the law's delays by shooting prisoners summarily without waiting for courts martial.[16]

The Sudanese had embarked at Alexandria in uniforms standard for the regular infantry: tarbush, white cotton slacks, jacket, and greatcoat with ammunition belt and pouch. Shortly after their arrival in Veracruz, these were replaced by uniforms based on those of the Tirailleurs Algériens. Their Egyptian uniforms were stored at Veracruz for use on the return voyage to Egypt. The initiative for this came from the intendance, which represented to the commander-in-chief that it would be most useful if the Negro battalion retained the Egyptian uniform as a reserve. General Forey issued an order to this effect.[17]

The ingenuity of the intendance provided a uniform that received wide approval:

Article	Number	Period of Issue
Cloth Overcoat	1	18 months
Monkey jacket, red cloth	1	18 months
Monkey jacket, linen	2	6 months
Trousers, linen	2	4 months
Zouave's turban	1	1 year
Waist sash (cummerbund)	1	1 year
Blue necktie	1	6 months
Skull cap fez	1	6 months
Tassel for fez	1	1 year
Shirts	2	4 months
Drawers	2	4 months
Slippers (babouches)	2	6 months
Stockings or gaiters	2	4 months
Haversack	1	2 years
Cartridge pouch and belt	1	indefinite
Rifle and bayonet	1	indefinite

The *arrêté* of 19 May also laid down the scale of daily pay:

Rank	Francs	Rank	Francs
major	16.66	sgt major	1.00
adjutant-major	5.20	sergeant	0.70
chief interpreter	5.20	corporal	0.45

captain	5.20	private 1st cl.	0.366 19
1st lieutenant	4.33	private	0.266
2nd lieutenant	3.50	[18]	

Article 3 regulated the gross daily pay of the entire battalion at 1,040 French francs. The troops were to receive their pay every fortnight, a regularity seldom attained in the Egyptian army. Campaign allowances were the same as for the French infantry of the line. Special pay rates were laid down for men in the hospital and on leave.

General Forey was promoted Marshal of France on 2 July and recalled to Paris on 1 October when he officially handed over the command to General François-Achille Bazaine, himself shortly to be promoted Marshal. During his last few days in command, Marshal Forey decided to show official gratitude to the Sudanese for their devotion to duty and to stimulate their zeal. By an *arrêté* of 28 September, a new military rank—that of private 1st class, for soldiers of outstanding ability—was created at a daily pay of 35 *centimes*.[19] The symbol of the rank was a distinctive yellow arm-stripe.

The total strength of these special troops was not to exceed one-quarter of the total battalion strength. Later in the campaign, the Emperor Maximilian added his own thanks by decreeing a further modest pay raise for holders of this rank. By an *arrêté* of 31 August 1863, the battalion—in common with all French and allied troops in Mexico—became eligible for the Mexican campaign medal.

By oversight in Egypt, the battalion arrived in Mexico without bugles, a serious deficiency, as signals during engagements were then given by bugle. However, it was discovered that several Sudanese soldiers "knew how to blow this type of instrument" and the intendance issued the battalion eight bugles. Though usually called bugles by writers in English describing the French infantry "clairon," the latter was longer and heavier than the standard British bugle of today.

The Sudanese formed a unit too small to support a full-time imām, and nothing in the record points to the existence of any exterior religious presence. A volunteer of sufficient literacy would always be available from among the troops to lead the prayers or read from the Koran at the funeral of a fallen brother.

Military Operations

After 40 years, the Sudanese troops of the Nizam were meeting the French again. Not the old drill instructors who remembered Napoleon I, but a generation of officers and men representing a new European culture, more literate, more worldly wise, more sensitive than their predecessors. Despite its intensive experience of war—the Crimea (1853-1855), Italy (1859), Cochin China (1858-1867), and Algeria continuously—the Second Empire allowed itself to fall behind Prussia in the modernization of its armament. Napoleon III was himself an expert in artillery on which he wrote a treatise while a prisoner at Ham. And, as Emperor, he actively shared in the design of a *mitrailleuse* machine gun.[20] But the overriding necessity was economy, and the French fighting services suffered.

It was national, financial stringency that delayed the replacement of the standard muzzle-loading rifle with a breech-loading successor. The shock of the French general staff to the lightning victory at Sadowa of the breech-loading Prussians against the muzzle-loading Austrians in 1866 galvanized the French government into urgent action. Production of the breech-loading rifle developed by Alphonse Chassepot, which had already been under leisurely testing for a year, was immediately put in hand. Urgent arming for a Franco-Prussian war, now held to be inevitable, left nothing for the army of occupation in Mexico. Only on the eve of evacuation could the war ministry spare a few experimental Chassepots for selected French units in Mexico.

To the north, the American Civil War had ended. With their greater industrial resources and technical ingenuity, the U.S. government had almost wholly re-equipped its armies when the Confederacy capitulated. It is a wry thought that, not long after the Sudanese battalion returned to Egypt, Khedive Isma'il, on his own initiative, provided them, and ultimately all the Egyptian Nizam infantry, with Remington breech-loading rifles, surplus stock from the U.S. conflict. And, as soon as the Franco-Prussian War was over, the Khedive negotiated the purchase of surplus Krupp breech-loading artillery.

The end of the American Civil War did not have an immediate, adverse effect on the French side, although officers noticed the growing number of American breech-loading rifles and carbines found in the hands of captured Mexican guerrilleros, particularly during the last year before the evacuation.[21]

As time passed, it was becoming clear that the French occupation of Mexico was limited to the principal towns and ports and control of the vital line of communication between Veracruz and the Plateau. It was in the small warfare of the countryside that the Republicans found their most effective reprisal.[22] Their well-led commandos roamed the Tierra Caliente on hardy, stringy horses or on mules, each consisting of about 300 mounted men, sometimes with a small backing of infantry. They had the tactical advantage of fighting in friendly country with ready access to intelligence, guides, and food provided by the villages. This increased their freedom of movement linked as they were to area commands which were in precarious communication with a nebulous national headquarters, always under enemy threat, somewhere in the north.

The documents assembled by General Jesus de León Toral in his *Historia documental militar* covering the entire intervention campaign from 1861 to 1867 make it clear that, except for a few months of chaotic uncertainty in 1863 when the Republican army was recovering from a series of French victories, the Republicans conducted their operations with a virtually decentralized command. Veracruz and the Tierra Caliente, for instance, came under the eastern command whose address was about as fixed as Robin Hood's. For most of the campaign, from 1863 onward, the regional commander was General Porfirio Diaz, a resourceful, if headstrong, leader who was popular with his men but incapable of working in harmony with his superiors.

In the conditions prevailing from May to August 1863, it was necessary to vary frequently the posting of the four Sudanese companies. This had the advantage of hardening the troops and familiarizing them with the terrain. Their first posting on active service was on the line of communication between Veracruz and the interior. The whole force came under the command of Chef d'Escadron J. M. Maréchal, of the Marine Artillery. He developed a deep affection for his Sudanese troops, whose qualities he reported to general headquarters with enthusiasm, and, in his last battle, died in their midst. Nos. 1 and 2 companies were posted to area headquarters at Veracruz. No. 3 was posted to La Soledad where it joined the French Contre-Guérilla. No. 4 was sent to guard the railway construction camp at La Tejeria, where it relieved two companies of the Foreign Regiment unable to withstand the climate.[23] It is No. 3 company who will have the duty of guarding 906 prisoner of war officers who surrendered at Puebla on 17 May. During the week-long French assault on the city the defense of communications between Veracruz and La Soledad was entrusted to the Sudanese. Forey entered Mexico City on 10 June. In Veracruz, the two Sudanese companies were accorded the place of honor in the celebration parade.

Their first patrol was a reconnaissance to Tlalixcoyan, a small, but strategically important, town on the left bank of the Rio Blanco, 32 km from its mouth at Alvarado. A column of 80 Sudanese, supported by a troop of Mexican Imperial cavalry (the combined force under the command of Captain Cazes of the Foreign Regiment),[24] marched out of Medellin on 6 July to show the flag. The country folk along the way to Tlalixcoyan seemed to be friendly.

The force had not long returned when, on 30 July, Captain Cazes received orders to make a second march to Tlalixcoyan with the same units as before, reinforced by the 2nd Sudanese company, the 3rd company of the 2nd battalion of the Foreign Regiment, and 20 reserve cavalrymen. To avoid the great heat of the day, the force advanced by night, with the cavalry pushing ahead. The enemy, forewarned, had already retreated, and Tlalixcoyan was occupied without resistance.

The return of the second French expedition to Tlalixcoyan left Medellin defenseless. The hostility evident among the villagers in the district might have encouraged some *guerrilleros* to attempt its seizure. To guard against the possibility, 30 Sudanese from No. 1 (Veracruz) company took up quarters there on 29 August. A month later a Sudanese reinforcement augmented the small garrison.

On 11 August, the 4th company joined a strong patrol escorting a consignment of 12 million French francs in transit from Veracruz to Orizaba for the use of the French army. The state of security in the Tierra Caliente may be gauged by the strength of the escort commanded by Sub-Lt Grincourt of the 2nd Zouaves: the whole of the French Contre-Guérilla infantry and cavalry, and No. 1 company of the Foreign Regiment in addition to the Sudanese. Once the convoy attained Chiquihite, the exposed plain was left behind and the foothills toward the mountains were the kind of country where cavalry are at home. Here the Sudanese and French infantry ended their unusual mission and returned to their bases.

In August, the Veracruz command sent an expedition to Minatitlan, a town and port on the Rio Coatzacoalcos, not far from the Gulf of Mexico, 160 km east-south-east of Veracruz. The government of the United States maintained a consul there whom the French suspected of being in contact with the fugitive Republican governor of the province.

To anticipate an armed descent upon the town by General Alejandro Garcia of the Republican eastern command, with the intention of seizing the customs revenue, Maréchal sent about 1,000 men, including 60 Sudanese of No. 1 company. Upon their arrival, after several days' march, the enemy retired without fighting.

The French occupied the town until 23 March 1864, with the ever-present danger of raids by lurking bands of *guerrilleros*. The garrison blockaded itself within the defended perimeter of the town. The troops felt keenly the constriction of movement and resulting boredom. There was one Sudanese casualty, a good soldier, Pte. 1st cl. Othon/Ittum Sudan, who had won distinction in the train ambush of 2 October 1863 and later joined the garrison. He died of fever, "his condition not improved by his addiction to the local liquor."[25]

5. The Railway

The railway defended by the Sudanese battalion had a recent and modest history. In 1855 the then president of Mexico, Antonio de López de Santa Anna, whose long career in and out of office manifested a genius for survival, granted a concession for the construction of a railway between Veracruz and

Mexico City to Rosso Brothers who transferred the concession to a Mexican financial grandee, Don Antonio Escandón. Under his patronage, the infant railway main line from Veracruz was completed as far as San Juan del Rio, a riverain village 40 km from the port, while a branch line of 18 km reached Medellin, on the left bank of Rio Jamapa, a strategically important point for the defense of Veracruz.

A colored sketch map of Veracruz by French military engineers depicts a railway issuing from the port at a mole built about half-way along the sea frontage of the town and aligned on a trace between the town wall and the sea in a west-south-westerly direction, still hugging the town wall, then turning south-west for about 2 km. There, the completed branch to Medellin left the main line.[26] Later, with the dredging of the harbor and building of quays for deep sea ships, the present railway terminus was constructed on the north-west side of the port under the limited shelter provided by the low coral island of San Juan de Ulúa.

The rolling stock of the railway company was ramshackle. The ancient locomotives of 2- 4-0 wheel formation and "haystack" fireboxes are unidentified by experts of locomotive history at the time of writing. The passenger coaches were obsolete stock from New York. The four-wheeled goods waggons *looked* British, but their origin is uncertain.

The further railhead was extended toward the foothills, the higher and healthier it became. The first station out of Veracruz, La Tejeria, at km 15, on the swampy dunes of the coastal plain, was only 36 m above sea level, a breeding-ground of disease. La Soledad, at km 42, stood at 47 m, only a little less unhealthy. But at Paso del Macho, 76 km, the railhead until the end of the French occupation, the altitude rose to 406 m, distinctly healthier. Cordoba, only another 30 kilometers ahead, was a veritable hill station, 850 meters above sea level.

At the time of the Sudanese arrival at Veracruz, the military commander at the port was pressing for the track to La Soledad to be made secure for the heavy loads of railway engineering material. This material was awaiting transport to complete the five-span wood girder bridge over the river Jamapa at the west end of the station. General Forey conducted the siege of Puebla on the plateau relying entirely on road transport to the siege works. He was now able to assure the war minister in Paris that the bridge would be open on or before 5 June.

The fall of Puebla and the enormous haul of prisoners of war from the city provided a serious problem of accommodation. Only the officers could be retained in custody. Other ranks were freed and eventually entered the Mexican Imperial army or rejoined the enemy or volunteered for railway construction work; Forey reported that 500 volunteers "well disposed for the moment" had signed on. On 13 July he announced that the crucial bridge at

La Soledad had been completed. Railhead advanced steadily toward Camaron and the provisional destination, Paso del Macho. The French engineers hoped that the line would be open for traffic from Veracruz to Paso del Macho by 31 August.

It was inevitable that this railway would be an attractive target for enemy attack. A traveller had written of one such raid on 10 June 1862 in which three French officers, seven other ranks, and two railway foremen and their wives had been killed on the train. More recently, the Veracruz command had reported two enemy raids on trains near La Tejeria, on 14 February and 12 March 1863, with one killed on each occasion. Dr. Chenu recorded an attack on the railway workshops at Veracruz on 31 March 1863 in which a number of workers were killed or wounded. On 6 April a more serious assault commanded by an able Republican officer, Colonel Honorato Dominguez, destroyed the railway construction camp at La Loma de la Rivera, 10 km from Veracruz.

By May 1863, the Sudanese had replaced the French troops guarding the railway, but it was not until 2 October that they had their baptism by fire. The daily train to La Soledad left Veracruz at 0700 carrying three French officers as passengers: Major Ligier of the Foreign Regiment,[27] Lieutenant Schérer of the Guadeloupe black Engineer Corps and Sub-Lieutenant Bontenaille of the Contre-Guérilla. Also among the passengers were several railway officials: Every Lyons, chief engineer, the chief mechanical superintendent, two mechanics, Fr. Savelli the priest of La Soledad, and several women and children.

The escort consisted of five armed Caribbean sailors, two sappers of the Martinique Engineers, and seven Sudanese:

Bakhit Badran, pte 1 cl., 1 coy, in charge of the squad
Bilal Muhammad, pte, 1 coy
Othon/Ittum Sudan, pte, 1 coy
Ibrahim 'Abd al-Rahman, pte, 1 coy
Muhammad 'Ali 'Abd al-Karim, pte, 1 coy
Muhammad 'Abdallah, pte, 4 coy
'Umar Muhammad, pte, 4 coy[28]

At 0720 the train reached a cutting in wooded country 8 k from Veracruz and 6 km short of La Tejeria, when the locomotive and the leading coach left the rails, which had been tampered with during the night by loosening the fishplates, the classic way to derail a train. At that moment the enemy, lining the lip of the cutting on both sides, poured volleys of lead into the stricken train while enemy cavalry closed in ahead and in the rear to prevent escape.

It was a desperate struggle. In the first few minutes Major Ligier fell mortally wounded; a Sudanese escort, Pte. Bilal Muhammad, was trying to lift the officer back into the train when he was killed, the first Sudanese to die in action in Mexico. As Ligier lay dying, Lieutenant Schérer took command. He later reported to the officer commanding Veracruz; "I was in the same coach as the escort when it happened. I at once assumed command and replied by a crisp fire. At the end of an hour of lively action the enemy fled and our little escort remained masters of the convoy. The enemy numbered about 150 men, 100 mounted and the rest on foot."[29]

In transmitting to the commander-in-chief the essence of Lieutenant Schérer's report, Maréchal wrote warmly of the Sudanese escort. "This engagement did the greatest honor to the Egyptians who fought it. These brave men, ably led by Lieutenant Schérer, who acted with remarkable courage and coolness, have nobly received their baptism by fire and repulsed with vigor an enemy nine times their number."[30] The affray claimed three dead and 14 wounded, the latter including Lt. Schérer and one woman passenger.

6. What Others thought of the Negro Egyptians

The official French designation for this overwhelmingly black unit of the Egyptian army was *le bataillon nègre égyptien*, a faithful translation of the official Arabic *al-orta al-sudaniyya al-misriyya*.[31] It must be borne in mind that in 1863 the relations between Europeans and Americans on the one side and Africans on the other were almost totally economic, with a dash of the fanciful and the patronizing. The real knowledge of the African peoples that reached the public in Europe and North America was small indeed. It is therefore to be expected that European and American travellers to Mexico would have nothing profound to write concerning the Sudanese.

Two such travellers make free with their ignorance. Charles Mesmer, who was passing through Veracruz, wrote that the Sudanese told him (presumably in Arabic with an interpreter) that the heat, dust, and mosquitoes there were as bad as they were in Egypt during the *khamsin*. He also makes the astounding statement that most of the Egyptian troops bore the French Crimean medal. On safer ground he noticed that a Sudanese escort accompanied each train in a special coach and that they were distinguished by the extraordinary cleanliness of their white uniforms.[32]

A second traveller, W. H. Bullock, who left Veracruz on 29 November 1864 on the same train as the papal nuncio, sheltered in his breast an unusual number of prejudices, some mutually contradictory. He was anti-clerical in an offensive way, a protagonist of Secretary of State Seward whose pronouncements on slavery, however well meant, were founded on ignorance. Bullock noticed the presence of a few companies of Nubians "borrowed against all international usage" from the Viceroy of Egypt. The author had evidently swallowed Secretary Seward whole.[33]

French opinion of the Sudanese in the field was not unanimous. A military medical officer, who may have spoken to or treated one of them, concluded on that frail basis that the Negro Egyptians were not Egyptians but Abyssinians. To press the point, he added a map of the Red Sea region.[34] Maréchal, the officer commanding Veracruz, wrote lyrically in a dispatch extolling the sterling qualities of the Sudanese under fire, calling them "these proud children of the desert" as though he were describing inhabitants of the Sahara. "A fine, well-disciplined body," wrote General Du Barail, "but most peculiar in their sleeping habits. They actually go to sleep exposed to the mid-day sun like lizards. And they awake without even a trace of migraine, whereas we, if we dared to commit such foolhardiness, would never wake."[35]

A French eulogist, short on ethnology, waxed romantic. Count E. de Kératry, a former officer of the French Contre-Guérilla, wrote

> this heroic detachment of Egyptians whose bearing and discipline do honor to their country. . . these brave children of the African desert, who have stubbornly stood up against enemy fire and fever in the most unhealthy parts of the hot regions, have earned the right to the gratitude of both Mexicans and French. Their uniform, entirely white, of exquisite cleanliness, is well known in the State of Veracruz and inspires lively terror.[36]

Indeed, the terror the Sudanese inspired in a romantic female mind can be appreciated from the experience of the Countess Paula Kollonitz, a lady-in-waiting to Empress Carlota. With greatly daring, she undertook the short but risky train journey from Veracruz to Medellin and back escorted by Sudanese troops; "tall and slender, dressed in white uniforms and armed with long guns and carrying daggers in their belts. As for me," she added, "I feel when I was in their hands less at my ease than I would have been had I no escort."[37]

Comment from the so-called Austrian Legion in Maximilian's service—officially the Austrian Volunteer Corps—was both serious and friendly on the one occasion in which Austrians and Sudanese fought, side by side, in the disastrous defeat at Callejon de la Laja in March 1865.

Citizens of the Austrian Empire rarely saw African blacks and then only as oddities at circuses and Punch-and-Judy shows. Or, if they happened to be bad as children, they read of them in the improving pages of Heinrich Hoffman's *Struwwelpeter*, about the Exemplary Blackamoor and the inky punishment meted out to the nasty little white bullies. Julius Uliczny landed at Veracruz in January 1864 as a private in the Austrian Legion. His ability later won him a commission, and after the war he published a history of the

Austrian-Belgian Legion in the Mexican campaign. In it he recounts the favorable impression given him by the Sudanese in their attractive white uniforms as they stared at the Austrians disembarking.[38]

Socially a world apart was Prince Carl Khevenhüller, an officer close to the Habsburg Imperial family and friend of Maximilian. He was bitterly anti-French and suspected Bazaine of double-dealing:

> The black battalion given as a friendly gesture to Napoleon by the Khedive Isma'il was stationed at Veracruz. They had already sustained heavy losses but they were forced to continue because, as French officers put it to me, they were for use simply as mincemeat. They were tall Nubians, black as soot, dressed in white uniforms with tarbushes on their woolly skulls. . .Only a few will ever see their fatherland again.[39]

Two final comments come from Americans, the first brief and friendly, by the author of a patriotic work for an American public: ". . . The railroad was guarded by Egyptians; superb black giants draped in the folds of their white robes and bearing themselves with proud dignity."[40] One gem from the treasury of pseudo-history must suffice: "the Legionnaires. . . were no more highly regarded by General Forey than such sorry outfits as the Egyptian Legion who wore fezzes and fell on their knees to Mecca and who were guarding the stores down on the quays of Veracruz."[41]

In welcome contrast is the testimony of an enemy prisoner of war, a cultured and generous Mexican, Lieutenant-Colonel Francisco de Paula Troncoso, a regular soldier who was captured after the second seige of Puebla. Troncoso (1839-1919) was a Veracruzano, a graduate of the military college. By 1868, he was a brigadier-general and later a professor at the military college. The following is an extract from his published diary:

> 8 June 1863. Finally. . .we reached La Tejeria where we were received by the wild Egyptians. These are some 150 Negroes who, they say, were presented as a gift by the Viceroy of Egypt to the Emperor Napoleon III—what a beautiful present! They are all black, young, very slim and very tall, without military training and as fierce as the crocodiles of their native land. They are clothed in white cotton cloth which makes their extremely black color show up all the more. The French officers told us that the officer commanding these Egyptians, a man of distinction, had died a few days before and we saw his horse, a most beautiful animal, richly caparisoned in the Arab style. In accordance with that officer's last will they embalmed his body in order to return it to Alexandria where his horse will also be sent.
>
> As there is no permanent housing in La Tejeria we are encamped in the open and the Egyptians surround us with a circle of sentries. These black

panthers do not know a word of French or Spanish and have been given orders not to permit anyone to take a single step beyond our lines. They do not speak to us but point their guns at us and, after this meaningful pantomime, we go back to our places. In the end a French officer told the commandant where these Egyptians should allow us to go, up to 50 or 60 meters outside the sentry lines. So, having become a little more humanized, some of the Crocodiles allow some French troops to go and buy us some bread, cheese, sardines and wine from the rickety canteen located 70 meters from our lines.

I pointed to a young Negro, a bugler, slimmer and even taller than his companions, toward the shop and gave him a peso. The Egyptian understood what was required of him and running up to the counter he helped himself, threw the peso over the counter and, still running, came away with a piece of sausage, a big hunk of bread, and a bottle of wine. One of the shop assistants followed him and got out of me another eight pesos. I gave two reals to my little Negro and shared with him what he brought me. He then began leaping up and down for sheer delight, making the most guttural noises I have ever heard. One of the guards was laughing with him but another, an austere one, did not approve. I ate with the greatest pleasure and so did Antonio Calderón, Angel Rodriguez, and others who were with me.

As soon as it was light I awoke and saw the Negro three paces away pointing towards the canteen. I gave him a peso and he brought me back a large mug of café au lait and a lovely bread roll. What joy! I wanted to reward him in some way and, while I was thinking about it, I noticed that his eye was fixed on my leather belt which was lined with blue and gold silk, partly frayed, a fact which was obvious because I had my waistcoat unbuttoned. I took it off at once and gave it to him, an act which left him eagerly admiring what was for him so magnificent a gift that he opened his eyes wide, put the belt on and started as he did last night to execute his leaps and somersaults, jumping up and down, shouting and laughing. Other prisoners also kept him busy.[42]

We are left to guess what the Sudanese thought of the Mexicans, if they thought of them at all. We cannot identify the pious vandal who scratched a graffito in Arabic of a passage from the Koran "In the name of Allah, the Merciful, the Compassionate" above a door in a church at Palacio Gomez, a good 550 km from the nearest Sudanese outpost. It could have been the handiwork of any Muslim soldier or deserter as an honest affirmation.

The only recorded incident of contact with Mexican Indians occurred when a posse of Sudanese mounted dispatch riders, including 'Ali Jifun, found them friendly and hospitable, warning the troops to be on their guard against enemy horsemen ahead and sending them on their way refreshed.[43]

We must not read too much into a single encounter, for in Mexican history there has long been friendly relations between former African slaves and Mexican Indians, with much intermarriage.

Once the Sudanese became accustomed to this strange land, their collective depression of spirit evaporated. Maréchal, their area commander, was well placed to weight their character. In a dispatch to the commander-in-chief he wrote, "Egyptian troops are carefree and contented. They see that we do all that we can for them and are grateful. For the rest they are grown-up children, easy to command and, if only you treat them gently, they will do anything you ask. From all the reports which I have received of them I can only write appreciatively." General Forey commented on their bearing under fire, "Ce ne sont pas des soldats, ce sont des lions."

Unfortunately their relations with the civil population in the state of Veracruz, who were mainly Republican, were embittered by an unexpected incident.

7. A Conflict of Laws

For the first few weeks after the arrival of the Sudanese in Mexico, the general opinion of their French allies was that they were disciplined soldiers, dignified in their bearing and, by European standards, exceedingly well-behaved. But European standards presupposed in French military minds a European way of thought and conduct. The Sudanese held to a different standard altogether in one important particular, the conduct of war.

In their Africa, war was all-out war. Quarter was neither asked nor given. The victors would cut off the head of the vanquished leader as a trophy of victory. The history of the Ottoman Egyptian regime in the Sudan abounds in stories of beheading by government troops. And when that regime was fighting its last battles, several Mahdist religious men were beheaded, and their heads sent to Khartoum for public display. The obscure Mahdist soldier who cut off the head of General Gordon at the fall of Khartoum took it to Omdurman in the belief that he had followed the traditional practice of war. In the ancient world the custom was widespread; David cut off the head of Goliath and bore it triumphantly to his people.[44] Islam inherited and embodied the ancient law in its own jurisprudence and, as in the case of the corporal at the goldfield on the Ethiopian border in 1839, Sudanese tribal opinion rejected an attempt to save the corporal's life by advancing extenuating circumstances which were inadmissible.

On a dark night in April 1863, a Sudanese sentry at the small fort at Medellin was shot. The bullet that killed him seemed to his comrades to have been fired from a group of detached houses not far from the fort. Next morning, at sunrise, the whole Sudanese detachment issued forth, attacked the houses, killed eight Mexican civilians, men, women, and children, and wounded others who escaped. In other words, the comrades of the dead sentry did exactly what they would have done if the sentry had been killed on the Ethiopian border or the Upper Nile. They were inflicting the appropriate punishment. If in the heat of indignation they had tilted the balance of retaliation too far, they recognized no other law.

Unluckily for the unsuspecting Sudanese, the law of retaliation formed no part of French military law, which recognized the legal rights of civilians. In the preliminary inquiry, the Sudanese freely admitted what they had done and asked only that all questions put to them by the court should be interpreted to them in Arabic.

After the preliminary hearing, eight soldiers were charged with murder or attempted murder. The court martial sat at Veracruz on 29 September and sentences were pronounced on the 30th.[45] The corrupt spellings of the names of the accused in the battalion roll (some barely identifiable) are here reconstructed:

Name, Rank and Coy	Sentence
Marjan Sudan Ballard [sic]	Death, reduced by Imperial decision to 20 years hard labor, later reduced to five years hard labor
Kunda 'Umar, pte, 2 Coy	Five years hard labor
Rihan Mikha'il, pte, 2 Coy	Five years hard labor
Sālim/Salīm Sa'id, pte, 1 Coy	Five years hard labor
al-Zubayr Ahmad, pte, 1 Coy	Five years hard labor
Rihan Hasan Rikabi, pte, 3 Coy	Five years hard labor
Kuku Muhammad Saghayrun, pte 1 Coy	Not guilty
Sa'id al-Hajj 'Abduh, pte, 1 Coy	Not guilty

In the absence of any record of the court martial, we are dependent on a note by J. C. Chenu:

> April 1863—Up to now the black Egyptians have given the impression of being men of gentle disposition although on occasion they have carried out their duties with some brutality. They also committed what must have been a premeditated crime which caused so much surprise among the French as to create a sense of outrage. The entire garrison of a small armed post at Medellin threw themselves on the inhabitants of some isolated houses near their fort with the intention of slaughtering them. Nine people, men, women and children, were killed, while several were wounded but managed to

> escape. In the courtroom the Egyptians manifested duplicity and pretended to know no other language than Arabic. Nine [six] of these men have been sentenced to imprisonment. . . . Their crime has been attributed to fanatical zeal.[46]

The opaque mind of Chenu rebelled at the insistence of the accused on using only Arabic during the trial proceedings. This, no doubt, led to endless delays and misunderstandings through faulty translating and interpreting by seconded sergeants and corporals from the Tirailleurs Algériens who were wrestling with the Egyptian interpreter over dialectical differences in the presence of an exasperated French court desperately trying to preserve its sanity.

These simple Muslim soldiers may not have known much Arabic, but what little they had was better than almost no French. The faithful of more than one religion derive strength from the infallibility of the written word. And when the written word is the language of the Koran, of their faith, they would have no other. By comparison French was merely the language of their non-Muslim allies, no more.

By the time of the French evacuation from Mexico, the prisoners had served more than three years in the prison of San Juan de Ulúa. A wise decision was made to return the prisoners to their companies, and all, with some relief, was forgiven. No evidence was found that the prisoners were subsequently pursued in the Egyptian military courts. It was a just solution to a legal impasse, for the French had shown legal naivety; they apparently assumed that everyone in Africa knew all about Grotius and the Law of War and Peace.

8. Did the Sudanese Serve outside the Tierra Caliente?

A reliable witness, Colonel Troncoso, whose diary as a prisoner of war we have just cited, wrote that the Sudanese patrolled the neighborhood of Veracruz together with a detachment of troops from Martinique and some marine infantry. He added however, that almost all these formations finished up at the siege of Puebla.[47] This, to an extent, is confirmed by ‘Ali Jifun, although his reminiscences were not always accurate and, not infrequently, were embellished. For instance, he claims to have been in the first advance on Puebla, an impossibility because that disaster to the French occurred several months before the Sudanese arrived in Mexico. He also claims to have gone on after the second, successful seige of Puebla to witness the surrender of Mexico City.[48] But Colonel Lahalle, who was serving there as a staff officer at the time, denies categorically that the Sudanese were ever in the capital, "not even the smallest detachment of them"; thus he never knew their officers. All that Lahalle did know about them for certain was that they spoke an unknown language, possessed great dignity in their carriage, and performed perfectly the duties assigned to them.[49]

'Ali Jifun's account of the capture of Puebla is of a different order of verisimilitude; on this he writes as an eye-witness, describing in graphic detail his part in the assault, his entry into the city with the triumphant Forey and Bazaine, the last house-to-house fighting, and the final clearing of the dead bodies from the streets. The battle order of the besieging forces omits the "*battalion nègre égyptien.*" Neither the French official papers nor the *Historique* of the battalion contains any reference to service outside the Tierra Caliente.

After these great events, 'Ali Jifun reveals his technique of narration. He recounts how he was sent with a detachment to flush out an enemy force near San Miguel. The enemy eluded them; but, in a deep gully, they captured a strange creature he described as "the daughter of a ghoul," which they crated and took down to Veracruz. There, during the absence of the Sudanese upcountry, he gravely assures his readers, public order had got so bad that the citizens petitioned Commander-in-Chief Bazaine to "let the Blacks go back." And so they marched back to the coast.[50]

The old man embroidered his narrative to tell a good story, to add vitality and color as though he were spinning a yarn at the camp fire. It would not have occurred to him that, in praising his battalion in the traditional way, he was bamboozling his present battalion commander who, had he been Sudanese, would have appreciated the dramatic bits and made allowances. It is also probable that the translator failed to understand all the 'Ali Jifun was dictating to him.

9. Liaison with Egypt: Isma'il Pasha

The ruler of Egypt during the four years of the Sudanese campaign in Mexico was Isma'il Pasha, grandson of Muhammad 'Ali Pasha. He succeeded his uncle, Muhammad Sa'id Pasha, ten days after the departure of the Sudanese for Mexico.

Isma'il's character has been exhaustively discussed, over-praised and over-vilified in a flood of books and newspaper columns in the European press. In brief, Isma'il could be charming and plausible to Europeans and Americans whose conversational patter and euphemisms he had learned to mouth with disarming skill. Inadequately educated for his role as ruler of

Egypt during a period of unprecedented technical change and foreign pressure, prodigally generous, he was brimming over with bright ideas imperfectly pondered. Sadly, he had no understanding of contemporary fiscal and banking principles and no self-discipline. He was removed from office in 1879 by the Ottoman government at the instance of his European creditors, leaving the Egyptians to repay a debt of over eighty million pounds sterling and to endure 60 years of foreign occupation.

That was the Isma'il of the foreigners' world. To the Sudanese in Mexico, he was to prove a considerate, even fatherly, master. He may be regarded as their last Mamluk father. His successor, Muhammad Tawfiq, was the servant of foreign masters. The Sudanese veterans served him well as his employees, but the family kinship was broken.

Notes

1. Noria, Spanish, from Arab. *nā'ūra*, a water wheel, appliance for raising water from a well or stream.
2. J. B. F. Fuzier, Extrait d'un rapport sur le service médical de Vera-Cruz pendant le mois de février 1863 (*Recueil de mém... militaire*, 1863, 3 sér., ix, 265-75). Médecin-major Francis Jean-Baptiste Fuzier (1824-80) studied medicine at Grenoble and Paris where in 1851 he presented his doctoral thesis on firearm wounds. After service in China and the Crimea he was principal medical officer at the military hospital of San Juan de Ulúa, Veracruz, where he served during the entire campaign without leave of absence. In the Franco-Prussian war of 1870-71 he was taken prisoner, escaped and joined the French army of the Loire.
3. L. Grandin, *Mémoires d'un chef de partisans de Vera Cruz à Mazatlán* (Paris, 1895).
4. Foret to War Minister, 24 June 1863 (S.H.A.T., G7, 1).
5. Same, 3 May 1863.
6. Du Barail, II, 343.
7. J. C. Chenu, *Aperçu sur les expéditions du Mexique*, 187, 210. Médecin-principal Jean-Charles Chenu (1808-80), a distinguished medical authority whose service began in the original French penetration of Algeria, 1830, and ended during the Prussian siege of Paris, 1871 as director of the Red Cross ambulance service for wounded troops.
8. Kousso, the dried panicles of the fertilized pistillate flowers of the tree *Bryera anthelmintica* growing in Ethiopia (Martindale, 28th ed., 94).
9. Chenu, 209-10.
10. See A Conflict of Laws, above.
11. Forey to War Minister, 30 May, 1863 (S.H.A.T., G/7, 1).

12. The Tirailleurs Algériens acquired the deceptive nickname "Turcos" after the Crimean War (1854).
13. Foret to War Minister, 24 June 1863 (S.H.A.T., G7, 1). Dispatch No. 360 was missing from this box.
14. We have not seen any postal documents of this battalion and do not know whether the men made use of the facilities offered.
15. Corps expéditionnaire du Mexique, bataillon nègre égyptien (S.H.A.T., G7, 224).
16. Charles Louis Désiré Du Pin/Dupin (1814-69) entered the Polytechnique, 1834 and was commissioned in the 61st Infantry Regt. After passing out of St. Cyr promoted Lt. 1839 and joined the topographical service, Algeria; Crimea, 1854, 1t-col. 1855; Italy (cavalry) 1859; Legion of Honour (cmdr) 1864; after return from Mexico col.; chief general staff, 16 division (Montpellier); unpublished memoirs now with S.H.A.T. His "réputation extraordinaire" acquired in Mexico ignored by DBF (art. E. Franceschini).
17. Arrêté du Commandant en Chef: Bataillon nègre égyptien, 19 May 1863. Plates 4-7.
18. The franc-sterling exchange in May 1863 was frs. 25.40 to £1 sterling, and frs. 26.00 to £1 Egyptian.
19. A base rate subject to adjustment.
20. For technical detail and illustration of models used in the Mexican campaign, see Willing, 56-70.
21. Maréchal to Forey, dispatch No. 31 of ?11 July, 1853 (S.H.A.T., G7, 124).
22. The French infantry were slow in adopting the tactical mobility of their enemy. A Sudanese cavalry troop was formed in late 1865.
23. Chenu, 211.
24. Jean-Joseph-Eugène Cazes, born 1832, cntered St. Cyr 1850, commissioned sub-lt., 65 Regt. 1852; transferred to For. Regt., 1860; capt. adj.-maj., 1863.
25. Chenu, 211.
26. Carte de la région aux environs de Vera-cruz, 1862, Brigade Topographique. . . 1:3600 (S.H.A.T., Génie, G7, III). For the site of the Veracruz railway terminus in 1863-67, see plate 15.
27. Jean-Jules Ligier (1824-1863) after one year in the ranks entered St. Cyr 1844; commissioned sub-lt., 39th Regt., 1846; Transferred to For. Regt., 1863.
28. *Historique*, 104-5 adds an eighth man, 'Abd el-Kal (?Āl, ?Khalīl) Yūsuf to the Sudanese escort. There was an 'Abd al-Āl, Yūsuf (No. 1 coy), but he does not appear to have been on the train.
29. Rapport, 3 October 1863 (S.H.A.T., G7, 124).
30. Rapport, 4 October 1863 (ibid.).
31. A word of mild caution here. The Egyptian Sudan was a political region which formed only part of the Bilād al-Sūdān, the immense geographical region extending from the Red Sea to the Atlantic, the savannah border or "coast" between the desert in the north and the tropical forest in the south and known by the Arabic word *al-sāhil* from the plural of which comes the

Arabic name of an inhabitant of the eastern, coastal, section of the region, *Sawāhilī*. In the present century the adjectival form *Sūdānī* (sing.), Sudanese, embraces all inhabitants of the Bilād al-Sūdān, yet it can still be taken in the political Sudan to mean "black Southerner" in a derogatory sense, so the use of the word in conversation has still (1991) to be tempered with discretion.

32. C. Mismer, *Souvenirs de la Martinique et du Mexique* (Paris, 1890).
33. W. H. Bullock (afterwards Hall), *Across Mexico in 1864-1865.*
34. S.S.A. Box 53, dossier 2, renseignements médicaux sur le régiment égyptien. Alexis Wolf, intendant-général of the French expeditionary force, introduced the Sudanese bn. to the readers of his reminiscences as Negroes from Abyssinia, "brave and disciplined, who were resistant to yellow fever and who rendered us a great service," (*Mes mémoires*, 298).
35. Du Barrail II, 344.
36. E. de Kératry, *La Contre-guérilla française*, 1869, 55.
37. P. Kollonitz, *Eine Reise nach Mexico*, (Vienna, 1867); tr. The Court of Mexico, (London, 1868).
38. J. Uliczny, *Geschichte des österreichisch-belgishcen Freicorps in Mexico*, 1868, 49.
39. B. Hamman, ed., *Mit Kaiser Max in Mexico; aus dem Tagebuch des Fürsten Carol Khevenhüller, 1864-1867*, (Vienna-Munich, 1983), 132-33.
40. M. Niles, *Passengers to Mexico: The Last Invasion of the Americas* (New York:, 1943), 248.
41. E. O'Connor, *The Cactus Throne* (New York, 1971), 79.
42. *Diario de las operaciones militares del sitio de Puebla en 1863*, 1909, 296-97.
43. 'Ali Jifūn, 326.
44. 1 Samuel 17-18.
45. Registre d'écrou du Fort Saint-Jean d'Ulloa, 1 Jan. 1865 (S.H.A.T., G7, 204 [bis]).
46. Chenu, 208.
47. Troncoso, op. cit. 295, entry for 5-7 June, 1863.
48. 'Ali Jifūn, 327-28.
49. O. Lahalle, "Mes souvenirs: extraits annotés par Suzanne Fiette" (Ph.D. diss., University of Picardy, Amiens, 1974), 426-27.
50. 'Ali Jifūn, 328.

War in 1864

1. **The Railway: Vulnerability and Progress**
2. **Combined Operations on the Rio Papaloapan; Fall of "Conejo"**
3. **Defense of Tlacotalpan; a Fight at Puente Garcia**
4. **Homesickness**

Chapter 4

War in 1864

1. The Railway: Vulnerability and Progress

The establishment of the Mexican monarchy gave illusory confidence to the international business world that an era of financial stability was approaching. A British company registered in London in 1864 as La Compania Limitada del Ferrocarril Imperial Mexicano (The Imperial Mexican Railway Co., Ltd.) acquired the perpetual concession to build and operate a railway between Mexico City and Veracruz from Don Agostino Escandón's firm.

Political stability was still deceptively far away. Veracruz and the railway were in a continual state of alert. The countryside around the port and on each side of the railway track was infested with guerilla bands, mostly Republican commandos actuated by patriotism. Others were driven by the lure of plunder, liable to be shot at sight by Republicans and French. These freebooters were known to erect checkpoints along the roads leading to the plateau and levy taxes on merchants carrying food to and from the port. Their mobility and the accuracy of their intelligence defeated the cumbrous efforts of the Imperial government agents and the French contre-guérilla to catch them. In the climate of sullen hostility in the villages of the Tierra Caliente, there could be no totally safe road or railway.

As everyone of any importance visiting Mexico City from abroad traveled by the most direct and relatively safest rail and road route, the Sudanese escorted a small procession of celebrities: the Imperial couple, generals, diplomats and churchmen, among them a papal nuncio. Some wrote gratefully of their warlike guardians.

On 29 May 1864, the Emperor Maximilian and Empress Carlota (Charlotte, daughter of Leopold I, King of the Belgians) disembarked at Veracruz and entrained to Loma Alta at km 61, the construction railhead at the time. The Imperial party numbered 85 passengers and 500 pieces of baggage. The Imperial train was escorted by a detachment of Sudanese. From Loma Alta, the party traveled in great discomfort in sturdy country diligences up the rough road to the capital.

Monsignor Pier Francesco Meglia, titular Bishop of Damascus, was sent by Pope Pius IX to confer with the Emperor Maximilian over the disposal of Church property confiscated and sold to the public by the former Republican government. The nuncio landed at Veracruz on 29 November, and on 1 December left the port in a special train composed of three "old-fashioned New York nine-passengers coaches," one for the nuncio and his entourage, one for the general public, and one for the Sudanese train escort. A fellow-passenger noted that the train had difficulty in clearing the wooden bridge over Rio Jamapa at La Soledad.

2. Combined Operations on the Rio Papaloapan: Fall of "Conejo" and Tlacotálpan

During a period of relative calm in the area, General Alejandro Garcia built an entrenched, fortified camp on a sandy summit in the range of low hills on the right bank of the estuary of Rio Papaloapan. The artillery commanded the river approach to the small city of Tlacotalpan. Great things were expected of the new, square camp with gun emplacements at each of its four angles and its complex entrenchment. Men called the place El Conejo, the coney, and by extension, the rabbit warren.

Lack of discipline was the greatest enemy; General Garcia was badly served by his officers there. The loneliness of the site invited illicit distractions. Comandante Campos was shocked to find prostitutes were admitted and valuable stores and equipment, such as a long chain for stretching over the river to bar the passage of French gunboats, were missing.[1]

The reduction of this inconvenient enemy barrier was entrusted to Major Maréchal who commanded a mixed force of 600 men. Of these 600, 234 were Sudanese participating for the first time in a combined operation with the French navy. With them was a detachment of 100 men of the Austrian Volunteer Corps, an unverified number of Martiniquais volunteers, and a troop of Mexican Imperial cavalry under Colonel Figuerero. Maréchal and his force sailed from Veracruz in the troopship *La Drôme* on the evening of 8 July. Next morning the troopship crossed the bar at Alvarado escorted by three armed warships—two gunboats, *Ste Barbe* and *Tactique,* and a small steam pinnace. Comandante Campos, to whom we owe this narrative of the battle, states that the force disembarked at a point opposite Alvarado at the foot of "Alto Liman," and that from there the column marched in an upstream direction toward Conejo by the sea side ("la playa del mar") on the right bank of the estuary. 'Ali Jifun, or his translator, who mispronounced it "Koneklia," well remembered the suffocating heat on the road, how he and his comrades slaked their thirst by mixing orange juice from the fruit growing by the roadside with the brackish water of the river.

Maréchal's dispositions clearly point to good intelligence: he knew where he was going despite the enemy's secrecy. At midday, the advancing column reached a lower outpost of the main work called l'Entrado del Miadero. The Republican commanders, Lieutenant-Colonel Juan Zamudio and Diaz Lagos, had been warned by the sighting of the French gunboats and at once opened fire.

From this moment, the French and Mexican reports of the action conflict. For Maréchal, all was plain sailing. The enemy put up a short resistance when Colonel Figuerero's cavalry galloped ahead while a detachment of Egyptians and Martiniquais volunteers sealed off the paths leading from the wooded summit. The enemy, now exhausted, abandoned its positions and left 65 prisoners, 5 of them officers, and about 100 dead. French and allied losses were light: 5 wounded. The Egyptians came through unscathed.

The gunboats were now softening the entrenched camp on the summit by continuous bombardment of the gun redoubts. At 1800 hours, the French entered the fortified camp and, without further fighting, seized six field guns, a mountain gun, and ammunition of various kinds.[2]

The next morning, 10 July, Maréchal, having a small garrison left, including 14 Sudanese, ferried the rest of the column to the left bank of the Papaloapan on the decks of the gunboats and occupied Tlacotalpan. This placed its considerable customs revenue in French hands. Finally, on 12 July, Maréchal placed a garrison of 214 men, 103 of whom were Sudanese, at Tlacotalpan under Lieutenant Lachaud,[3] the officer commanding Medellin; while Maréchal himself, with the remainder of the force, returned to Veracruz on 13 July after an absence of four days.

In his dispatch on the operation, Maréchal particularly mentioned Captain Husayn Ahmad (No. 1 coy) who was later decorated with the Legion of Honor; Lieutenant Faraj Muhammad al-Zayni (No. 3 coy), and his own aide de camp, Lieutenant L.J.F. Waldejo. Waldejo had "crossed impossibly exposed positions under a hail of lead to carry out my orders" and finally led the Sudanese in the actual assault, the first to enter the camp.

On the conduct of other Sudanese ranks during the assault, he recommended Sergeants Hadid Farhat (No. 1 coy), Marjan 'Ali al-Danasuri (No. 4

coy), and Private First Class Sa'id Muhammad al-Hajj (No. 2 coy) for the award of the Military Medal. On the conduct of the "Egyptians," Maréchal waxed eloquent: "these Egyptians, who give quarter reluctantly, have made an enormous killing, I have never before seen so much energy put into fighting, and all in absolute silence. Only their eyes spoke; they were admirable in courage as in spirit."[4]

The destruction of "Conejo," on which so many hopes had been placed, plunged the enemy in gloom. Towns and villages on the navigable river Papaloapan were now exposed to bombardment by French gunboats based on Alvarado.[5] The Republican command decided to abandon Tlacotalpan and retire into the interior. The citizens of the small city were permitted, if they wished, to abandon their homes to escape what Comandante Campos calls "the savagery of the Egyptian Legion."[6]

The comandante dramatized the moment when he wrote of the last retreating Republican rearguard catching sight in the distance of the enemy flotilla ascending the broad river in line astern led by a steam pinnace followed by the gunboats *La Foudre*, *Le Tonnerre*, *La Tempête* and the last one whose name he cannot recall.[7] Some moments later, at a signal from *La Tonnerre*, the line of ships anchored, the boats were slung out on davits and lowered into the water to be immediately filled with Egyptian infantry. The Egyptians were landing in front of the market place as the last Republican officers were galloping south to join their retreating army. Unable to rid himself of the memory of the Sudanese massacre of Mexican civilians at Medellin two years before, the comandante added that his men were doing everything possible to avoid another disaster at the hands of the "ferocious, cruel, and savage enemy."[8]

3. Defense of Tlacotalpan: A Fight at Puente Garcia

On 14 July, the day after Major Maréchal's column returned to Veracruz, General Garcia mounted a swift attack on Tlacotalpan from the south, over a bridge across a small stream running east to west, upstream of the little city. The action began at 0700. Garcia led about 500 men into battle, mostly regulars of the Zaragoza battalion whose base at that time was at Cosamaloapan, 50 m upstream. Lieutenant Lachaud went forward with little more than a detachment of 65 Sudanese and 75 cavalrymen of the Imperial Murcia regiment, taking up his position 300 m from the bridge. The Republican force, hidden in an impenetrable wood nearby, received the French force at point blank range. Without delay, Lachaud led his infantry into the wood with a bayonet charge for which his cavalry could render them no support.The two sides fought in close combat. In the scuffle, Pte 'Abdullah Husayn was observed to run a Mexican through with his bayonet and hold him at arm's length in the air. Shortly after, when the fighting had slackened a little, Lieutenant Lachaud, who already had had his horse shot out from under him, fell pierced by a bullet which entered his right eye and came out by his right ear. Sub-Lieutenant Vauclair at once took command.

After an hour of fighting, both sides drew off exhausted. The cavalry were unable to take part in this infantry free-for-all and remained powerless in the rear. According to the French, it had been a bloody affair: the enemy had lost an uncounted number of dead and abandonded 121 wounded on the field—not miscellaneous *guerrilleros* but hardened regular soldiers. Four Sudanese died and 17 wounded. The dead were Cpl. 'Abdallah Husayn and Ptes Faraj Muhammad Kan'an (3 coy); Nasib 'Abdallah and Sid Ahmad (4 coy).

Maréchal reported to the commander-in-chief that every man had nobly done his duty. "Outstanding were Lt. Faraj 'Azazi (1 coy) who commanded his men exceedingly well during the action; Sgt. Hadid Farhat (1 coy); "Agui Sa'id Mohammed al-Agha 'Abdallah Husayn Pacha" [sic] (3 coy); Pte 1 cl. Kuku Sudan Kabbashi (1 coy); Sgt Marjan al-Danasuri (4 coy) and Pte (now Cpl) 'Abdallah Husayn (3 coy) for whom I ask the award of the Military Medal as much for the energy which he had displayed in the combat as for the serious wound which he has received and the number of men whom he has killed."[9]

A backstairs view of the action came from E. Serdan, the Imperial town magistrate of Alvarado, in a letter to his superior, the Imperial prefect of the Veracruz district, dated 14 July:

> Just recently I heard from the captain of the Martinique troops here that 500 Republicans had attacked the Imperial forces at Tlacotalpan and at 11.00 a.m., when an officer came to bring the news, the fight was still going on. It seems that there were some tragic casualties among our men including a captain [Lieutenant Lachaud] who was shot in the forehead. . .Praise God there were no further casualties. The gunboat *Santa Barbara*[10] will probably reach Tlacotalpan by 6 o'clock this afternoon.

The most graphic account of this untidy, heroic action comes from the enemy. With patriotic fervor Comandante Campos wrote:

> The republicans attacked and routed the Egyptians. The idiots had completely destroyed the commemorative stone on the Garcia bridge and dug out the metal lettering thinking that it was silver when it was simply lead. Captain Rodriguez swore "I'm not leaving until I get one of those Blacks" and he fired into a group of them who were taken completely by surprise and covered with

> confusion rending the air with savage and most disagreeable yells all the more ferocious because they were uttered in their guttural language, their surprise sharpened by their not knowing whence the shot had come. Rodriguez and his officers started firing and called for reinforcements as more Sudanese commanded by Lachaud arrived. Firing now became general.
>
> A big black man, truly handsome in spite of his ugliness and the fantastic appearance of his uniform, clambered up a coconut palm near the bridge, his rifle slung on his shoulder, squatted among the fronds and began shooting at the Republicans below but was himself shot down by a sergeant from Tlacotalpan. This was the last shot in the action as the remaining Egyptians ran off. Our men who suffered only a few wounded retired taking with them trophies which they removed from the bodies of the Sudanese dead such as Mameluke short jackets and fezzes from the uniforms and, as curios, some long rosaries of rare large beads, some like relics, and a very strange kind of guitar with a long neck and a body made as though from a large gourd with only three strings. . . .Such was the encounter at the bridge called El Puente Garcia, a triumph of little practical military importance but of great moral value to [Republican] troops and civilians alike.[11]

Another version of the French bombardment of the armed camp of Conejo and their first occupation of Tlacotalpan comes from a little-known denunciation of the brutalities committed by the invaders on the inhabitants. As for the Egyptians "They entered houses and dragged out bedsteads, carpets and mosquito nets which they piled up in the main square making it look like a Bedouin camp." Under orders from Commandant Maréchal "they burnt several factories upstream of the town." But the writer insisted that "truth and justice demand record that the Egyptians, however perverse and cruel, fought in the action of Puente Garcia with determination and courage."[12]

By early August, the 17 wounded men had recovered sufficiently to travel, and on August 7th the small garrison was ordered to leave the town and arrived at Veracruz on the next day. The French attributed the lightness of their wounds to the *guerrilleros'* habit of overloading their small arms with a bullet plus a miscellany of lead pellets, which lessened the accuracy of the bullet's path and weakened its ballistic force. With the short effective range of a poorly maintained rifle, the object was to produce a spraying effect simulating the action of a shot gun. The operation had taught the French a hard lesson; there were not enough troops available to maintain the luxury of an outer defense perimeter for Veracruz as far distant as the Rio Papaloapan, deep in enemy country. Hereafter, until a few weeks before the evacuation, the Rio Blanco was to become the southern limit of French deployment. The sheer ubiquity of the *guerrilleros* prevented anything approaching an enemy-free zone around Veracruz.

Travelers through Veracruz in 1864 repeat a story that a band of Republicans rode up to the town gates, lassoed the "Nubian" sentry and carried him off with them. There does not appear to be any official confirmation, and the battalion nominal roll does not contain any endorsement to the name of a soldier disappearing in this way at that time.

3. Homesickness

Disease, if not the enemy, had taken a heavy toll on the battalion in its first year away from Egypt. The French military medical service reported that what they diagnosed as typhus killed 24 Sudanese; next came lung infections with 11 deaths; and dysentery and diarrhea claimed 11. The only battle casualty until July 1864 was Pte Bilal Muhammad (No. 1 coy) killed in the defense of the ambushed train on 2 October 1863.

A more insidious malaise was homesickness. By August 1864, the continued dispersion of the battalion in small detachments was fostering a feeling of isolation among the men. They had been passively homesick all along, but isolation had fostered brooding among small groups. And if they were mercifully free of yellow fever, they were still prey to various other diseases which, although in decreasing severity, nevertheless continued to erode the morale as well as the bodies of these increasingly lonely soldiers. As their battalion *Historique* states with a touch of unction: "most of them being married and the fathers of children, one can imagine the desire which they have of returning to the land of their birth for which the Negro race has so intense a love."

To distract them from worrying about their families, Maréchal kept them continually on the alert with frequent new postings and patrols. But, no matter how homesick they felt for the Nile, they never slackened their military efficiency, but officers and men felt that they needed a rest. The battalion commander addressed their petitions to Isma'il Pasha who replied:

> We have received your communication bearing news of the actions of yourself and the officers of the Egyptian Sudanese Battalion proving your bravery and resolution in battle in the face of the enemy. Your courage and skill have won the admiration of the French nation. We are exceedingly grateful to you for the way in which you have cherished the honor entrusted to you by the Egyptian government. You and your officers have won high praise and renown. You have fulfilled our expectations by your alertness and good discipline in carrying out the orders of the French commander-in-chief. Our gratitude is dependent upon your winning by your deeds the gratitude of that same commander and his French army; indeed the cordial relations between the

Egyptian government and the French depend upon favorable actions and mutual help. So that, since you have been sent by the Egyptian government, your duty lies in doing everything possible to earn their gratitude and win their acclaim. If God Almighty wills, when your mission is concluded and you return home, we shall be best disposed and most willing to show our gratitude for your praiseworthy services. He who treads the path of trust and high endeavor, may he with joy attain his aim. And now we have given orders on the petitions of the officers who are waiting for replacement for the fallen. These petitions are returned to you for distribution, each to its author, together with a suitable expression of our gratitude to each for his trusty service.[13]

To the Director of the War Office the Khedive wrote:

We have received your communication of 15 jumada 1, 1281 [16 October 1864] and the attached report by the French officer Ségur concerning the Egyptian battalion in Mexico, and its translation. We are aware from the diary of the battalion adjutant-major that they have lost 68 men out of the original strength of 446 excluding the civilian interpreter, leaving 378 alive. Please inform the French officer how pleased we have been to receive his report. You are also to arrange pensions for the orphaned children of the fallen officers and men in accordance with established custom. . . .[14]

Notes

1. Campos, 133-34, "Conejo," Spanish for rabbit (English cony), a military password for the entrenched camp, a rabbit warren in two senses. Dr. Chenu (*Apérçu,* 173) casually remarked that all Mexican troops were followed by great numbers of women "*soldaderas*" who perform the duties of "*cantonières maraudeuses.*"
2. Campos, 135-40; 'Ali Jifun, 186; *Historique*, 110-11.
3. Lt. Lachaud, 7th Infantry of the Line, *Historique*, 111, 113.
4. Louis-Joseph-Ferdinand Waldejo, born 1830; enlisted as a pte. 1854; commissioned sub-lt., For. Regt., 1863; lt., 1865.
5. *Historique*, 111-13; Toral, 203-4; information from captured Mexican Imperial documents.
6. Campos, 145.
7. Ibid., 149.
8. Ibid., 153.
9. Two names mistakenly written as one. Cpl. Sa'id Muhammad may have earned the title Hajj through having made the Pilgrimage, and the agha at the

end of his name would be appropriate, if then unusual, for a cpl. 'Abdullah Husayn's assumption of "Pasha" is unexplained. Maréchal added that the Sudanese killed twice their own number of the enemy.

10. [sic = Ste. Barbe]. Toral, 294, from captured enemy documents.
11. Campos, 161. The "guitar" would be one of the many Sudanese adaptations of the classical Arabic *rabab* widely known in the Sudan as *rababa* ('Awn al-Sharif, 420; art. Rabab; *The New Grove Dictionary of Musical Instruments*, London and N.Y., II, 117; 'Abdallah Muhammad 'Abdallah [and others], *Traditional musical instruments of [the] Sudan* [Arabic and English], Khartoum, 1985, 51).
12. See *Apuntes para la historia de la civilización Francesa*, Appendix 2(3).
13. Khedive Isma'il to Muhammad Almas Agha, *wakil* of the Sudanese battalion, 23 Jumada 1, 1281 [29 October 1864] (Taqwim, 575). Muhammad Almas was addressed *wakil* (in this sense acting) until his rank was made substantive. After his promotion had been confirmed he was henceforward addressed as *efendi*.
14. *Nāzir al-jihādiyya* (not wazir, minister, frequently accorded by foreigners). The nazir was a military or naval officer, a bureaucratic manager of a department with no political standing or cabinet office. His successors retained this status until the introduction of cabinet responsibility after the First World War. The term *jihādiyya* (organization for conducting Holy War) was supplanted in 1882-1883 by *ḥarbiyya* (war office) as closer in line with contemporary European usage and less offensive to non-Muslims. Coinciding with the increasing militancy of Middle Eastern states after the Second World War the designation changed to Ministry of National Defence, a euphemism already fashionable in Europe.

War and Weariness in 1865

1. First Expedition to Cocuite; Three Actions

2. Second Expedition to Cocuite; Disaster at Collejon de la Laja (Tlalixcoyan)

3. Siege and Relief of Cotaxtla

4. An Egyptian Cavalry Troop Raised

5. A Train Raid; Action at Las Palmas; Defense of Cocuite

6. Escorting the Empress Carlota

7. 'Ali Jifun Lassoed

Chapter 5

War and Weariness in 1865

1. First Expedition to Cocuite; Three Actions

The year began with constant pin-pricks by an audacious enemy leader named Garcia, "a clever miscreant" in the eyes of the French command. Had they known, he was not the unsavoury *guerrillero* of this name but Colonel Antonio Garcia, commander of a force of regular Republican troops. Comandante Campos, who was no flatterer, described him as "calm and calculating, skilled in the military arts."

The command at Veracruz mobilized a punitive patrol to "chase Garcia and his band with instructions to kill every enemy armed bandit they found." The force was commanded by Lieutenant Chesneau of the Foreign Regiment, the commandant of Medellin. It was composed of 70 Sudanese under Sub-Lt. Baron and a detachment of 40 Mexican Imperial Mounted Police. The column set out from Medellin on the evening of 21 January 1865 and arrived by forced marches at Paso del Limon on the Rio Blanco at 15.30 hours on the 22nd. The river was almost fordable at that time of year, so they crossed two at a time each man holding the stirrup of a swimming cavalry horse. Two Sudanese were drowned in the crossing.[1] The enemy had prepared to defend it. Chesneau's force went forward at once and, after a lively defense, the enemy retired. Chesneau had hoped to arrive that evening at Cocuite but, after an exhausting march, he did not arrive until 22.00 hours that night. The men had already been in action that day and had marched 68 km. They were dead tired, so they bivoacked for the night.

At dawn on 23 January the force advanced; Sub-Lt. Baron with 35 Sudanese were on the left flank of the assault. The enemy doggedly resisted, disputing every tumble-down hovel. Some tried to escape into the surrounding woods; these the Sudanese dispatched. Twenty-two Mexican bodies were counted when the assault was over. Only then was it disclosed that the enemy commander was not Garcia but the guerrillero "Pillardo" Sala, "notorious for his ferocity." A French innkeeper in Cocuite told Chesneau that the enemy force they had defeated numbered at least 300 men, but there was a second unit of about 350, well disciplined and well equipped, led by Colonel Antonio Garcia himself.

It had been a hard fight; the Sudanese and their Mexican allies each had had two men killed and three wounded. Chesneau had his horse shot under him.

On the strength of this action, Chesneau decided to carry out a reconnaissance up the left bank of the Rio Blanco. He re-crossed the river at Paso del Limon, again crossing two at a time with each man holding on to the stirrup of a swimming cavalry horse.

During the rest of January 23 the enemy lay low. A curious thing happened. As the column marched through the villages they noticed that there were no men to be seen, only weeping women. When questioned, the women, after much prevarication, admitted that their menfolk had been forced by the enemy to take up arms and join them. So after threatening some of them, Chesneau learned that Antonio Garcia's force had been reinforced by the survivors of their battle that morning and by other small groups and were ready to bar the passage of troops in the gorge of El Palmar.

At 0600 on the 24th January, Chesneau led his column toward the enemy whose dispositions showed clearly that their commander was a competent soldier; Chesneau estimated his enemy at 300 infantry and 100 well-mounted cavalry. He was at last convinced that he was in the presence of a unit of the Republican regular army.

Chesneau immediately attacked. At the outset of the battle of El Palmar, the Sudanese soon dislodged the enemy from the heights of the defile and the latter took cover in a grove, nearly 5 km long, of royal palms. There, for close to two hours, the enemy kept up their fire in a sniper's combat. Then they drew off and, with their wounded, made for the nearby woods and disappeared. Altogether they left 62 dead of whom three were regular officers with epaulettes, a rare sight in the Tierra Caliente. Among the casualties on the French side were two Sudanese killed[2] and three wounded. Baron had his horse shot under him.

On 25th January the column returned to Medellin. Lt. Chesneau had had his first experience of leading Sudanese into battle and wrote enthusiastically in his report to Veracruz. In his report to general headquarters Maréchal incorporated Chesneau's praise:

It is difficult to render full justice to the bearing of these excellent men in the face of the enemy, their patience in putting up with privation and fatigue, their enthusiasm under fire and on the march. As every man among them has done his duty admirably in these three actions, Lieutenant Chesneau thinks that each Sudanese in his column is worthy of praise and, in the presence of merit shared equally by them all, he has confined himself to submitting to me the names of three soldiers who were the most seriously wounded. But I feel I ought to cite Lt. Faraj Muhammad al-Zayni (3 coy), Lt. Muhammad Sulayman (2 coy), Pte 1 cl. Jaddayn Ahmad (2 coy), Pte 1 cl. Idris Na'im (2 coy), Pte 1 cl. 'Abdallah Sudan (2 coy), and Pte Muhammad al-Riqq (2 coy)."3

2. Second Expedition to Cocuite: Disaster at Callejón de la Laja (Tlalixcoyan)

In all the fighting the Sudanese experienced in Mexico, this was the only action which involved them in the international politics of Napoleon III. Commandant Maréchal commanding the Veracruz area led an expedition that, for a few days, brought the Sudanese into contact with another nation having a strange resemblance to their own: the Österreichische Freicorps, the Austrian Volunteer corps, which had been recently recruited from all parts of the Austrian Empire to support the Hapsburg emperor Maximilian in Mexico.[4] Both Austrians and Egyptian Sudanese were drawn from heterogeneous ethnic and linguistic backgrounds and each was united politically by an official language: German for the Freicorps, Arabic for the Sudanese. During off-duty hours the men of both forces would speak their own native languages among themselves. Each force professed a common religion: the Freicorps Christianity, the Sudanese Islam.

The Austrian Legion,[5] as it was popularly called, was an integral part of the Mexican Imperial army; the detachment under French command had the same allied status as the Sudanese. Two officers were in charge of the 96 Austrian volunteers: Lt. Hugo Codelli (Baron Codelli von Fahnenfeld-Sternengreif) in command, and Lt. Friedrich Mickl. Each officer led a half-company. Codelli was the better educated, the more literate, the more restrained; Mickl a bad speller, more expansive, and a draughtsman who illustrated his combat report (Gefechte Relation) with three field sketches from one of which our colleague, Erich Korger, has devised a diagram of the engagement (plate 13).

The 100 Sudanese commanded by their *chef de battaillon*, Capt. Muhammad Almas, entrained with the Austrians in the evening of 26

February for Medellín where they joined a French artillery detachment of Martinique Engineers with a mountain howitzer and a troop of Mexican Imperial cavalry. The French commander of the column, Commandant Maréchal, was accompanied by his aides de camp, Sub-Lts. Waldego and Baron.

At 0600 hours on 27 February the combined column marched south to Rancho de Vaqueros where they rested for the night. In his action report, Codelli remarked on the presence of enemy scouts hovering in the distance during the march and the accuracy of their intelligence of the French column's movements.[6] There were slight brushes with enemy scouts hovering in the distance along the route to Tlalixcoyan, which the column reached at noon on 28 February. Here Maréchal learned that the enemy were entrenched and waiting for them at Paso de Vaqueros, 6 km south on the further bank of the Rio Blanco. After a two-hour rest at Tlalixcoyan, the southward march resumed and at 1500 hours reached the river bank opposite the enemy's trenches amid a hail of bullets from two solidly built redoubts delivering a troublesome crossfire at the ford. A few shells from the howitzer—Maréchal himself pointed the range—penetrated a corner of one of the redoubts. Lt. Mickl reported: "after ineffectual rifle fire I and 20 men plunged into the river and reached the further bank at the same time as the Mexican cavalry and some of the Egyptians. We suffered one Austrian dead and three Egyptians wounded."

The enemy immediately abandoned both redoubts along with a dump of firearms and ammunition.

The troops crossed the river mainly with the help of the cavalry horses and a boat, demolished the earthworks and set fire to the huts left by the enemy. The column then marched an hour in the direction of Mistiquilla and bivouacked for the night on open grassland outside Cocuite. Lt. Mickl wrote:

> We did not now meet with the least opposition from the enemy even though the entire countryside was hostile. The French commander, Maréchal, had a fleeting notion that the aims of the expedition had now been completely fulfilled and he toyed with the idea of dividing the column in order that he, the Egyptians and the cavalry, should make the homeward march to Medellin in one day leaving the Austrians to make the homeward march in two days. However, in the course of the night he dropped the idea."

Early on 2 March, having burned the quarters that had housed the enemy infantry and cavalry in Cocuite, the column reformed. Passing through Tlalixcoyan they found all the houses locked against them except the priest's and he, according to the official dispatch confirmed by Codelli, refused to give information on the enemy's whereabouts. The column marched from Tlalixcoyan at 0600 hours in the following order:

Vanguard	20 Egyptians
Main body	95 Austrians
	80 Egyptians
	The howitzer and gun crew
	Staff and baggage
Rearguard	40 Mexican Imperial cavalry

'Ali Jifun denied that the priest at Tlalixcoyan had refused to give information about the enemy's position but simply warned them not to return to Veracruz by the more direct route which they were taking, as the road was most unsafe. 'Ali Jifun continued:

> Our commanding officer, however, considered that there was no danger, so the priest's advice was disregarded. Our path now lay through a forest in which there was a dense undergrowth of brushwood. The path was narrow and difficult, and the guide had the misfortune to fall from his horse and break his neck. Presently we heard shots and bullets coming through the trees. I was with the rear of the long, straggling column, and now a man marching near me was shot through the head. The order was passed along for the rear to close up and when we reached the remainder we found that [Maréchal] our commanding officer, a Frenchman, had been killed and all the gunners shot down. We attempted to form up and open fire in the direction from which the shots came, but the enemy were too many for us and we drew off until we succeeded in getting clear of the woods. Then Muhammad Almas Bey rallied us and urged that we could never go back without our commander's body and our gun. So we re-formed and succeeded in bringing out the gun and all the killed and wounded and finally we returned, much shattered, to Veracruz.[6]

The battalion *Historique* carries a story that, during the short halt at Tlalixcoyan, Maréchal had learned from a guide that the Republicans had prepared an ambush on the road ahead and were lying in wait in the gorge of Callejon de la Laja. In fact, unknown to the French commander, the enemy had been feverishly working all the previous night constructing an ambush in the narrowest part of the gorge. The *Historique* goes on to affirm that Maréchal decided to go forward and dislodge the enemy. This astounding statement, supported by 'Ali Jifun, was denied by Lt. Codelli, the Austrian commander, who was close to Maréchal until the French commander's death. In his report Codelli states that neither Maréchal nor he was aware of any ambush in the gorge ahead; both officers had been taken by surprise.

For an experienced officer to make so disastrous a decision is almost beyond belief. To enter the gorge without preliminary reconnaissance was risky enough but to go deliberately into a suspected ambush in a narrow gorge to dislodge an enemy of unknown strength by a frontal assault would have been an act of gross military irresponsibility.

It would seem that the authors of the *Historique*, seeking a heroic explanation, invented a bogus rationale for Maréchal's action.

The Austrian version was less melodramatic. Codelli writes:

> The gorge was so narrow and the enemy's fire so unexpected that the Egyptian advance guard gave way exposing the Austrians who were following and who now formed the front line which continued under heavy fire raining down on them from both ridges of the ravine. I found a gap in the abatis which barred our way forward and screwed myself through followed by my men. It was here that we and the Egyptians suffered our heaviest losses.[7]

Meanwhile Lt. Mickl found a small gap in the log barrier through which he and his men from the second half-company wormed their way to level ground and rejoined Codelli's half-company.

> Once the shaken column was able to extricate itself from the gorge on to the plain Lt. Chesneau, now in command of the column, fearing that the enemy would attack again ordered us to retire immediately.[8] There was no time to bury the dead and even Commandant Maréchal's body was left in the bushes with the weapons of the dead. Our troops marched on under the great heat with no water for two hours which we somehow survived when some of our men began to drop. Lt. Codelli pleaded with the commanding officer for a longer rest but Lt. Chesneau was obsessed by the danger that the enemy, "four times as strong as we, would be following us; it was vital to get to Medellin that day."

Chesneau also insisted on taking a longer, westerly, route to minimize the risk of being followed by enemy cavalry. He had no means of knowing that the enemy were so exhausted after a sleepless night of ambush-building that they could only limp back to Tlalixcoyan.

Lt. Mickl describes the march with moving realism:

> So we marched on and by 2200 hours reached Calentura on Rio Jamapa [sic, read Rio Atoyac] with half our men left behind on the road. Sixteen men caught up with us later having been revived in the coolness of the night but left the bodies of seven burnt-out, dead comrades along the road and saved themselves only by urinating in each others' mouths. At 0300 hours on 3 March we marched from Calentura and at 0700 hours arrived at Medellin. Here we entrained for Veracruz arriving at 1300 hours.

So the Austrian contingent had fared badly. Nine were killed in the ambush, seven died from exhaustion and thirst during the retreat. Six who were seriously wounded were abandoned in the gorge. Three superficially wounded men were able to march back with the column, and three previously unaccounted for were reported taken prisoner by the enemy.[9] The Austrian medical officer with the contingent, Senior Physician Capt. Unger, was wounded in the knee during the fighting and died in the military hospital at Veracruz on 28 March of the wound aggravated by typhus.[10]

The Sudanese casualties were all from No. 1 Company. The dead were Sgt. 'Uthman Abu Bakr, Cpl. Khayr 'Abd al-Fattah, Pte 1 cl. Khayrallah Ahmad, Ptes 'Abdallah Muhammad, Eimara [?'Umara] Marmi, Fadlallah Ahmad and Mursal Muhammed. The wounded were Cpl. Marjan Matar, Ptes 1 cl. Ramadan Kuku and 'Ali Idris, Ptes Kuku Sudan al-Kabbashi and Angalu Sudan (alias Angalu Habiballah). All five were mentioned in dispatches and awarded the French Military Medal.

The French deaths included Commandant Chef d'Escadron Maréchal and the ten gun crew from the Martinique Engineers; three officers were wounded, 25 other ranks killed, and 24 wounded.

Lastly, an enemy version from the very human but not always reliable memories of Comandante Campos:

> At 0500 on the 4th [read 2nd] March Antonio Garcia the commanding colonel and his adjutant walked up and down the Mexican lines quietly encouraging his men in an extremely tense situation. Soon they could hear the footfalls of marching men. Suddenly came the order to fire.

From here Campos's narrative broadly confirms the French and Austrian reports that all the gunners and then Maréchal himself fell dead by the side of their gun, and the Republican fire power then drove the French column out of the gorge and on to the plain. He admits that the French (including, of course, the Sudanese) returned and retrieved Maréchal's body but is loath to acknowledge that they also retrieved the gun. The Republicans recovered the bodies of Captain Camporada, who had commanded the Republican infantry from Boca del Rio, and another soldier; the only Republicans, he proudly writes, who were killed in the action, and then the victors retired exhausted to Tlalixcoyan. After their arrival there a Captain Garcia of the cavalry was summarily relieved of his command on a charge of mutilating, or condoning the mutilation of, Egyptians who died in the fighting by cutting off their ears from which was made a "disgusting, nauseating and bloody necklace."[11]

The hardship of the retreat revealed the contrast between the Sudanese and Austrian troops in respect of their health, and therefore their immediate military value in the Tierra Caliente.

To give them their due, the Austrians were only now undergoing the same harsh apprenticeship in adjusting their bodies to climate, dietary, and environmental changes which the Sudanese had survived two years before. Most of the Sudanese had been slaves acquired by the government for military service either by direct purchase or in lieu of taxes. They had been passed or rejected for military service by the regimental medical officer. Only the minority, "swept off the streets of Alexandria by the police at the last moment before sailing" would probably have received no medical examination.

The Austrian volunteers had been recruited in great haste with superficial medical checks. Several arrived with venereal disease contracted in Europe or in Martinique on the voyage to Mexico.[12] They were also subject to the same common fevers that afflicted newcomers to the fever belt, and they were not resistant to yellow fever. One of their officers wrote without malice of his hotch-potch of all manner of men including ambiguous patriots and self-seekers.[13] The author might also have cited the usual mixture of good and "less good'' to be found in every volunteer legion campaigning in other causes in Europe at that time.

The most consistent evidence for the cause of the disaster is that of Lieutenants Codelli and Mickl in their reports of the action. 'Ali Jifun's overriding loyalty to his dead commander was his chief concern. Comandante Campos was always a noble enemy who never wrote spitefully of the Sudanese. The least reliable version is the Sudanese battalion's *Historique* whose authors represented the action as a victory.

In his report to Paris, Marshal Bazaine made no judgement on what appeared to have been the dead commanders lapse in leading his column into a prepared ambush or alternatively in failing to reconnoitre the gorge before committing his force to unnecessary hazard. The commander-in-chief could not ignore the likely effect on public opinion in France of any official admission of military incompetence in a campaign widely unpopular at home.[14]

Emperor Maximilian, in a gesture expressing his good intentions, ordered the village of Camaron, on the railway between La Soledad and Paso del Macho, to be renamed Villa Maréchal. Camaron was already hallowed in French military memory in April 1863 by the heroic stand to death of a detachment of the Foreign Regiment against a Republican force many times its size. The Emperor's gesture was politely ignored. Callejon de la Laja was best forgotten.

3. Siege and Relief of Cotaxtla

Cotaxtla, a village on Rio Atoyac, was in two senses a post advisable to deny to the enemy: it was, like Tlalixcoyan, a useful advance post for the defense of La Soledad and for keeping an eye on the Rio Blanco Valley. The nearest enemy concentration was at Cocuite on the right bank of the river. Moreover, the villagers of Cotaxtla were known by experience to be hostile to the French.

It was therefore decided to place a small garrison there. Lt. Berge, military commandant of Paso del Macho, took command of a force consisting of 40 Sudanese from Veracruz and Paso del Macho, 30 Guadeloupe Engineers with a howitzer, 20 Mexican Imperial Exploradores (light infantry), and a troop of cavalry. They marched out of Paso del Macho late on June 23rd and arrived at Cotaxtla at dawn on the 24th where they found the village clear of the enemy. The gun and 30 Sudanese under the command of Lt. Gonsalve of the Foreign Regiment were left to man the post; the rest of the force returned to their base. Gonsalve and the Sudanese were there because the previous commander, a Mexican ally, had been found both careless and feeble and had been removed.

On 12 August the small garrison was strengthened by 20 more Sudanese. They had no sooner arrived at Cotaxtla than the post was set upon by 200 Republicans from Cocuite. The Sudanese resisted but judged it better to stay on the defensive and wait for help. When news of this emergency reached La Soledad next day, another party of 20 Sudanese was dispatched at 2100 hours to relieve their beleaguered brothers at Cotaxtla. Next morning, Lt. Bosler, military commander of La Soledad, received another 50 men from Veracruz and at once led them to Cotaxtla. The garrison was now led by Lieutenants Gonsalve and Salih Hijazi who had commanded the first reinforcement of 20 Sudanese. The men had taken refuge in a redoubt and, aided by their howitzer, had already beaten off several assaults. Only a lack of food and ammunition would have forced them to surrender, but the timely arrival of Bosler and his Sudanese saved them.

The defeat at Callejon de la Laja and the increasing calls on the Sudanese for service outside their appointed function—to defend the line of communication—intensified the desire of the French command for the relief battalion promised by the Khedive Isma'il for summer 1865. Now, in the middle of the rains, enemy bands had been crossing Rio Blanco from their bases on the right bank, and there had been several minor clashes in which the Sudanese had proved their worth. As Central Africans they accepted rain as a gift from God, as an element in the natural order; without rain they would die. To sheltered, urban Europeans assured of sufficient water, rain was simply a nuisance. On

15 September the officer commanding Veracruz reported that "these proud children of the desert [sic] show on these occasions a rare intelligence and devotion. They waited a whole night in ambush without budging, in pouring rain, to take some bandits by surprise." For another thing, "once these bandits were in the hands of the Egyptians they were well guarded. Never has it been reported that the Egyptians ever let their prisoners escape."[15]

4. An Egyptian Cavalry Troop Raised

The superior tactical mobility of the Mexican enemy over the more sedate French army was due primarily to the high proportion of Mexican mounted men to their total strength. In addition to a few squadrons of Republican thoroughbred cavalry recognized in Europe, there was the far greater number of what Europeans would loftily call mounted infantry riding local horses or, at need, mules, which the French used only as pack animals, and carrying an assortment of small arms including, toward the end of the war, breech-loading rifles and carbines from the United States.

It took the French two years to begin copying the mobility of the Mexicans by training part of their infantry as horsemen. Orders came from general headquarters to convert three companies, one from each of the three brigaded formations, to mounted cavalry squadrons: first the Foreign Regiment in June 1864, next the 2nd Tirailleurs Algériens in September 1865, and lastly the Sudanese Battalion during the autumn and winter of 1865. The Sudanese troop was intended to provide mounted scouts for patrolling the railways. Each man was to receive the same extra pay of one *rial* [? half peso] a day to be paid by the municipality of Veracruz in recognition of his contribution to the security of the town and port.

'Abd al-Rahman Musa (2 Lt., No. 4 coy) who had evidently received some mounted training before he came to Mexico, was put in charge of the training of the cavalry troop of 45 men, too few to rate in English military parlance as a squadron. These erstwhile infantrymen were not just a detachment of mounted infantry but cavalry in the classic sense, mounted on local-bred or U.S. horses and equipped as light cavalry with sabres and carbines. Their sabres were captured enemy stock.

5. A Train Raid; Battle of Las Palmas; Defense of Cocuite

On 7 October the line was cut and a train derailed at Arroyo de Piedra on one of the curves between La Purga and La Soledad. Aboard the train were Lt. Friquet and two unnamed Martinique soldiers, Loubet the sergeant in charge of the train, Pte. Vanderbendt of the Foreign Regiment acting as guard, a sergeant, and a corporal from Guadeloupe carrying a large sum of money mostly for engineering works.

It was a horrible affair. A band of about 200 *guerrilleros*, led by Sotomayor, a former prisoner of war freed by Emperor Maximilian, lay in wait for the morning train from Veracruz. The band had already been observed on the move between La Soledad and paso del Macho but there was no information that they were heading in the direction of Veracruz. At 0800 the train derailed. The enemy shot the unarmed driver, pillaged the rolling stock and robbed the passengers. The latter were taken some way off and sorted out; most of them, civilians, were released; but nine soldiers were killed in cold blood, among them Lt. Friquet of the Engineers, one native of Martinique, and Loubet.[16]

As soon as news of this attack reached Lt. Bosler, Military Commander at La Soledad, he relayed it to Veracruz and without waiting further set off with a small force to the scene of the attack. He succeeded in surprising the raiders who drew off in disorder, but not before they killed a Martinique soldier of his force and wounded nine others, one seriously.

Meanwhile at Veracruz on the night of 7-8 October, the Commander, Maj. Kermarek, collected all available troops and dispatched them by a relief train which left at 0100 hours, carrying 50 Sudanese under Sub-Lt. Baron, 18 Mexican Imperial cavalry under Col. Figuerero, 10 Sappers of the Martinique Engineers, and 90 Marines. On arrival at the derailed train, the Marines were sent back to Veracruz as no longer required. The Sudanese and the Figuerero detachment were detained for the pursuit of the bandits.

Lt. Bosler left with this mobile force to cut off the enemy's retreat. At 0700 hours on 8 October the vanguard, a detachment of 15 Sudanese cavalry led by 2 Lt. 'Abd al-Rahman Musa, charged the enemy in the ravine of Las Palmas followed by the main body under Lt. Bosler. After 10 minutes of brisk fighting, the 250 enemy, taken by surprise, broke off the action and decamped. Their flight was encouraged by the Sudanese whose blood was up at the crimes committed by this band in its raid on the train the day before. Bosler reported later that he had completely dispersed the band.[17] A Mexican, Manuel Mayoral, was recognized by a Sapper of the Martinique Engineers as having been a member of the band that attacked the train on 7 October. He was arrested and tried by a court martial at Veracruz on 1 November 1865.

The Sapper was the only witness; on his testimony Mayoral was sentenced and shot.[18]

Comandante Campos gave his version of the motive behind the raid. A brother officer had told him that a son of the guerrilla leader Molina had accused Colonel Dupin and his "imported bandits in French uniforms" of killing his father and two brothers in a raid on Molina's secret hide-out in the forest. In revenge for their deaths, the youth swore that he would kill all Frenchmen, all Mexican traitors, and all traitorous peasants. "If they want blood," he shouted, "they'll have it!" The raid on the train was the direct consequence of the youth's vow.[19] This story was known in the French camp. Both French and Republican versions suggest that Molina's widow, a woman of substance, provided the funds to mount the operation.

Colonel Dupin soldiered on until his conduct toward the Mexican guerrilleros became a liability to the Mexican Imperial cause and Emperor Maximilian asked Marshal Bazaine to remove him. However Bazaine had not lost confidence in Dupin's military ability and appointed him to succeed Maréchal temporarily as Acting Officer Commanding at Veracruz. Both men had a leading place in the Republican demonology; if Dupin occupied the role of Satan, Maréchal, the "callous ransacker of Republican widows' property," in Comandante Campos's words, ran him close.

6. Escorting the Empress Carlota

In December 1865 the empress paid a brief visit to the state of Yucatan, a short distance by sea across the Bay of Campeche. She had come from Mexico City by road and joined the railway at Paso del Macho where she was welcomed by the political prefect and notables who, with the empress's train escort of 30 Sudanese, had traveled from Veracruz the day before. Three detachments of Sudanese, each of 45 men, were based on La Soledad, La Purga, and La Tejeria for patrolling the railway track throughout its length.

The empress arrived at Veracruz to the roar of a 101-gun salute fired by Sudanese artillerymen trained in their art by the commander of the artillery park. The town garrison, made up of French marines with Sudanese and Austrian riflemen, lined the street from the railway station to the empress's quarters where the Sudanese mounted troops formed her personal escort. At 0400 hours on the following morning the empress's escort preceded the imperial *cortège* to the waiting steamer.

After a few days the empress returned from Yucatan when the same ceremonial order in reverse was observed. After her arrival in the capital, the empress made known to the emperor the fine service rendered to her by the

Sudanese battalion. In gratitude Maximilian issued a small supplement to the daily pay of the battalion of 1 medio (half a peso = fr. 0.33) and decorated three Sudanese officers, Acting Maj. Muhammad Almas, 1 lt. Faraj 'Azazi (1 coy) and 2 lt. Khalil Fanni (2 coy), with the Mexican Imperial Decoration of Our Lady of Guadeloupe. The Municipality of Veracruz gave the Sudanese a further daily allowance in recognition of their help in maintaining the safety of the citizens and their property.[20]

7. 'Ali Jifun Lassoed

'Ali Jifun recounts a wild west adventure:

> During the time when my company was garrisoning La Tejeria, a section was sent one day to look after the train which had been stopped at a place called Khor Limoon because the line had been destroyed at that point. I was cook to the company that month and while I was looking after my work a Mexican came in and told our officer that a large party of the enemy's horsemen was coming down with a view to looting the train before the line could be repaired. So the officer ordered me to get on his horse and gallop away to warn the section to be on the alert. I mounted as I was and hurried off with nothing but my knife on my arm, to carry out my orders.[21]

When I drew near I saw that the shawish [sergeant] in charge of the party had evidently been warned, for they were formed up in readiness when I arrived, and almost immediately after, the enemy's horsemen appeared. The shawish ordered me to gallop off for reinforcements, as the enemy was in considerable force; so I galloped off and almost immediately some of the enemy turned to pursue me. I urged my horse to his utmost but one of my pursuers, who was mounted on a fine white horse, drew away from the remainder and rapidly gained upon me. In spite of all my efforts this man drew closer and closer, and now I heard his companion urging him to lassoo me. Presently, coming still closer, he threw his rope and caught me straight across the shoulders. Then he turned his horse and I turned mine in order that I might not fall. But my captor rode faster than I could and I felt my arms pinioned into my sides until the knife I was wearing inside my elbow cut into my ribs. This drew my attention to the fact that I had a knife[22] which I could perhaps use; so, snatching it from its scabbard with my right hand, I cut the lassoo in two and went on my way toward the fort. My enemy also turned and endeavored to follow me; but by this time the fort was near and, my comrades coming to my assistance, the enemy retreated.[23]

Notes

1. 'Ali Jifūn, 186, gives their names as Ptes Kuku Bashir, (No. 2 coy) and Abd Elahi [sic = 'Abdallah] Kunjari, (No. 1 coy).
2. Their names were inadvertently omitted from Maréchal's dispatch to general headquarters (*Historique*, 121).
3. Appendix 1. cn. See names under coys.
4. A similar contingent of Belgian volunteers was recruited in honour of the Mexican Empress Carlota. There were no official Belgian-Sudanese military contacts.
5. Österreichisches Staats Archiv/Kriegsarchiv, Vienna: Mexikanisches Freiwilligen Corps, fasc. 11, 20 Nov. 1864, fo. 525 Codelli's dossier reveals that, as a private aged 17 he had fought against the Franco-Sardinian army at Magenta in the war of '59, and was soon after promoted 2 lt., i.e. military cadet.
6. 'Ali Jifūn, 186-87.
7. The obstacle which beset Codelli appears from his description to have been an abatis of felled trees and branches pointing outward, a military defence known in the Sudan as a *zarība*. Mickl's barrier proved to be a stockade of perpendicular logs.
8. Diagram, Plate 19.
9. Codelli and Mickl, combat reports with annexes. Brief description of the combat in *Der Kamerad, Oesterreichische Militär Zeitung*, Vienna, IV Jahrg., no. 31, 263-64, 21 April 1865.
10. Ibid., nos. 31, 264 and 36, 300.
11. Campos, 206-7.
12. Chenu also reported 40 cases of purulent ophthalmia.
13. Maj. von Schönovsky, *Aus den Gefechten des Österreichischen Freicorps in Mejico. . .1865* (Vienna, 1873), 108. Intendent-Général Wolf tersely described the Freicorps: "a mixed lot, well led."
14. Bazine to War Minister, 27 August 1865 (S.H.A.T., G7, 2).
15. *Historique*, 179-81.
16. Ibid., 183.
17. Campos, 60 n. *L'Estafette*, daily newspaper, Mexico City, 15 October, carried an account of the raid with detail from *El Monitor Veracruzano*, (o.c. Veracruz to Bazaine, 8 and 9 October 1865, S.H.A.T., G7, 124).
18. *Historique*, 184-85. A copy of Bosler's report was enclosed with Montholon's dispatch to foreign minister, Paris 7 July 1865 (A.M.A.E. corr. pol. Mexique, 4 fos. 169-70).
19. Justice Militaire (S.H.A.T., G7, 204).
20. Campos, 60-61.
21. *Historique*, 321-32.
22. Worn in its sheath strapped to the left arm above the elbow.
23. 'Ali Jifūn, 238-39.

Mutiny of the Relief Battalion in the Sudan

1. Organizing a Relief Battalion for Mexico

2. Mutiny at Kasala

3. Suppression of the Mutiny

4. Responsibility for the Mutiny

Chapter 6

Mutiny of the Relief Battalion in the Sudan

1. Organizing a Relief Battalion for Mexico

On 3 December 1864 the British ambassador at Istanbul cabled his prime minister, Lord John Russell, to the effect that the French government had applied to Isma'il Pasha for reinforcements to replace casualties among the Sudanese sent to Mexico two years earlier. On hearing of this the Ottoman government, in a mood of reproof, advised Isma'il Pasha to refer the French government to Istanbul.

There was no unusual delay on Isma'il's part. On 6 March 1865 he ordered the governor-general of the Sudan, Ja'far Pasha Sadiq, to send to Egypt a battalion of Sudanese infantry at full strength under the command of Colonel Adam Bey al-'Arifi.[1]

In selecting Kasala as the most suitable garrison town in which to raise the relief battalion for Mexico, the Egyptian war office could not have made a more unfortunate choice. For some years the governor, Ibrahim Bey al-Mahallawi,[2] had presided over a province in shocking administrative disorder. Discipline among the troops was weak, their officers had grown corrupt and, to add to the chaos, there had been little rain, a bad harvest and, in consequence, a virtually empty provincial treasury. Troops' pay and allowances were payable not by the central government at Khartoum but by the provinces. Since the provincial treasury was depleted, pay was greatly in arrears.

2. Mutiny at Kasala

In October 1864 there had already been a mutiny of 500 unruly black troops while they were about to set out from Kasala to raid the Basen, a fiercely dissident tribe on the Ethiopian border. The only member of the column to receive his pay was its commander, whom the governor had paid in secret. When his troops heard of this skulduggery, they were outraged, refused to march, seized a stock of arms and ammunition, and vented their rage on an innocent third party by looting the village of Sabdarat. The governor, now thoroughly frightened, begged Sayyid al-Hasan Muhammad 'Uthman al-Mirghani, the prominent religious notable of Kasala and head of the Khatmiyya brotherhood, to persuade the mutineers to return to duty. The Sayyid arranged a truce between the governor and his mutinous troops. The governor issued an installment of 4,000 Maria Theresa dollars toward their pay. The men sullenly accepted the money and marched.

Ignorant of any trouble in Kasala, the Khedive continued his plans for the transport of the relief battalion to Mexico:

> We have given orders for the ship *Ibrahimiyya* to proceed to Sawakin to transport the battalion of Sudanese troops comprising 1,000 officers and men. This battalion will sail to Mexico to replace the Egyptian Sudanese troops there. . . . As soon as this battalion reaches Egypt you are urgently required to issue to each soldier two vests, two pairs of trousers, two pairs of stockings, one tarbush, two pairs of shoes, two belts, two sets of clothing of good, hard-wearing material, one short, single-breasted linen coat as issued to the infantry, sleeping bag, and burnous. Officers are to be issued with the infantry officers' uniform with braiding according to rank. Choose clean new tents for issue to them. . .have recourse to your own expertise in the detail of clothing, equipment, and weaponry, for we may have overlooked some essential items. Postscript: You should at once inform the French consul-general in writing. The firearms to be issued will be the model *shishkhana*. Officers and men will receive three months' pay; no ammunition will be issued.[3]

On the same day the Khedive issued a further instruction: "the battalion should be sent on from Alexandria to Toulon in the *Samanoud* or other large ship of the 'Aziziyya Steamship Company with an extra pilot in case the master had not made this particular voyage before."

Whether 'Umar Bey Fakhri, the acting governor-general in Khartoum, or Ibrahim Bey al-Mahallawi in Kasala, was responsible for taking three months to fulfil his Khedive's order is not known: at the end of three months, on 29

June, Ibrahim Bey wrote to the war office with excuses for delaying the mobilization of the required battalion.

On hearing of their destination overseas, the troops became suspicious and petitioned to be allowed to take their families with them. This was refused by the governor who lied to them that their mission would be too short to make this practicable. About 1 July the newly-formed battalion, without its colonel, who was to join them later, set out on their 500 km march to the port of Sawakin where they would embark for Suez.

They had not gone far when they met another black unit that had been told (or had invented) the alarming news that the relief battalion was going to be put in chains and deported. So far as is known no one had received any information good or bad about the battalion already in Mexico: how it was faring, the food, the drink, the women, the enemy? Nothing. What had the war office in Cairo or the regimental officers in Kasala done to anticipate the possibility of false rumors circulating and step in first with authentic news? Apparently nothing.

The two units returned together to Kasala and made a savage, undisciplined assault upon the citadel. The garrison commander, Colonel Hasan Bey Arna'ut, with a few faithful troops reinforced by 150 loyal black soldiers and their officers, strongly resisted. The mutineers, delirious with excitement, fired thousands of rounds into the air but were uncertain what to do next. The Albanian and his beleaguered force resisted until, once again, the religious leader, Sayyid al-Hasan al-Mirghani, persuaded the mutineers to suspend their attacks.

Meanwhile, on 4 July, in ignorance of the mutiny at Kasala, the French foreign minister sent the minister of the navy a copy of the apologetic letter from Isma'il Pasha explaining the delay in bringing the relief battalion for Mexico from the Sudan. Cholera had broken out at Sawakin, and it was dangerous to send a troopship there to embark the battalion. The men bound for Mexico would instead proceed on foot by easy stages toward the Nile for onward passage by river and rail to Alexandria.

3. Suppression of the Mutiny

Colonel Adam Bey al-'Arifi with 400 men from the black regiments at al-'Ubayd and Khartoum arrived at Kasala on 30 August. Intermittent fighting continued. Steadily reinforcements from towns on the Nile, from Berber to Wad Madani, converged. In the end the mutineers lost their nerve.

At that point they were crushed in blood: 1,637 mutineers of the 4th Regiment, chiefly Dinka from the upper White Nile Valley, were killed in the fighting and in the massacre which followed, while losses among the loyal defenders amounted to 312 dead and 83 wounded. After all resistance had been put down, the surviving mutineers who had surrendered were tried by court martial resulting in the execution of a further, unrecorded number. The black colonel Adam bey al-'Arifi lodged a strong protest to the Egyptian war office against the trickery by which the mutineers were induced to surrender. His protest got no further than Khartoum.

The rotting bodies of nearly 2,000 mutineers lay unburied all over the town, causing an outbreak of fever to which many loyal troops who survived the fighting fell victim. Among them was the commander of the garrison troops, Hasan Pasha the Albanian.[4]

Halfway through November a rumor of the mutiny of the battalion bound for Mexico reached the U.S. consulate-general in Egypt. In a dispatch dated 13 November the consul-general triumphantly announced to Washington that the Egyptian government's plan to send a contingent to Mexico had foundered partly, if not wholly, because of the detestation entertained by the people, and especially among the conscripts themselves, for service in distant lands. The consul-general's optimism was short-lived. On 16 November the Egyptian foreign department advised him that "the insurrection in the Soudan' had been repressed." A relief battalion would be transported to Mexico after all.

In spite of Isma'il Pasha's efforts to carry out his promise to the French government, it was the French who cancelled the move. Napoleon was at last convinced that his policy for Mexico had failed.

4. Responsibility for the Mutiny

Who was responsible for the mutiny and the ensuing butchery of the mutineers? Where the world outside noticed the mutiny at all, it was shrugged off as unimportant. The only foreign eyewitness to record the incident was Count Raoul du Bisson, a professional adventurer who had come to the Sudan with a small band of French and Levantine *desesperados* to found an agricultural colony on the Egyptian-Ethiopian border and who were heavily armed. J. A. W. Munzinger, the future general governor of the Eastern Sudan but at this time French consul at Musawwa', reported that du Bisson and his men had valiantly assisted in the defense of the Kasala citadel.

There is some confusion here. Douin, our principal authority for the mutiny, accepts Munzinger's statement, but the Count du Bisson himself, in a salacious narrative of his impressions of the Sudan (a work of no merit), *Les Femmes, les eunuques et les guerriers du Soudan* (1865), makes no mention of the mutiny, and we can only guess the reason. Nine years later Sir Samuel Baker wrote that, since the mutiny of the blacks at Kasala "when they murdered their officers and committed many atrocities" [sic], the Egyptian officers had always distrusted them. Baker added that his own chief of staff, Maj. Muhammad Ra'uf, had told him that,if a black who happened to be a general favorite was punished, his comrades would probably mutiny.[5]

Baker missed the point. The officers of the Turco-Egyptian establishment never troubled to understand their black soldiers, in particular the Dinka, a highly-strung people who, as the British after them found out, needed very sensitive handling. The Turks were therefore incapable of winning their confidence and loyalty. History had bequeathed the Turks a prejudice against blacks whom they treated as inferior beings, lacking intelligence and unfit for command. The presence in their midst of a Sudanese officer of field rank, Colonel Adam Bey al-'Arifi, a first-rate officer and a champion of the black soldiery, did not remove their prejudice.

Color prejudice, color antipathy, as is well known, does not incapacitate a multiethnic institution from governing a region so tribally fragmented as the Sudan with its own peoples of varying degrees of black and brown. The conquerors of 1820-1821 had as complicated ethnic roots as the people they conquered: ethnic Turks from Anatolia, the Caucasus, the Crimea and the Balkans, Circassians, Kurds and Laz from the Anatolian eastern border, Slavs, Hungarians, Greeks, Albanians, and smaller groups from Inner Asia and North Africa. A modern observer, denied a chastening sense of history, might be led into the illusion that this rich genetic blend would have brought great benefits to the land it governed.

Unfortunately not. With the passing of the centuries the Ottoman ethnic constituents were being fused into a recognizable rough uniformity aided by the Muslim marriage practice which in time blurred the outward distinction of ethnic origin. By the mid-nineteenth century this haughty feudal governing class was assuming an approach to an Egyptian identity deeper than simply the arrogance of ownership; a few were marrying into the native Egyptian population whom as a whole they still regarded as of servile standing. There was no spontaneous, communal amalgamation with the native Egyptians whose resentment at the Ottoman monopoly of government, wealth, and land grew with the years.

At the apex of this privileged land-owner pyramid, Isma'il Pasha himself became the victim of its limitations. For all his theoretical enthusiasm for the Sudan, he had never been there and was dependent on written and verbal information that he could not verify. His draconian punishment of the mutineers by decimation was useless as an example for black mutineers. He furthered his folly when, for a time, he drastically reduced the establishment of black formations in the Sudan, and, in their place, ordered the transfer of several white

Lower Egyptian *fallahin* replacements dismissing any possibility of the unsuitability of the Sudan climate by instancing the practice of the English in sending white troops to garrison India.

Isma'il's treatment of the Turco-Egyptian officers responsible for incurring, and then repressing, the Kasala revolt demonstrated his ignorance of sound military education and his remoteness from the true causes of the mutiny. He demoted 'Umar Fakhri Bey for dilatoriness in transacting the paperwork at Khartoum, but the nucleus of inadequacy, the entire Ottoman military command, he left alone.

The mutiny demonstrated the lack of trust between the Turks and the blacks, a limit to the credibility of troops filled to bursting with a sense of injustice. When their fears were not dissipated, they exploded.

By contrast, it is not easy to explain why the Sudanese campaigning in Mexico found the French so congenial. Personal contacts may have contributed, for it had become a basic maxim of good military management in North American, and rather later in European, armies that men will place confidence and loyalty only in officers who look to their men's welfare in practical ways, not simply in correspondence or by mouthing high-sounding words at regimental parades. The good officer listens to complaints; if they are justified, he tries to satisfy them; if they are not, he explains why not. An important part of the good officer's duties is to allay anxiety by supplying correct information, convincing reassurance. An attempt to establish some form of liaison devised for a largely illiterate soldiery between the troops in Mexico and the garrisons in the Sudan would have helped. The stories from the front might even have penetrated the war office in Cairo with the notion that there was merit in having officers who cared for their men yet nevertheless kept good discipline.

In some ways the French officers were not altogether unlike those other young foreigners whom veterans of the Sudanese battalion were to meet in the years ahead when they fled to Egypt from the destruction of the old Egyptian army. There, for the first time, they encountered the English[6] who, like themselves, were mostly illiterate in Arabic and spoke it even more barbarously then they but, with all their faults and eccentricities, looked after them, paid them on the nail and meant what they said.

Notes

1. Also known by the diminutive al'Irayfī. from the 'Arifiyya branch of the Dār Hāmid (Baqqāra) tribe of central Kordofan who pasture among the Nuba Mountains. He is further, but mistakenly, recorded as Adam Bey al-Duwālābī

and, less improbably, as Adam Bey al-Taqalāwī inferring that he originated from the native population of Jabal Taqalī.

2. Of Lower Egyptian stock, Ibrahim Bey was born at Mahalla al-Kubra and received his military education in Cairo.
3. Khedive Isma'il to Director of the war office, 24 muharram 1282 [19 June 1865]; *Taqwīm*, 612. As Isma'il must have known by then that the calibre of this rifle was incompatible with that of the French forces in Mexico, their issue may have been to avoid any action which might unsettle the morale of the troops.
4. The fate of the governor, Ibrāhīm Bey al-Mahallāwī, is disputed. Douin III, 1, 209, states that he died in the epidemic. But a descendant of the mudīr, a former colleague of the writer, assured him that Ibrāhīm Bey lived on in retirement in Kasala and died of natural causes during the Mahdist siege of the town in 1885 (R.H.).
5. Baker, I., 355-56. Muhammad Ra'uf, a future governor-general of the Sudan, had a long service commanding black troops and spoke from experience. For his Egyptian service career, see Zaki, 107-8.
6. *Injlīzī*, was, and is, the popular Sudanese Arabic word for British. The correct term, *Birītānī*, is used in official documents.

A Diplomatic Confrontation: The Government of the United States versus the Sudanese Battalion

Chapter 7

A Diplomatic Confrontation: The Government of the United States versus the Sudanese Battalion

In the preceding chapter we attributed the mutiny of the relief battalion at Kasala primarily to weaknesses in the Ottoman officer corps. There was also an element of color prejudice or racism, long evident in the Nile Valley. However, in the Ottoman world at large, there was no scruple about slavery itself or slave enlistment of soldiers being *wrong*. In the United States the attitudes were very different; a civil war had just been fought in part over this very issue. We now turn to the involvement of the United States in the aftermath of the Kasala mutiny.

A confrontation between the U.S. Secretary of State William Seward and Edouard Drouyn de Lhuis, French minister for foreign affairs, occurred in the autumn of 1865 and was forgotten soon after the end of the year. It must have been one of the most bizarre incidents in Sudanese history and, though it concerned the Sudanese battalion, its troops may never have heard of the rumpus or, if they had, they would not have understood what the fuss was about.

On 20 September 1865, acting on information from Charles Hale, the U.S. consul-general in Egypt, Secretary Seward sent the following instructions to John Bigelow, the U.S. minister in Paris:

> Since the original transaction [the dispatch of the Sudanese battalion to Mexico in 1863] occurred the United States have abolished slavery. The attention of Congress as well as that of the executive department and of the country, has been steadily fixed upon the course of events in Mexico which, I need not say, form a subject of serious apprehension with regard to the safety of free republican institutions on this continent; an object which we are accustomed to connect with the desired ultimate consequence of the abolition of every form of compulsory civil or military servitude in this hemisphere.

> You are instructed to bring this matter to the attention of Mr. Drouyn de Lhuis, and state to him that the renewal of the transaction alluded to [a reinforcement or relief of the existing battalion] could not be regarded with favor or even without deep concern by the people of the United States or by their government.[1]

Or, as briefly mimicked (with a touch of mock sanctimoniousness) by Muhammad Sharif Pasha, chief of the Egyptian foreign department, in correspondence with Consul-General Hale:

> in the opinion of the cabinet of Washington, the Egyptian soldiers who form part of the French expedition to Mexico are to be regarded as slaves and their stay there as contradicting the great measure of humanity which has freed all their brethren in America.

Having stated the fallacy, Muhammad Sharif Pasha proceeded to knock it down:

> Permit me Sir, to protest on my side against the expression of an error so clear. Slavery no longer exists in Egypt. It was abolished there long before it was abolished in the United States. . . . The Negroes in the Egyptian territories are subjects of His Highness by the same title and with the same rights as the other natives of the country. In serving under our flag they obey a law of conscription equal for all. . . . In virtue of a principle made applicable as long ago as the reign of our illustrious Mehemet 'Ali, all slaves enrolled under the flag became free in full rights."[2]

The victorious Union, which had opposed the French presence in Mexico from the start, next opened a diplomatic war to hasten the French withdrawal and with it the hard-pressed empire of Maximilian. In a technical sense, all that the French wished to do was to send a relief unit to allow the war-weary battalion to come home, not to add to the existing establishment already in Mexico.

Seward was not unduly cynical in voicing his government's desire for "the abolition of every form of compulsory civil and military servitude in this hemisphere."

One rigidly legalistic critic, Francis Dainese, accused the secretary of state of gross diplomatic irregularity and favoritism in appointing William Thayer instead of himself, Dainese, as U.S. consul-general in Egypt. He published a bitter attack on both Seward and Thayer indignantly entitled *The History of Mr. Seward's Pet in Egypt, his Actions Denounced, and his Usurpations Condemned by the Courts* (Washington, 1867). The book was addressed to the American Congress in the form of an indictment.

1. Officers taking the oath of allegiance, from a copy in ʻUmar Ṭūsūn, *A Military History of the epoch of Muḥammad ʻAli al-Kabir* (Arabic), Cairo, Dar al-Maʻarif Press, 1950, 290. Source not stated.

2. Troopship *La Seine* (photo copyright, Musée de la Marine, Paris)

3. The Egyptian Sudanese Battalion disembarking at Veracruz, from a sketch by J.A. Beaucé (*L'Illustration*, Paris, XVI, 1863, 244).

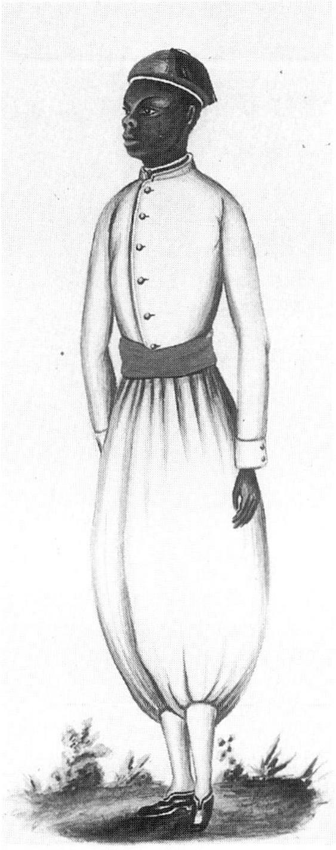

Plate 4. Full Dress

Plate 5. Active Service Order

4-7. Four tailor's designs of a uniform and equipment for the Egyptian Sudanese Battalion made by the Intendance branch, (this copy from Archives historiques, Service de Santé des Armées). (Photo copyright, Musée du Val de Grâce, Paris).

Plate 6. For Cold Weather: The Overcoat

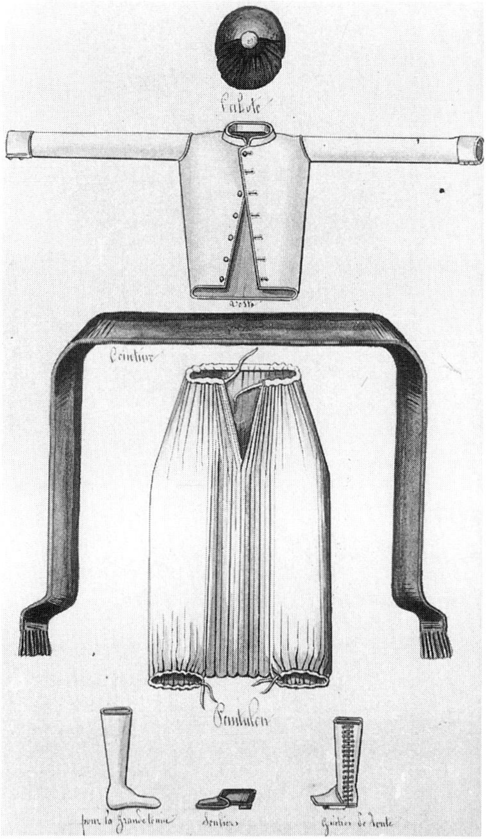

Plate 7. Military Apparel

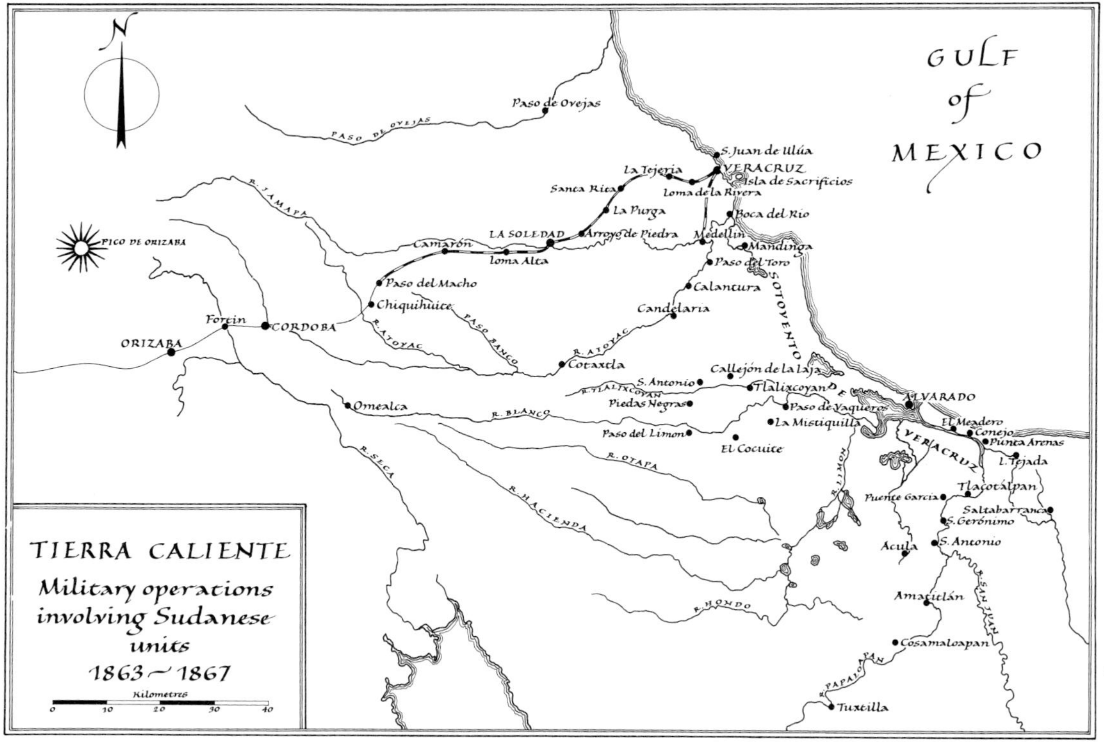

8. Tierra Caliente: land and river operations involving Sudanese units. Topographical additions for the Sotavento de Veracruz supplied by Architect Humberto Aguirre Tinoco.

9. Railway Bridge, constructed by French military engineers at La Soledad, 1863. The slightly anachronistic locomotive, a British Fairlie double engine, was introduced to Mexico shortly after the French evacuation (from A. García Cubas, Album del Ferrocarril Mexicano, view by Casimiro Castro, Mexico City, 1877). (Copyright, if any, unknown).

FERRO-CARRIL

De Orizava á Veracruz.

AVISO AL PUBLICO.

Todos los dias saldrá un tren de esta ciudad para la Purga á las............ 7 h. de la mañana.

Dicho tren regresará saliendo de la Purga á las......................... 9 h. de la idem.

Los trenes estraordinarios no tienen hora fija.

Tarifa de los precios.

BOLETOS.

Un boleto de Veracruz á la Purga y viceversa....................	en 2.ª	clase	$ 1 50
	en 3.ª	„	„ 1 00
Un boleto de Veracruz á la Tejería y viceversa..........................	en 2.ª	„	„ 0 75
	en 3.ª	„	„ 0 50
Un boleto de la Tejería á la Purga y viceversa.............	en 2.ª	„	„ 0 75
	en 3.ª	„	„ 0 50

WAGONES.

De Veracruz á la Purga y viceversa..	1	wagn	grande	„22 50
	1	„	chico	„20 00
De Veracruz á la Tejería y viceversa.	1	„	grande	„15 00
	1	„	chico	„12 50
De la Tejería á la Purga y viceversa.	1	„	grande	„15 00
	1	„	chico	„12 50

A ninguna persona será permitido penetrar en el Patio de la Estacion sin enseñar anticipadamente su boleto al portero. A la llegada de los trenes ningun viajero podrá salir del Patio sin entregar su boleto.

El director ingeniero en gefe.—M. E. Lyons.

FERRO-CARRIL

10. Mexican Railway timetable from the *Eco del Comercio*, Veracruz, 16 July 1863 (courtesy Public Record Office, London).

11. Ambushed train defended by Sudanese and French West Indian escort, 2 Oct. 1863 (*L'Illustration*, Paris, XLII, 1863, 340).

12. Gunboat *Ste Barbe* (photo copyright, Musée de la Marine, Paris).

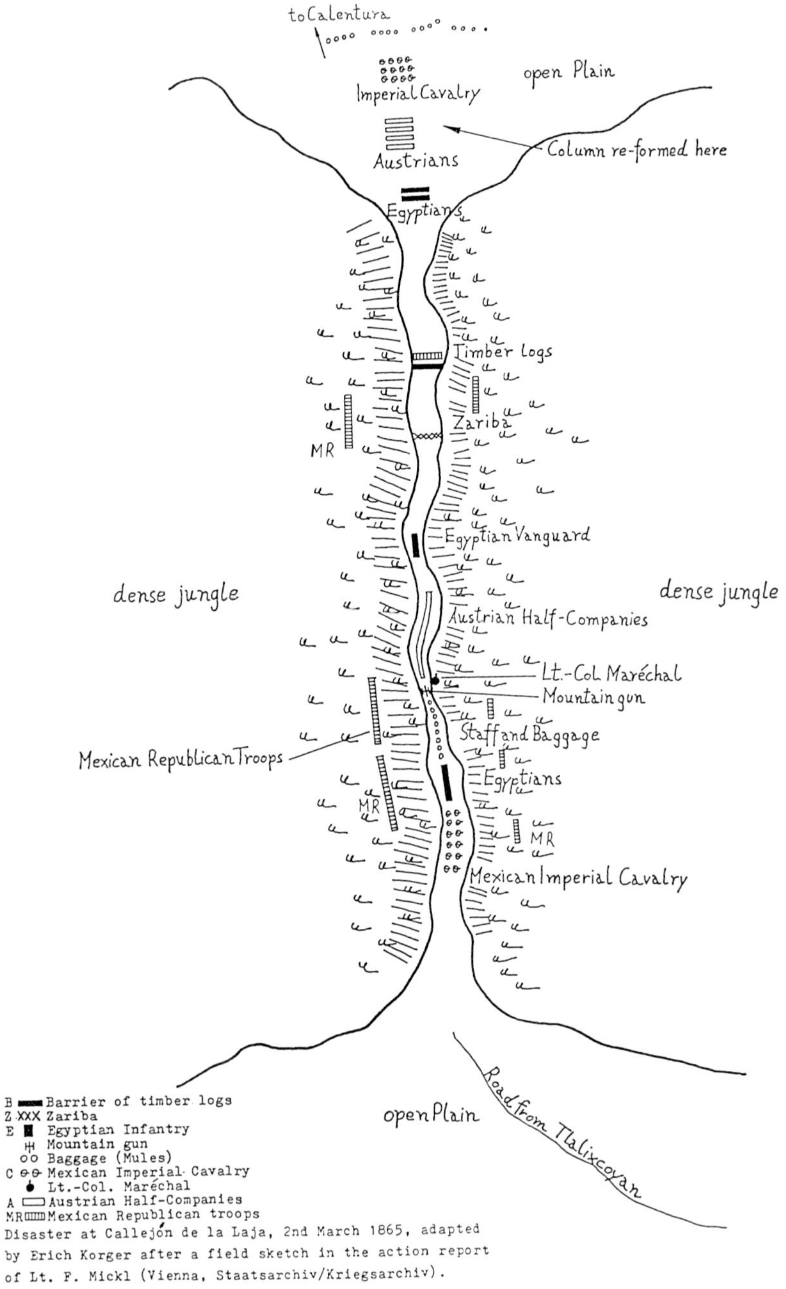

13. Diagram showing successive phases of the disaster at Callejon de la Laja, near Tlalixcoyan, 2 March 1865, based on a field sketch by Lt. F. Mickl, Austrian Volunteer Corps, by Erich Korger.

14. Captain ʻAbd al-Raḥmān Mūsā, commanding the Sudanese mounted troop (photo copyright Musée de l'Armee, Paris).

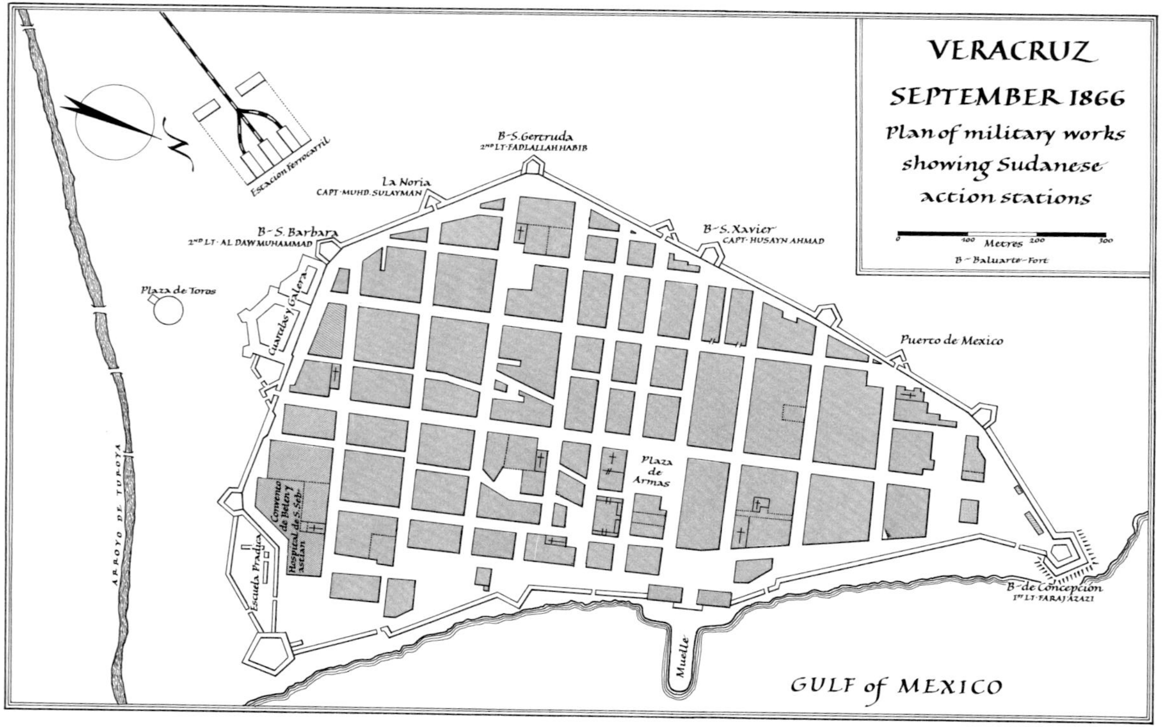

15. Veracruz, Sept. 1866. Plan of military works showing Sudanese action stations.

16. Arrival of the Egyptian Sudanese Battalion in Paris from Mexico, an impression (*Le Monde illustré*, Paris, II, 1867, 300).

17. Group of Sudanese officers from the Battalion recently returned from Mexico to Egypt, with Dr. Charles Gaillardot Bey, 1867, from 'Umar Ṭūsūn, Buṭulat al-orta al-sudaniyya al-misriyya, 1 (courtesy of the Moḥamed Ali Foundation).

18. Unmarked burial place of Brig.-Gen. Muḥammad al-Mas Pāshā, Governor of Khartoum, formerly commanding the Egyptian Sudanese Battalion in Mexico (courtesy of Ian Cliff).

19 Dr. E.C.O.T. Schnitzer, the future Emin Pāshā, from a complaint of his alleged behavior toward the widow of his employer, by Abüzzīya Tevfīk in *Nevsale marifet*, Istanbul, 1889, 210.

The thrust of Dainese's allegation is that, Seward, in his haste to appoint Thayer to the consulship-general in Egypt, breached diplomatic protocol by directly accrediting him to the Khedive Isma'il instead of proceeding, as he should have done, through the U.S. minister at Istanbul. Through this lapse he had given Isma'il Pasha the standing of a sovereign prince, which encouraged him to commit acts of defiance against his master, the Ottoman Sultan, including "the raising, equipping and furnishing of an armed regiment of Arabs [sic] for His Imperial Majesty Napoleon III in 1862 to assist in establishing the Archduke Maximilian in Mexico."

This fiery interlude apart, Secretary Seward in his dispatch to Paris was doing no more than repeating what had become one of the great popular slogans in Europe and the Americas: the pursuit of freedom and the abolition of its antithesis, slavery. Philosophers in Europe had been wrestling with the theory; the Romantic Movement clothed it with emotion. In 1776, Britain's American colonies had the glorious effrontery to put the theory into practice; Seward now proclaimed its extension to the slaves. But it was not just freedom from slavery that caught the imagination of the rising urban middle and lower-middle classes of Europe and America; it was a vision of freedom of trade and industry, freedom of the press, freedom of association, freedom of religion; there seemed no limit to the possibilities of freedom.

Of the two protagonists in the dispute, Seward had the better excuse for his ignorance of any form of slavery except that which had been legally abolished in his own country. Not only was there no interest in Islamic institutions in the United States which might possibly have sharpened the awareness of the politicians, but Seward suffered the further disadvantage of living in a society devoted to the separation of politics and religion, a doctrine that would have made it difficult for him or his cabinet colleagues to have understood the working of any civil and military institutions whose direct appeal to authority lay in a scripture and tradition other than Christian. Seward was therefore denied even the oratorical possibilities of a yet more alarming imaginary threat posed by the presence on the United States' southern border of vigorous, mobile Muslim units such as the Sudanese and the Tirailleurs, trained troops ready and eager to join some fanatical anti-Christian insurrection of American Negroes disillusioned by their social ostracism from the white community after their legal liberation.

Seward's opposite number, Drouyn de Lhuis, represented the foreign policy of a nation with a relatively long awareness of the Middle East. He should have known better than to have accepted Seward's mixing up of the Sudanese with American slaves. But Drouyn de Lhuis' hands were tied; he now knew of the certainty of the French withdrawal from Mexico, but he was not yet authorized to make an official pronouncement.

Seward's brusque intervention, however, had little to do with ideology: his aim was *Realpolitik*, to get the French out of Mexico. Ideological considerations were not for him nor, for that matter, for the American people. In January 1866, Bigelow in Paris notified Washington that the French foreign minister had assured him that his government had no intention of sending more troops to Mexico. Seward had got what he wanted, and the incident he had created was closed. His British contemporary, Lord Palmerston, a kindred soul, could not have worked it better.

Notes

1. Seward to Bigelow, 264, 20 September 1865; U.S. Congress, Mexican affairs, pt. 2, H. Doc. 75, p. 431.
2. Muhammad Sharif to C. Hale, 16 November 1865, enclosure A to dispatch Hale to Seward, 18 November 1865, T.45, roll 5. Mehemet/Mehmet defers to the Turkish pronunciation, Muhammad to the Arabic; the spelling in Arabic is the same. See D. Perkins (DAB XVI, 1935) for a view of Seward's *Realpolitik* as that of a lawyer rather than a politician.

War in 1866

1. ‘Ali Jifun Carries the Dispatches
2. Another Combined Operation: Captain Testart’s Patrol
3. The Loss of Tlacotalpan
4. The Growing Insecurity
5. The Enemy Within
6. The Republican Threat to Veracruz
7. Two Celebrations
8. The Sudanese Surprised
9. Problems of the Evacuation

Chapter 8

War in 1866

1. 'Ali Jifun Carries the Dispatches

In the new Sudanese cavalry detachment was Trooper 'Ali Jifun who describes his adventures as a mounted man on a dangerous mission:

> Fifty of us under an Egyptian officer, by name 'Abd al-Rahman Efendi Musa, were now formed into a troop of cavalry for patrolling and general duty on the lines of communication. . . .While I was [based] at Veracruz employed as a trooper I used to carry the mail between the railhead at Paso del Macho and Cordoba, and, being a *wakil ombashi*,[1] usually had charge of a small party of men. Originally the mail had been entrusted to Mexican irregular horsemen, but these had been so often intercepted that the General decided to try the Sudanese.

Just as we started on our first expedition several dispatch-riders had been cut off and killed, so that at this moment it was practically impossible to get the letters through. Bazaine gave orders for us to do the work, and on our bey calling for volunteers, we all stepped forward and said we were willing to go. Finally I was selected to go in charge of five picked men mounted on the best horses of the detachment and one evening at sunset we started off.

We rode all night, taking care to keep well clear of the beaten track, and so soon as dawn came we hid in the forest. Next night we traveled on as before and in the morning we found ourselves in the middle of an Indian village. The Indians however, turned out to be a friendly tribe who had wandered into this hostile district; so after giving us food and warning us that we must not stop for fear of being seen by the Mexicans, they sent us on our way. Presently we met a single Mexican who told us that we would certainly be taken as the whole road to Cordoba was beset by horsemen. So we turned off into the wood and hid once more till night.

At sunrise we started again and rode until morning when we found the forest ended and, far away on the great plain stretching out before us was Cordoba. So we put off our disguise and waving a white handkerchief on a spear we galloped in. The commandant was greatly pleased with our successful ride as he had been unable to get his dispatches or to hold any communication with the base for several days.[2]

2. Another Combined Operation: Captain Testart's Patrol

In his report on 28 March to the war minister, Bazaine explained his plan for a combined operation to land troops from the sea to reinforce Tlacotalpan and connect with a second force. These would advance from Cordoba by way of Omealca via Cosamaloapan to meet Commandant Cloué's gunboats waiting at Tlacotalpan.

The object of this land and river movement was to attempt to clear the vast delta of enemy forces commanded by General Alejandro Garcia, second in command to the prestigious Porfirio Diaz, chief of the Republican eastern military zone.

Bazaine informed Paris that he was determined to place a more permanent, reinforced, garrison in Tlacotalpan by dispatching from Veracruz by sea 200 Egyptians and 100 Tirailleurs. Tlacotalpan would never be safe until the enemy had been ejected from the countryside round the town. Meanwhile, to distract the enemy from sending reinforcements from the interior, the Imperial commander-in-chief, General Count Thun, from his headquarters at Puebla, would threaten the country round Tuxtepec, the riverhead for navigation by the smallest craft on the Rio Papaloapan.

Captain Testart[3] in command of the land column set out from Cordoba with a force composed of 100 Sudanese, 100 Tirailleurs, a section of light artillery, and a troop of Imperial cavalry under Colonel Figuerero. They crossed the bridge over Rio Blanco at Omealca and, following the river, passed through Cosamoloapan, which the enemy had abandoned, and arrived at Tlacotalpan simultaneously with three gunboats: *Pique, Tactique,* and *Diligence* sent from Alvarado by Commandant Cloué, commanding the French naval squadron in the Gulf of Mexico. Testart had taken only two days on the march. By 9 May, Bazaine could inform Paris that the combined operation had been completed and that the units involved had returned to their posts, the Sudanese to Veracruz.[4]

Captain Testart was among the finest French officers with whom the Sudanese came into contact. A brilliant graduate from St. Cyr, he passed out just in time to see service in the Crimea in 1855. He served against the Austrians in the war of 1859 and in 1860 was transferred to the Tirailleurs Algériens. General Yusuf of the Algerian army, himself a former mamluk of the Bey of Tunis, wrote of the young Testart as "a most distinguished officer, intelligent, well educated, well brought up, would make an excellent company commander."

3. The Loss of Tlacotalpan

The continuous and implacable efforts made by the Republicans to recover Tlacotalpan is understandable. No ordinary Mexican town, it was a customs post of attractive revenue to any holder of the place. Far more important was its heroic niche in Mexican national history. Its resolute resistance to the American invaders of 1847 earned for the cozy little town the honorary dignity of city (ciudad) conferred by a grateful government. Tlacotalpan had become the lively symbol of Mexican resistance to the invader; it was their Verdun.

With the onset of the summer rains, the Imperial garrison began to lose heart. They were subjected to almost daily assaults, although the waterlogged tracks made it difficult for the Republican artillery to bombard the defenses effectively. The Imperial garrison was not only discouraged but ill. Colonel Marino Comacho, the Imperial commander, was faced on 8 July with a sick list of 180 men. He decided to evacuate the town and asked Marshal Bazaine for transport by gunboat for his garrison and himself. The commander-in-chief authorized the arrangements and informed Paris.[5]

Comacho was a good soldier; he was also a diplomat. His adversary, General Garcia, found it necessary to explain to the Republican minister of war the complicated diplomacy to which he himself resorted to winkle the Imperial garrison out of its defensive lines. Shortly after Garcia's force had made an assault on the town, the battered defenders were looking for an opportunity to retire before the Republicans made a second attack on them. "I was convinced about this," he wrote,

> as I was preparing a second assault on this position in a few days. The result of this attack would have been the reconquest of the town. Yesterday, however I received an invitation from the Imperial commander, Don Marino Comacho, to a conference in which, after explaining the position, he proposed to hand over the town that day provided that I would not attack his

troops during their withdrawal to "Conejo." He also stressed that with this guarantee he wished to avoid the shedding of blood; but, if he did not obtain such a guarantee, the commanders of the four French gunboats by the town would open fire if so much as one man was wounded during the passage to Conejo. These gunboat commanders would be only too willing to make such a murderous attack.

The editor adds in extenuation of this unusual transaction:

Although the threat of destroying Tlacotalpan if the Imperialists were attacked during the crossing to Conejo could have been a trick by Comacho to obtain the best possible terms for evacuating the place, the mere possibility that such a threat could be made effective justified General Garcia's acceptance of this condition.[6]

4. The Growing Insecurity

A gifted and extremely elusive enemy commander, Lt-Col. Prieto had escaped from French custody as a prisoner of war and took to roaming the countryside accompanied only by his servant, to collect money, food, and intelligence from the villagers for the Republican bands now venturing nearer and nearer to Veracruz. On 1 June, at the head of 30 mounted men, he raided Boca del Rio, almost under the walls of Veracruz, and kidnapped two Imperial officials: a magistrate and a district administrator. A detachment of 20 Sudanese detailed to watch for Prieto arrived too late to intercept him.[7]

On 8 July, the six Sudanese troopers who daily patrolled their allotted section of the railway arrived at a point between the stations of La Purga and La Soledad when they disturbed an enemy band obviously intending to tamper with the rails. The Sudanese at once bolted for the nearest fortified post, La Purga, but not before they had killed one Mexican without loss to themselves. On 27 July, Prieto's band had a skirmish outside La Purga with another Sudanese patrol which cost the Republicans two killed and fourteen wounded.

The Sudanese garrison at Medellin had its turn on the night of 25-26 July when, at about 0200, a Republican force of infantry and cavalry commanded by Prieto assaulted the fort on the edge of the town.[8] Through sheer laziness the Mexican captain of the Rural Guard was surprised and taken prisoner. His men fled, abandoning their rifles to the enemy. Two Sudanese sentries keeping watch on the fort were quietly seized and their throats cut before they could cry out. The alarm was at last sounded and the Sudanese—there were now only 26 of them—took up their battle stations under the interpreter Prince who commanded the fort. The engagement lasted until 0530 when Prieto and his men drew off, suffering one killed and two wounded. The Sudanese losses were two killed at the beginning of the fight and two wounded: Bakhit Ibrahim al-Shirbini seriously, and Bakhit Baraka superficially; the latter was reported to have been most unwilling to quit his post because, as he told his officer, "The enemy have promised to return and I shall wait for them."[9]

With the uncertain political situation and the approaching end of the French occupation, the Tierra Caliente became cluttered with what the French dispatches described as adventurers and criminals of all kinds. There was growing insecurity on the roads, and there were repeated cases of banditry. The work of the Sudanese battalion in the maintenance of law and order was becoming more vital day by day. Veracruz was so depleted of troops for general garrison duties that the Sudanese were again called upon to form a guard of honor for the Empress Carlota as she made her way to Europe on a desperate mission to seek aid for the collapsing Empire. On 12 July, the day on which she drove through Veracruz from the railway station to her ship, 25 Sudanese were taken off their duties to form a guard of honor while a salute of 101 guns was fired.

5. The Enemy Within

A dangerous result of troop shortage was uncovered at Veracruz early in July by the Marquis de Montholon, French ambassador to the Imperial Court of Mexico, as he was passing through the port. When he discovered that the Sudanese were being employed as prison warders, a role for which they had neither the aptitude nor the training, the ambassador wrote curtly to Rolland, military officer commanding Veracruz, regarding an incident in which the Sudanese guards fired on and wounded convicts in their charge. There had been a conspiracy among the convicts to make a collective escape from their prison, which was next to the fort of Santa Barbara and surrounded by walls easy to climb. Some wounded by Sudanese bullets had been taken to the hospital from which three escaped. Six were held in prison. These had succeeded in passing a message through the lines to Prieto or some other rebel leader to the effect that they wanted nothing more than to place themselves at his service. It was arranged that Prieto would take the prison, called "The Galera," by surprise and arm and free the prisoners.

Montholon did not mince his words:

I ask you, Colonel, to stop employing Egyptians as prison warders. After what has happened these troops have been proved unsuitable for guarding criminals just as the civil police here are useless for this duty. To allay the fears of the townspeople the civil prefect has a ship standing by to transport these convicts to Yucatan.[10]

'Ali Jifun recounts an incident vividly illustrating the danger from enemy agents inside the town. He never spoils a story with fussy dates; by now he was out of touch with the Islamic calendar and was not familiar with the Gregorian. But his story has every appearance of occurring at this time of insecurity:

One night while I was at Veracruz I was on guard over the Port Mexique [Puerta de Mexico], Baraka Ahmad[11] was on sentry duty and was suddenly set upon by a Mexican with a knife. Baraka was a powerful man and succeeded in preventing his assailant from doing him any injury. But as the guard turned out, the man escaped."

Presently it came to my turn to relieve Baraka Ahmad and I took his place. This night was very dark and it was raining heavily, so I determined to take every precaution against being surprised. Straight in front of my post was a large palace,[12] and, high up, a small window with a light in it. Presently I saw someone looking out of this window. Shortly after, a door below was opened and a man came out. One of our men had already been killed while on sentry duty in Veracruz and our orders were to fire at once upon any person who, we believed, had the intention to attack us. But I feared wasting my shot in the dark and placing myself at my assailant's mercy, as he would be upon me before I could reload.

So I pretended to be asleep and, when the man came quite close I drove the butt of my rifle into his chest. He was a very big, strong man and seized me; but I resisted with all my strength, and we struggle together until the guard came to my rescue and seized him. We found that this man had a long sword underneath his cloak, besides a pistol and knife. Next day it was proved that he killed the former sentry some time before, besides another soldier, a Martinique Negro. So his house was destroyed and all his property confiscated, he himself being sentenced to death. Before he was executed he made a special request to be allowed to see the man who had taken him prisoner, and I went to see him in prison. I was given a reward of £10 and each of the guards received a small amount in recognition of his services."[13]

6. The Republican Threat to Veracruz

By the middle of 1866 it had become evident that Maximilian's empire had failed to win the support of the politically influential classes in Mexico, the Imperial government was bankrupt, and the Emperor Maximilian lacked the drive essential for the control of the desperate situation. Napoleon III had become disillusioned with Mexico as his scheme for French intervention had gone wrong; he was already cutting his losses and actively planning the withdrawal of his army of occupation. To speed the French on their way, the Republicans were intensifying their attacks on the French lines of communication and making constant pinpricks in the defenses of Veracruz and two fortified posts on its defensive periphery, La Tejeria and Medellin. On 3 July, Bazaine was informed that the Veracruz command had uncovered a plot to seize the town and arrested five men.[14]

Veracruz was the only port capable of handling an orderly evacuation of men, equipment, and stores. The Veracruz military and naval commands therefore prepared a plan for the defense of the city and port. Under the plan the Sudanese were to be placed in charge of four redoubts as well as the principal internal water supply to the town, La Noria.[15] The role of the Sudanese in the plan is shown in the following directive issued to cover the event of an attack on the city from outside or by a rising within:

Situation (1)

EMERGENCY ORDER IN THE EVENT OF AN ENEMY ATTEMPTING TO SEIZE VERA CRUZ BY ASSAULT

Fort San Xavier (west wall) 25 men commanded by Capt. Husayn Ahmad.

La Noria post (west wall) 36 men commanded by Capt. Muhammad Sulayman.

Fort Santa Gertruda (west wall) 25 men commanded by 2 Lt. Fadlallah Habib.

Fort Santa Barbara (south wall) 25 men commanded by 2 Lt. al-Daw Muhammad.

Fort Concepción (east wall) 25 men commanded by 1 Lt. Faraj 'Azazi.

Egyptians not included above will parade under arms inside the barracks.

The battalion commander Muhammad Almas will assume command and be prepared to send reinforcements to the point which will be indicated to him.

Situation (2)

EMERGENCY ORDER IN THE EVENT OF THE ENEMY ATTEMPTING A SURPRISE ATTACK WITH THE TOWN

Capt. Muhammad Sulaymān will proceed to take command of La Noria post which will be reinforced by 15 men.

2 Lt. al-Daw Muhammad will take command of the Galère[16] which will be brought up t strength of 25 men.

Sub-Lt. Baron will proceed to the barracks with the Egyptians present in Veracruz. He will hold himself ready to march with all available Egyptians to any threatened points.

The post occupied by the senior officer commanding the town will be reinforced by 11 men.

In both situations (1) and (2) the Navy will defend the southern part of the town.[17]

7. Two Celebrations

During August 1866 the Sudanese were worked as never before. Their military value to the French was in sharp contrast with the smallness of their number. Fifty was the irreducible minimum required to cover administrative duties and the sick and wounded in Veracruz. The remaining effectives were required for the most pressing duties of patrolling the railway, escorting trains, and acting as dispatch riders.

The anniversary of the birthday of the Emperor Napoleon III on 15 August was celebrated by a parade held in the Plaza de la Constitución of all troops who could be spared from the defense of Veracruz. The troops of the garrison formed a double line from the square to the parish church where Mass was solemnized. After the service Lt. Col. Rolland, the commanding officer, at the head of his staff, reviewed the troops and presented to the recipients the crosses of the Legion of Honor and Military Medals.[18]

On 16 September, the military command at Veracruz was presented with another celebration, on this occasion rather less welcoming: a Mexican national holiday to mark the anniversary of independence from Spain. The populace was less than friendly, and the command took the greatest care to prevent any Republicans from trying to profit from the effervescence to insinuate themselves into the town to attempt an armed rising. Throughout the night armed patrols of ten men led by an officer patrolled the streets hour by hour. The night passed without incident.

8. The Sudanese Surprised

On the night of 4-5 September an enemy band [attacked?] the fort protecting the railway station and village of La Tejeria. The attack took place after the small garrison had been weakened by the departure of the daily patrol of the line. The *Historique* explained that four other Sudanese had left the fort to recover their horses, which had taken fright at the noise of an approaching train. Catching them unawares the raiders fired, killing one Sudanese, wounding another, and probably capturing the third. The small detachment left in the fort under 1 Lt. al-Daw Muhammad at once charged after the bandits who scattered after leaving several dead.[19]

'Ali Jifun has a less heroic recollection of the incident:

> Another day a few of our horses were grazing close outside the fort and four of our men were out in charge of them. Nearly all our duties at this time were by night and we used to sleep as much as possible during the day. A band of rebels suddenly descended upon our horses and killed 'Abd el-seed [possibly 'Abd al-Sayyid 'Abd al 'Aziz] and Muhammad Simbil and took prisoner Idris Muhammad Sandaloba and Rizq Tamrow [unidentified]. The sentry on duty at the fort gave the alarm but, by the time we turned out, the horses were gone and the men had been killed.[20]

9. Problems of the Evacuation

By the beginning of February 1866, the French had shed all reticence concerning their planning for eventual evacuation though a precise timetable had not yet been drawn up. A serious problem for the Mexican Imperial government was the maintenance of a secure line of communication between Mexico City and Veracruz. The Sudanese battalion would be leaving with the French expeditionary force, and it was essential to plan for its replacement; not only had the Sudanese proved immune to yellow fever, they were also first-class soldiers.

The next-best substitutes would be Caribbeans or U.S. Negroes; both groups, though not immune to yellow fever, had a higher resistance to the disease than Mexicans from the Plateau. This solution was proposed by Elliott, a railway contractor, and supported by General Thun, the Austrian commander-in-chief of the Mexican Imperial army. On 22 February 1866, Emperor

Maximilian's government broached to Marshal Bazaine the feasibility of enlisting a force of Negroes, about 400 men, to take over from the Sudanese.

Bazaine politely damned the suggestion with faint praise. He could see nothing wrong in principle in raising such a force, but he pointed out that the suspicion of the U.S. government would certainly be aroused if the proposed force were to be commanded by ex-Confederate officers and manned by emmancipated American slaves. Such an amalgam of potentially discordant elements was unlikely to have any military value once the word had got around that the Sudanese battalion they were replacing was officered entirely from its own ranks since the beginning of the campaign. Maximilian dropped the proposal.[21]

The Marquis de Montholon, French ambassador at Maximilian's court, wrote to his foreign minister that the enemy was closing in on Veracruz and that 1200 rebels [i.e. Republicans] were threatening the town which would soon be without a garrison. The Egyptians, he went on, were guarding the road from Cordoba to Paso del Macho while the Tirailleurs Algériens were replaced by a disciplinary company.[22] The commandant at Veracruz was nervous and Commandant Cloué in command of the naval squadron on the Atlantic coast had requested a reinforcement to the town garrison, recommending that Marshal Bazaine should be pressed for a decision in order to avoid a disaster.[23] Bazaine needed no prompting. He ordered Commandant Cloué to concentrate all his ships at Veracruz to help protect the town and communications if the need arose.

Meanwhile Maximilian was living a dream in the fond belief that, once the French forces left Mexico, and it was seen by the public that he no longer depended on foreign aid, they would accept him. His attitude toward Bazaine cooled and some members of his government went out of their way to be obstructive, even rude, to the French commander-in-chief. Bazaine had more to do than be sweet to the fading Mexican Imperial government; he had to ensure the safe departure of his army and navy from the country, and he was encouraged by the understanding shown by two Republican leaders, General Porfirio Diaz and Vincente Riva Palacio. He opened negotiations with those two local commanders, whose words he believed he could trust, to effect the exchange of prisoners of war but, even more immediate, to come to an understanding with them for a peaceful withdrawal of the French forces.[24]

The year ended with an element of relief in the Mexican theatre of war after the continuous violence of 1865. What fighting there was seemed meaningless in the growing certainty of French army and navy withdrawal from the country. In the outside world great events were happening.

The civil war which had torn the United States apart had ended in May 1865 with the surrender of the Confederacy. In November the U.S. Congress protested against the French intervention in Mexico. If Emperor Napoleon III needed further proof of the failure of his Mexican policy, here it was; the battle for the domination of the American continent had been won by the United States. The financial and political agony of continuing the occupation of Mexico was becoming too great for the Second Empire to bear.

Notes

1. i.e. lance-corporal, a British rank, no U.S. equivalent. See *Summary Concordance of Military Ranks*, page xvii. He was a private 1st class, much the same. 'Ali Jifun's use of "bey" here was simply politeness.
2. 'Ali Jifūn, 326-27.
3. Zacharia Maria Testart (pronounced Tétar, spelled Testard in *Historique*, 234, 236, which may have mislaid the careful Dabbs, (Dabbs, 204, 337). Both spelling are current.
4. Bazine to Minister of War, Paris, 20 August 1866 (S.H.A.T., G7, 3). Not long afterward Testart was seconded to the Imperial Mexican army to command the 8th battalion Cazadores (light infantry, chasseurs) and was killed in action in October.
5. Bazaine to Minister of War, Paris, 20 August 1866 (S.H.A.T., G7, 3).
6. Garcia to Republican Minister of War and Navy, 8 September 1866 (Toral, 577-78).
7. Bazine to Minister of War, Paris, 9 June 1866 (S.H.A.T., G7, 3).
8. Ibid., 27 July 1866.
9. Bakhit Baraka (3 coy) was promoted sgt.
10. Montholon to Rolland, 7 July 1866 (A.M.A.E., corr. pol. des consuls, Mexique 4, fo. 1691).
11. Probably Pte. 1cl. Baraka Ahmad.
12. Palace (Arab. sarayya) rustic Sudanese word for any house of more than one story.
13. 'Ali Jifūn, 329-30.
14. Dabbs, 173, citing BA XXII fo. 4253.
15. See Chapter 3, note 1. The noria here was protected by a bastion with a barbette (handing-over notes of military installations by the French to the Imperial Mexican authorities, procès-verbal, 4 March 1867 (S.H.A.T., Génie, IV, No. 96).
16. Galère (Spanish galera) a prison "consisting of three rooms in bad condition" (handing-over notes).
17. *Historique*, 240-41. Each strong point would receive its quota of artillery. Projet d'armement, place de la Veracruz, Commandement Supérieur, 1 June 1866 (S.H.A.T., G7, 89).
18. Ibid., 241-42.
19. Ibid., 243.
20. 'Ali Jifūn, 329.

21. Dabbs, 162, citing BA XVII, fos. 3504, 3512.
22. A company formed from military prisoners on parole.
23. Montholon to Foreign Minister, Paris, 20 October 1866 (A.M.A.E., corr. pol. Mexique, 68).
24. Col. E.I.M. de Maussion to Bazaine, 16 January 1867 (Dabbs, 209 n.113, citing BA XXVI, fo, 5112).

The Mission Completed

1. Some Last Impressions of Veracruz and of the Sudanese
2. The Line of Communication under the Strain of Evacuation
3. Among the Last to Leave
4. The Reckoning

Chapter 9

The Mission Completed

1. Some Last Impressions of Veracruz and the Sudanese

The last and most colorful impression of the Sudanese on the eve of their departure from Mexico came from Colonel Henri Blanchot, the staff officer whose reminiscences gave generous scope for a romantic pen. Veracruz had been in French hands for six years and had changed beyond recognition. The disease-laden, ruined buildings in which lived a sordid populace, the festering hearths of misery and material and moral putrescence, had disappeared, he wrote. The French military had taken the town in hand, transformed the Paseo into a fine public garden and the parade ground into a delightful square planted with sweet-smelling shrubs to the great despair of the scavenging birds who no longer sought their daily food among the heaps of dung.[1]

The ideological significance of sewage disposal was not lost on the U.S. military. *Terry's Guide to Mexico*[2] informs its readers that the Americans who bombarded and briefly occupied Veracruz in 1914,

> cleaned the port, eliminated all the pest holes, beautified it in various ways. . .the bluish bubbling sludge which anciently meandered along the open sewers. . .has permanently vanished; the loathsome. . .*zopilotes* [scavenging birds] now have to scratch for a precarious living and as a consequence the port is. . .free from the dread vomito.

It is only fair to the *zopilotes* to add that some are still there perching on the roof tops, looking morose as ever, as though waiting wearily for publicity from the next invader.

Colonel Blanchot reflected,

> Strangest of all was the appearance of the Egyptians who formed the town garrison. These black children from Upper Egypt had come under the French flag. Under the burning sun of the Tierra Caliente they had relieved the French troops who were being annihilated by the merciless climate. Among these memories may I add a word of gratitude to these friends of yester year who have generously rendered us so important a service. They were superb, those ebony sculptures draped in white cashmere, those descendants of the warriors of the ancient Pharaohs, who impressed the onlooker with their height, the pride in their posture and the dignity of their bearing. They exhibited a self-respect eager to win the admiration of the French soldiers; their manner of saluting the officers and presenting arms were an eloquent characteristic deeply flattering to France.[3]

2. The Line of Communication under the Strain of Evacuation

The railway might just hold out. In a report on the functioning of the line during the second half of January, the Veracruz command wrote that the transport of troops and materiel on the railway was going smoothly "though you have to be prepared for occasional delays arising from accidents, only too frequent on our line, which signally lacks the order common in Europe."[4]

The railway had been over-used and under-maintained. The military had pressed for quick construction; the result was the laying in haste of a level, serpentine trace to avoid delays in digging cuttings and building embankments. Another hazard was the bridge at La Soledad, five timber girder spans each 64 feet long, carried on tall stone piers and abutments, a positive incitement to arson.

The last enemy raid on the bridge was a providential failure. Some irresponsible Republican faction tried to set fire to the bridge. Fortunately for the French and Republicans, the bridge timbers were too wet to burn; so railway communications continued, but with care.[5] After the departure of the French, the Republican government made a new agreement with the London-based railway company for the supply of a fleet of Fairlie double-ended locomotives shown in plate 9.

The evacuation of French civilians and their families added to the hazards of the railway permanent way. In several places, where the roads crossed and re-crossed the railway track, continuous convoys of heavy Mexican road vehicles were damaging the rails and sleepers and halting troop trains.[6]

Yet in the middle of the tremendous activity and stress inevitable during the last few days of the evacuation, the French military engineers were engaged in the bureaucratic process of formally handing over the fixed military assets of the railway and port to the representatives of their Mexican Imperial allies. Thus Major G. A. Dormont of the French Engineers and Señor Ansel Arnaud of the municipal commission of Paso del Macho for the Imperial government signed a *procès-verbal* on 1 March 1867 covering the fortification of the railway terminus.[7] Similar documents were signed for Veracruz and the main stations on the line.

It proved an empty gesture as the Mexican Imperial government was entering upon its final phase of dissolution.

3. Among the Last to Leave

Regular evacuation by naval transport began on 10 February 1867 and ended on 12 March when the last transport left the shore for the anchorage at the island of Sacrificios off the south end of the town. During the actual troop evacuation, each column usually entrained at Paso del Macho in the morning and arrived at Veracruz in the evening. Here the column spent the night under canvas and went aboard its allotted ship in the early morning. Transports generally sailed from the port at sunset. Captain Peyron, the port commandant, directed the embarkation.

Several officers wrote with variations on the theme of Captain Paul Laurent of the 3rd Chasseurs; "From Paso del Macho to Vera Cruz the line is guarded by the Egyptians whose constitutions resist the murderous climate better than the Europeans."[8] His own convoy left Paso del Macho by the night train at 2300 hours and arrived in Veracruz at 0600 the next day.

With a sense of drama, for time was slipping away, the commandant in charge of entraining at Paso del Macho wrote on 2 March: "I leave Paso del Macho this evening with the last Frenchmen."

By 7 March, there remained at Veracruz only the 7th Regiment of the Line, a section of the general staff detailed for port embarkation duties and the Sudanese battalion reputedly but improbably guarding to the last moment the line to the port. A member of the Belgian Legion who claims to have entrained at La Soledad as late as 7 March saw the Sudanese still patrolling the whole railway to Veracruz.[9]

On the 12th, the last three ships steamed from the port to their concentration anchorage under the relative shelter of the island of Sacrificios. Marshal Bazaine embarked in the troopship *Le Souverain* with his family and some of his staff. The liner *Castiglione* followed with the rest of the staff. *La Seine*, the ship that had brought the Sudanese from Egypt in 1863, was to take them home. Shortly before they went on board, Bazaine himself reviewed them and, in the name of France and her emperor, thanked them for their services and devotion. They had all been lucky; only two cases of yellow fever occurred during the period of evacuation; neither was Sudanese.

By the morning of 15 March, the Republican forces were already closing in on Veracruz. General R. Benavides reported that his column of 400 infantry and a cavalry brigade had arrived near the southeastern perimeter of the town. Looking over the sea to Sacrificios three km away he noticed 17 loaded French transports still anchored, ready to leave.[10]

4. The Reckoning

The permanent bequest of the Sudanese battalion to the history of Mexico was nil. There were officially twelve deserters but, according to the records, only six failed to return to camp. Of those who returned, having weighed the possibilities of a new life in Mexico or their old life in Africa and having chosen the latter, none served more than a few months in prison; two were pardoned and one was promoted to sergeant on his return to Egypt. Of those who preferred to stay in Mexico, we know nothing. Inquiries made in the Tierra Caliente in 1981 and 1989 were in vain. After all, descendants of deserters are not overly anxious to recall their great-grandfathers' renunciation of their heritage, and great-grandchildren forget. Whether they settled down happily among their fellow African and former slaves and founded families that flourish today or whether they died and left no memorial, it is not our present intention to inquire: *Requiescant in pace*.

It was rather Mexico that made its impress upon the Sudanese and provided the topic of conversation for gatherings of old soldiers for many years to come. In Mexico the Sudanese had been transformed by four years of service with one of the best armies in the world. For the first time in their lives they had met foreign officers who took the trouble to know them, to attend to their comfort, to laugh with them, to maintain discipline by example.

Fate dealt less kindly with the French. The war which brought high military honor to one small Sudanese battalion was for the French a disaster. The five years and three months of their intervention in Mexico brought the French only profitless expenditure, loss of men and money, discredit in Europe, and the damaging ill-will of the United States. The accumulated expenses and losses of the military and naval establishments fatally crippled the French in their financial preparations for the war with the Prussians which the French government with incredible folly precipitated in 1870. The French entered that war with their resources depleted, severely limiting the number of divisions deployed at the front and the supply of equipment and stores to maintain them in the field.[11]

Thus the decision of Napoleon III to lead France into military intervention in Mexico proved to be the prelude to the fall of the Second Empire and to his own ruin.

For Mexico there was no respite. The French occupation and the French association with Emperor Maximilian, though less than cordial toward the end, indirectly brought discredit to the Church and to the Mexican Conservatives who supported the Church. The departure of the French forces and the collapse of the Mexican Empire signalled a return of the country to its chaotic norm. The Republic floundered on through constitutional disorder during nearly 40 years of enforced discipline at the hands of General Porfirio Diaz, the former Republican commander of the eastern zone now turned dictator. On Diaz's fall, chaos speedily returned and it was not until the Americans seized Veracruz in 1914 that a politically adult, national government was at last within sight.

Notes

1. Blanchot, III, 468.
2. ed. 1930, 472-73.
3. Blanchot, III, 368-69.
4. Montholon to Foreign Minister, Paris, 10 February 1867 (A.M.A.E., corr. pol. Mexique, 69, fos. 10-11).
5. Blanchot, III 465.
6. Dabbs, 214, citing BA XXVI, fo. 5197.
7. S.H.A.T. (Génie), Expédition du Mexique.
8. P. Laurent, *La Guerre du Mexique*, 342.
9. E. Amiable, *Légionnaire au Mexique, 1865-1867*, Bruxelles, 1942, 105.
10. Report to the Republican Minister of War and Navy on the siege and occupation of Veracruz, 5 July 1867, cited in Toral, 791.
11. Willing, 72, 73.

The Voyage Home

Chapter 10

The Voyage Home

1. The Atlantic Passage

On 12 March 1867, *La Seine,* with Frigate Captain Pagel[1] in command, left the foreshore at Veracruz to join the concentration of French troopships at anchor nearby: on the 16th of March she steamed out into the Gulf of Mexico. On board were the remaining 299 officers and men of the Sudanese battalion, with Algerian and French troops and 18 civilians including several women and children.

The homeward passage in the spring was a happier experience for the black Egyptian contingent than the grim outward voyage into the unknown in 1863. This time no Sudanese died en route. Passengers, civilian and military, were nevertheless under strict naval discipline. Officers and their families were a superior category, seated "at the commandant's table." At thc top of the list of precedence were the two senior officers on board, Colonel Boleslawski, an Austrian, and the chef de bataillon, Muhammad Almas. Accompanying the colonel was his wife, their infant daughter, tragically named Maximiliana, with the family servant, Widow Collin. Below them were nine Sudanese officers (they had left Egypt with three) and four sergeant-majors.

The Egyptian contingent was under the administrative care of Lieutenant Baron and a small establishment of two French staff clerks, Corporal Voirin and Fusilier Bruyneel, and three interpreters: Staff Sergeants Muhammad b. Ahmadi and 'Ali al-'Arabi with Second Class Staff Interpreter 'Amr b. Muhammad also recorded as a tailor. Lt. Baron and his staff had been with the battalion almost since its arrival in Mexico in 1863.

Pagel's original orders were to proceed directly to Alexandria but, a week before the troops sailed from Veracruz, Marshal Bazaine urgently besought the war minister to favor the Egyptians "whom I routed via London in order to visit Paris which would have an excellent effect on the battalion." Finally, however, it was decided to disembark the troops at Toulon. *La Seine* used her engine only in the Gulf of Mexico to reach the southerly crossing of the Atlantic where greater use of wind and current afforded economy. On 13 April, she called at Horta on the Azores island of Faial where she encountered quarantine restrictions that were not lifted until the ship berthed at Toulon at 0800 hours on 30 April. Her transit time from Veracruz had been 48 days, indicating once more the forced dependence on sail.

2. Paris

One or two soldiers were found unfit to travel by rail after the long, slow sea voyage. The fit entrained for their nine-day spree in the capital as a gift from the Emperor. Lt. Baron who had accompanied them from Mexico would be with them.

During the stay in Paris, the battalion was placed in the care of the marshal commanding the Imperial Guard and were accorded pay and allowances on the same scale as the prestigious 1st Infantry Regiment of the Imperial Guard. Each day parties of nine Sudanese were conducted round the city on sightseeing tours by French non-commissioned officers. 'Ali Jifun was among the Sudanese military tourists to the capital.

Amid the international festivities the Sudanese battalion was not forgotten. *Le Monde Illustré* of 18 May 1867 carried a fanciful engraving of the battalion marching over the Pont d'Austerlitz past a row of Parisians reinforced in an improbable coincidence by a Mexican onlooker in a Sombrero.[2] The journal added that the arrival of the battalion in Paris had excited public curiosity. "The language spoken by these black warriors is a mixture of Coptic, Turkish, Arabic and Persian," wrote *Le Monde Illustré* in a crescendo of speculative linguistics, "Only their interpreters can understand their language. It was said that the battalion was going to stay in Paris to serve the Viceroy as a guard but it seems that other arrangements have been made. It has been disclosed that the battalion left Paris on Monday last."

The climax of the Paris holiday was a review by the Emperor. At 3.00 P.M. on 9 May, Napoleon, accompanied by Shahin Pasha, the commanding general of the Egyptian army, reviewed the battalion in the court of the Tuilleries Palace. For four years in Mexico the battalion had rendered the greatest service in the Hot Lands and at Veracruz. A goodly number of officers bore the

Cross of the Legion of Honor while the other ranks wore on their breasts the French Campaign Medal. After the review, Shahin Pasha individually presented those upon whom decorations and awards had been conferred to the Emperor.[3]

'Ali Jifun's version of the ceremony introduced a personal element, sadly lacking in the official account in *Le Moniteur*:

> Shaheen Pasha had been sent from Egypt to meet us and he now attended as interpreter to the Emperor, who called out some of our names from a list, and said a few kind words to each as he came to the front. Napoleon first addressed us all generally through Shaheen Pasha first, and then, one by one, called up those of us who were on the special list. He said he was very pleased with our gallant conduct and hard work in his service in Mexico, and, while lamenting the loss of those who had not returned, welcomed the survivors and wished us all success. Every non-commissioned officer and man was promoted one step in rank on the spot, and thus I became a bash shawish [company sergeant-major]. We all received the French medal for the Mexican campaign, and I myself was specially brought forward to receive the gold decoration "Pour Valeur et Discipline." The Emperor told us through Shaheen Pasha that my name had been specially submitted to his notice on account of my bravery in many actions and my steady devotion to duty, so he now himself pinned upon my jacket the insignia of the highest honor he could confer upon a soldier. Whenever I was wearing this decoration in the streets of Paris, guards and sentries presented arms as I passed.[4]

3. Alexandria

The Sudanese entrained for Toulon. *La Seine*, still commanded by Captain Pagel, and a second frigate, sailed for Alexandria on 16 May with the battalion and a mixed cargo consigned by the Overland Route via Suez to Cochin China[5] which the French had recently begun to acquire.

The homecoming of the battalion to Alexandria on 27 May—*La Seine* had arrived on the 26th—was announced in a flurry of official publicity.

Consul-General Outrey informed his minister in Paris that, after disembarking, the battalion was given two days' rest. On 30 May, the Khedive held a review of the Alexandria garrison in honor of the Sudanese battalion, which marched past the saluting base at the head of the parade.

In the evening a double banquet was held at the Khedivial Palace of Ras al-Tin; the first, inconspicuous, for the other ranks of the battalion, the other, for the officers, presided over by the Egyptian director of foreign affairs, Muhammad Sharif Pasha, and the commander of the navy. Among the guests were the French consul-general, the commander of a French naval squadron (then paying a call at Alexandria), the senior officers of each French warship in the harbor, the senior officers of the Egyptian garrison and, of course, the officers of the Sudanese battalion.[6]

At an investiture held at the Ras al-Tin Palace, Consul-General Outrey introduced Lt. Baron to the Khedive who conferred on him the grade of officer of the Majidiyya decoration. He thanked him with all his heart for the generosity which the French army had shown to his Egyptian troops.

The French consul-general was at pains to correct some widely exaggerated stories being spread in the town as to the extent of Sudanese casualties in Mexico. He asked Lt. Baron for the correct figure. In brief, the Lieutenant told him, the battalion never had more than 447 men including officers. Of these 20 had been killed in action, 28 had died from wounds, 64 had died of sickness, two had disappeared during battles, 12 had deserted, 7 convicted prisoners had been serving their sentence in the fortress of San Juan de Ulua and had been sent home with the rest of the troops,[7] and 1 man was still in hospital in France.[8] The total loss to the battalion was therefore 133 men, of whom 112 were dead.

The battalion strength on its return to Alexandria was 321. The consul-general added that he would have those figures published in the local press.[9]

Officer promotions were published *en bloc* on 28 May 1867. The promotion which raised the battalion commander, Lieutenant-Colonel Muhammad Almas Efendi, to colonel and bey was announced in the relatively exalted form of a *buyuruldu*.[10]

By ceremonial tradition, Queen Victoria conferred honors accompanied by brevets drafted with an economy of words. Her contemporaries, the Khedive Isma'il Pasha and his titular sovereign, the Ottoman Sultan, followed an opposite tradition and garnished their benevolence with mellifluous literary set pieces, hierarchically graded in length and formulation according to the importance of the recipient. To illustrate this contrast we have translated in full the brevet addressed to the Sudanese major conferring on him promotion to colonel and elevation to the grade of bey, because it exemplifies a relationship between ruler and ruled which then had no parallel in the United States or Britain:

> The glory of the magistrates and the nobility, Muhammad Almas Bey, former major of the Sudanese Egyptian battalion in Mexico and promoted colonel—may his greatness increase!
>
> Whereas it is Our usual custom and known nature to reward the diligent, loyal and upright, and to cause them to achieve their desire; and I am pleased

> by the performance of the Egyptian troops in Mexico, where their discipline has been perfect, and the general report of their proficiency on the battlefields in the arts of warfare and their skill, which hoisted the army's banner and proclaimed the nobility of the Egyptian forces in spite of their absence from their homelands and their remote station. I am pleased at the confirmation of their splendid characters, good conduct and complete rectitude; as also I am now pleased at the return home of this unit, raising the banners of glory, happiness and rejoicing.
>
> Wherefore I have granted you the rank of colonel to honour your status, to promote you amongst your colleagues and friends, to show appreciation of the good services you have rendered, to reward you for your zeal you have displayed, and to testify to my great consideration for you and my continuing regard.
>
> Wherefore acknowledge fully this favour, and continue your accustomed loyalty and rectitude as a mark of gratitude for it. Show the utmost diligence in the increased duties of your exalted rank, wealth and promotion to the attainment of your hopes.[11]

These were elegant but not empty words. They implied the historic Mamluk family relationship between patron and freedmen which forged a bond of mutual obligation. Nine years later the recipient of his Lord's confidence loyally fulfilled an obligation, after his fashion.

4. Promotion with a Purpose

The Khedive now fulfilled a promise of double promotion. After the first few days ashore, 33 officers of the battalion received double promotion in their commissioned ranks, while 34 non-commissioned officers were commissioned as 1st and 2nd Lieutenants. Eight buglers and drummers and 173 privates 1st class were promoted sergeants. Isma'il ordered the director of the war office to accord the promoted personnel the appropriate pay, rations, and uniform and to allocate a site at al-Tura for officers' retirement accommodation and settlement.[12]

In ordering this extraordinary mass advancement, the Khedive was not imitating the military excesses of Gilbertian Opera but was motivated by his concept of sound military sense. Their French allies and Mexican enemies had between them converted the Sudanese into a highly-trained, battle-hardened force capable of fighting an intelligently led, well-trained, modern army. The French consul-general's explanation of Isma'il's action is convincing: to distribute these disciplined and trained soldiers in such a way as to make the fullest use of their theoretical and practical knowledge derived from four years of hard campaigning with their French allies. To have kept the battalion intact as a military show-piece would have defeated the advantages of its distribution throughout the Egyptian Sudanese Infantry of the Line. There is no evidence that Isma'il's decision was induced by fear that this privileged unit might get above itself and make trouble. The effect of the returning Sudanese on the Egyptian scene did not escape the attention of the U.S. consul-general in Egypt who reported to Washington:

> I have reason to believe that, in spite of their discontent when they set out, the other ranks no less than the officers have come back well satisfied with their campaign and appreciate the attention of which they have been the object. They have a great admiration for France and for the French military administration. Nearly all of them have learnt to speak French and have adopted the way of life of French soldiers. If these men are distributed over Egypt the French influence in this country will be greatly increased.[13]

The Sudanese had returned to Egypt a *Corps d'Élite*.

Notes

1. Louis Antoine Alexandre Pagel (born 1810, retired 1868), not to be confused with Frigate Captain Victor Jean Pagel (born 1821, retired 1873). The former's report on the voyage to the Ministry of the Navy was untraced. What follows has been derived from the correspondence between Bazaine and the Minister of the Navy, Paris (S.H.A.T., G7, 71, 950) and S.H.M.T., (Hist/91 -007).
2. By M. Vauvert, article by Ryckebusch (plate 16).
3. *Le Moniteur Officiel*, 10 May 1867.
4. 'Ali Jifūn, 330. The branch of S.H.A.T. charged with the administration of decorations and awards explained that, although the metallic content, and hence the color, of the French M.M. varied from time to time, the status and symbolic value remains constant. For gold read gilt.
5. al-Waqā'i' al-miṣriyya 30 May 1867, 109. rpr. in *Taqwīm*, 707.
6. A.M.A.E., corr. pol. des consuls turcs d'Alexandrie, 1 June 1867, fos. 217-19.
7. See chap. 3, sect. 1.
8. Three more returned later: Idris Muhammad Sandaluba and Rizq Ahmad (both ptes. of No. 1 coy), prisoners of war released by the Mexican Republican government on the conclusion of peace and returned to Alexandria, 2 September 1867. Sgt. Nasim Sulayman (No. 2 coy), a patient in a French hospital, missed his ship and rejoined his unit later.

9. Consul-General Outrey to Foreign Minister, Paris, 1 June 1867 (A.M.A.E., corr. pol., Alexandrie, 39, fos. 217-19).
10. Arab *buyuruldi* or, by metathesis, *buyulurdi*. In Turk. the word simply means "Let it be executed accordingly."
11. Khedivial decree of 28 May 1867, rpr. in *Taqwīm*, 705-6.
12. Tura, on the right bank of the Nile 13 km south of Cairo, was a depot for the black regiments.
13. U.S. Consul-General Egypt to Secretary of State, Washington, 8 June 1867.

The Veterans from Mexico in African History

1. Thirty-One Years of Active Service

2. In the Equatorial Command, 1869-1888

3. In Dar Fur, 1874-1876

4. In Defeat against the Ethiopians, 1875-1876

5. A Brush with the Egyptian Nationalist Movement, 1881-1882

6. In the Mahdist Revolt: Destruction of the Egyptian Army in the Sudan, 1881-1885

7. In the New Egyptian Army: Among the last Survivors from Mexico

Chapter 11

The Veterans from Mexico in African History

1. Thirty-One Years of Active Service

The climax of four years of fighting a clever army in Mexico was the battalion's triumphal reception in Paris as the Emperor's guests, followed by a hero's welcome and double promotion for most of them in Alexandria. This was the sweet foretaste of the bitter years ahead.

The disbandment of the battalion[1] and the dispersal of its personnel throughout the Sudanese regiments brusquely ended four years of discipline and shared hardship. All but a few veterans from Mexico lived on in a condition of statistical and biographical oblivion. A few, but not all, depended on rank. Of the 321 officers and other ranks who survived the campaign, officers fared best in the written record. General officers were, after all, the most publicized. Then, in declining order of biographical attention, came field officers, junior officers, and lastly, scarcely noticed at all, non-commissioned officers and men.

The poverty of documentation discovered so far—we lack the permanent contact with the military archives possessed by our Egyptian colleagues—is partly explainable by the devastation of war in the Sudan during the first four years of the Mahdist military triumph (1881-1885). It is also explainable by the more enduring preference of the people, in a land of low percentage literacy, for profitable documents such as land title deeds rather than military biographical records. For instance we know that two field officers, both from the Sudanese battalion, both first-class men, deserted to the Mahdist cause, but we know the name of only one non-commissioned officer, Sgt Fadl al-Sid Abu Juma' (No. 3 coy)[2] who sought salvation by changing sides.

In following the Sudanese veterans from Mexico back to the Africa which formed them, it is not difficult to rediscover that the strength of their inner convictions was unaffected by their four years of contact with a friendly but alien culture. While serving with the French army they were subject to military law and in particular to the sentences of courts martial in the event of alleged wrongdoing. These courts administered a law of war and of peace which accorded rights to enemy civilians. This was a concept which these Sudanese soldiers found was contrary to their traditional ways of conducting war as was evident in the trial for murder described in chapter 3(7).

With a few savage exceptions, the Mexicans did not kill their enemies who had surrendered their arms. The Sudanese were not accustomed to taking prisoners of war; in Africa they usually had no means of accommodating them. On their return to the Sudan, the battalion must have sighed with relief to be back with people who recognized the rightfulness of the law of retaliation without pettifogging foreign palliatives, the law which all Sudanese adults understood and practiced. Even during the massacre of soldiers and civilians after the Mahdist forces had breached the defenses of Khartoum on the night of 25-26 January 1885, the motive of many killings was alleged by witnesses to have been private revenge which did not recognize courts martial.

2. In the Equatorial Command, 1869-1888

Unlike some Ottoman sultans and European sovereigns of the past, Isma'il Pasha did not indulge in topographical exaggeration to amplify the booming resonance of his territorial claims. In the year A.H. 1282 [A.D. 1865-1866] his official *laqab* accurately defined what was his before he began his plans for territorial aggrandizement:

> Ruler [*hākim*] and Lord of Egypt, Possessor of its boundaries and frontiers, its citadels and the Sudan with the Governorates of Sawākin and Muṣawwa', namely, His Highness Isma'il Pasha, son of Ibrahim Pasha, son of Muhammad 'Ali Pasha the Great, of Kavala.[3]

Despite the Khedive's idea of placing the Sudanese veterans from Mexico throughout the Egyptian black regiments as military paragons for the rest to imitate, he ended by sending most of them where his territorial ambitions called for them: to the Equatorial region and the Eastern Sudan. Out of thirty-eight officers *en disponibilité* in May 1867, thirteen were assigned to Sir Samuel Baker Pasha's expedition to the Great Lakes (Lakes Region of

Central Africa), and eleven to garrisons in the Eastern Sudan to support Egyptian authority along the Somali coast and into the continually disputed borderlands of Ethiopia.

The mid-nineteenth-century Euro-American West expected its heroes in black Africa to conform to its own perception of black Africans: mentally and morally children incapable of profitable land use or mineral exploitation, waiting for leadership and guidance from men of an inherently superior civilization motivated by altruism; upstanding, decisive, insensitive yet sentimental men.

Such was the British railway manager, big game hunter, explorer and author of distinction whom Isma'il Pasha appointed to lead a military expedition to extend the Egyptian influence on the Upper Nile toward the Great Lakes. Sir Samuel Baker[4] accepted a four-year contract with the rank of major-general and the dignity of pasha as general governor of the unoccupied territory between the southern limit of White Nile navigation and the Great Lakes, with the mission of opening them to commercial development and—as a sop to politically powerful anti-slavery interests, chiefly in Britain—an obligation to suppress the slave trade.

On this issue, Isma'il deceived Baker and Baker deceived Isma'il. Isma'il had inserted the anti-slavery clause in the contract because the topic was fashionable in Europe and almost topical in the United States but relied on Baker's sophistication not to emphasize unduly what to him was a foreign whim impossible to realize in real life. Baker on the other hand wildly upset the balance of his contractual obligations by overdoing the abolition of the slave trade which made him popular at home and sold his books but which also involved him in continuous war with the riverain tribes and did nothing to develop the country. In a perverse way this suited Baker who loved a fight and came to regard his mission as largely a military exercise. Meanwhile, his demands on government stores had alienated Egyptian officials on his line of communication with Khartoum; Ja'far Mazhar Pasha, governor-general of the Sudan, complained to the Khedive of Baker's intemperate demands.

In effect Baker found the direction of a complex, cooperative command uncongenial and wisely resigned. He was most in his element with fighting men and the veterans from Mexico won high praise in his book *Ismailïa*: Lieutenant "Farritch" (not a bad guess for Faraj Ahmad Hāshim) was now in Baker's bodyguard[5] and Lieutenant Marjan 'Ali al-Danasuri who as a major was killed in 1885 in resisting the Mahdist advance into the Equatorial province.[6] 'Abdallah Salim al-Faqi was promoted commander of the Sudanese detachment with rank of adjutant-major.[7] Another of Baker's officers, Adjutant-Major 'Abdallah al-Dinkawi,[8] commanded the fort at Fatiko. Baker admired the courage of Captain Marjan Sharif[9] in a fight with Bari tribesmen.

Colonel C.G. Gordon, the future general, who was to die in Khartoum along with his senior staff of veteran officers from Mexico, succeeded Baker. Col. Muhammad Ra'uf Bey, another future governor-general of the Sudan, held the post *ad interim*. Baker's violent treatment of the Bari people had soured any welcome they might have given to his successor. In 1875, they killed both Captian Marjan Sharif and his commanding officer, Major Ernest Linant de Bellefonds, in a pitched battle.[10]

In the course of his two years as general governor, Gordon first met the survivors of the Sudanese battalion from Mexico. Through the French consul-general in Egypt, he obtained replacements for the faded ribbons of their decorations and medals and, having himself acquired some French, may well have talked with them. Gordon developed a respect for the men of the Sudanese battalion which he retained throughout his life.

A former Confederate States officer, Colonel Charles Chaillé-Long Bey,[11] now an officer on the Egyptian general staff, was on duty in the Equatorial province as second-in-command to Gordon Pasha in 1874-1876. Gordon sent him on a reconnaissance to the Ruler of Uganda to test the feasibility of an Egyptian advance toward Lake Victoria.

Chaillé-Long had already tried his hand in journalism in the United States and had developed a flair for graphic popular writing, which he applied only too professionally to his books on his African experiences. Like most of Khedive Isma'il's American and British appointments, he was illiterate in Arabic, the language of government, and demonstrated his ignorance of both Arabic language and Islam by blissfully writing "Abdel" (the servant of) as though it were a man's name. He maddened Sir Harry Johnston with his imaginary plurals for African place names.[12] But at least his familiarity with French might have enabled him to talk to Sudanese who had themselves been exposed to four years with the French army at Veracruz. He writes with human intimacy of two remote garrisons of veterans from Mexico in the heart of Egyptian Equatoria who gave him hospitality on his journey into Uganda.

On his way south in 1874 to King Mutesa's hutted capital, and again on his return northward to Lado, he received a warm welcome by the commanders and men of two fortified posts at the furthest edge of Egyptian penetration. At Fatiko he found a garrison of 200 men, smartly turned out, many wearing their medals from their Mexican campaign, commanded by Adjutant-Major 'Abdallah al-Dinkawi who wore the ribbons of the French Legion of Honor.[13]

At Foweira, another military post on his route, there was a second contingent of old "Mexicans" commanded by another veteran adjutant-major decorated with the Legion of Honor. His name, Chaillé-Long writes, was Baba Tuka, Daddy Tuka. It was only natural that these African troops, at last living in congenial surroundings away from the superficial cultural constraints of the Arab North, should revert to easygoing informality, and to calling their commander Baba Tuka rather than Adjutant-Major Tawakkul Muhammad.[14] Or, as a Sudanese colleague asks, was it Chaillé-Long's mis-hearing of a western Arabic nickname Baba Tukiyya, Daddy Waistbelt, a possible reference to his girth?

The Foweira garrison of 190 officers and men included 76 who had served with Bazaine in Mexico. In the evenings the officers entertained the visitor with stories of their adventures in Mexico and their holiday in Paris on the way home. It was the event of their lives and the Francophone Chaillé-Long clearly enjoyed this Franco-African encounter.

The last general governor of the Egyptian Equatorial province was Edouard Carl Oscar Theodor Schnitzer, a former medical officer in the Ottoman service, who had adopted Islam and the name Muhammad al-Amin, the Arabic original of the Turkish form Emin.[15] He was appointed in 1878 and was later elevated to the rank of brigadier-general and the grade of pasha of the fourth class.

Whatever Emin's other troubles were, most of his troops were content in their isolated paradise on the Upper White Nile; they were (except for two Mahdist invasions from the north) reasonably out of danger, and quite out of reach of the discipline of Cairo.

In an almost cheerful letter to Cairo written in 1886,[16] Emin explains:

> The great part of my men, especially the [Sudanese] officers, have no desire to leave the country. . . .The greater part of our soldiers, coming as they do, from our own district. . .naturally prefer, to remain here and live as their fathers did while the Negro soldier sent hither from Egypt whether he be an officer or a private soldier has forgotten in the lapse of years what strict discipline means and further has adapted himself to the country.

Emin Pasha was the only general governor of the Egyptian Equatorial Province who possessed any real capability for surviving in the hard conditions of isolation. Neither Gordon nor Prout[17] was put to the test. Alone, of the three general governors, Emin was literate in Arabic and Turkish. The more cultured Europeans who were his guests at Lado or later in one of his several field posts further south understood his enormous difficulties of keeping the Ottoman flag flying in the face of insubordination and mutiny among his men. He suffered the final ignominy of being more or less forcibly "rescued" by the insensitive, able, ruthless, and celebrated H.M. Stanley to the greater glory of the latter and to remove one of the final obstacles to the British occupation of the southern portion of the Egyptian Equatorial province. The blow was softened by a dispatch from the Khedive Tawfiq authorizing him to leave his post and come away. Egypt, the pioneer of what was now called "the scramble for Africa" had ceded to her mighty rival.

3. In Dar Fur, 1874-1876

The Egyptian government did not conquer the independent sultanate of Dar Fur; a powerful Northern Sudanese trader, al-Zubayr Rahma Mansur, conquered it for them in 1873-1874 with his private army.[18]

This incident did not involve many veterans from the Mexican campaign. One of the few identified was Major Salih Hijazi[19] who began his military career as a subaltern in No. 4 company of the Sudanese battalion. Salih had returned from a short turn of duty in Egypt about 1873 when al-Zubayr (from his territorial base in the prairie country south of the Bahr al-'Arab) seized Dar Rizayqat in southern Dar Fur within the territory claimed by the Sultan and offered it to the Egyptian government with the additional offer to conquer the rest of the sultanate in compensation for his having killed Muhammad al-Hilālī, the officially appointed governor of the territory where his own business interests were centered.

Khedive Isma'il affected to accept al-Zubayr's offer, made him a bey, and helped him with some troops and ammunition. However, the Khedive did not trust al-Zubayr and ordered Isma'il Ayyub Pasha, governor-general of the Sudan, to make an urgent invasion of the sultanate in order to prevent al-Zubayr from seizing it for himself. al-Zubayr, indignant at this treatment, hurried off to Cairo to complain to the Khedive who, by a master-stroke, permanently prevented him from returning to the Sudan. Thus Isma'il Pasha Ayyub and his Egyptian army made an easy, if only superficial, occupation of the fallen sultanate.

Dar Fur was now organized as a standard general governorate like the Equatorial province and the Eastern Sudan. The Sultan's capital at al-Fashir was retained as the administrative center and main depot for the army while at Qulqul on the trade and pilgrim route from the Chad basin 200 km west of al-Fashir and at Dara 120 km south of it, two subsidiary garrison posts were established. Major Salih Hijazi was promoted lieutenant-Colonel (*Qā'im makām*) and appointed governor of the *Qā'im maqāmiyya* of Dara.

He was soon occupied with a conspiracy by the sons of al-Zubayr Pasha, as related by old soldiers to Prince 'Umar Tusun.

> al-Zubayr already had about 12,000 soldiers commanded by his son Sulayman Bey, a foolish young man angry with the Egyptian government who had summoned his father to Cairo and refused to let him return to Dar

Fur to achieve his ambitions. So, when Sulayman heard that General Gordon was coming to Dara he plotted to murder him, attack the Dara garrison, press on against the other garrisons and govern Dar Fur for himself while holding all the Egyptian officers and officials hostage to force the Egyptian Government to return his father to the Sudan.

Now Sulayman had with him two officers more farsighted than himself: al-Nur [Bey Muhammad] ʻAnqara and Saʻid [Pasha] Husayn al-Jimiʻabi.[20] They advised him to forget his scheme but, as he would not listen to them, one of them wrote secretly to General Gordon advising him of the plot. Gordon then wrote to Salih Bey Hijazi to be on his guard.

Salih Bey at once began to construct walls, a ditch and bastions and made such ostentatious preparations against attack that the conspirators realized that they had been betrayed and abandoned their plot.

Salih Bey remained Governor of Dara until his death there about 1878. He was succeeded by another volunteer veteran from the Mexican campaign, Major Muhammad Sulayman (No. 2 coy) who was promoted Lieutenant-Colonel to qualify for the post. By 1879, he was transferred to command the garrison at Kulkul. For his service against the Mahdi Muhammad Ahmad in his stronghold at Jabal Qadir and his death in the ensuing battle (See Appendix 1 [No. 2 coy]).

4. In Defeat against the Ethiopians, 1875-1876

There were two brief Egyptian invasions of northern Ethiopia during the reign of King John IV.

The first expedition clashed with an Ethiopian army at a locality named on maps as Gundet and Guda Guddi about 70 km northeast of Axum, the King's capital, on 17 November 1875, and was crushed with great slaughter. The second expedition, bigger and better armed than the first and intended to avenge the disaster, was itself defeated at Gura, about 50 km south-southeast of Asmara, on 7 March 1876.

The scale of the first disaster was hysterically reported and details of the massacre are still not fully known. A reinforced Egyptian battalion from Keren probably contained a number of veterans from the Mexican campaign. The second disaster was made known to the world in an apologetic literature published in English by American officers of the Egyptian general staff drawing attention to the shortcomings of their Turco-Egyptian employers and to the savagery of the Ethiopian enemy. If ever there was a tragi-comedy of military mismanagement, this was one.

Ever since 1827, each successive ruler of Egypt from Muhammad 'Ali had waged monotonously unsuccessful war against the Ethiopians. By 1871, Isma'il Pasha's modernization of his armed forces had reached a stage which convinced him that he could make active preparations for the kill. To deny his enemy access by sea to foreign military aid, he created a single, straggling, frontier province called the Eastern Sudan which extended from al-Qallabat in the Nile Basin to Berbera on the Somali coast opposite Aden. It was to be an autonomous general province under a general governor.

Isma'il appointed to the post Werner Munzinger,[21] a German Swiss, formerly of the French consular service. This able, sardonic, diabolically hyperactive man developed a rabid, personal hatred of King John to such an extent that he became the architect of his own destruction along with that of his Tigrean wife and all but a handful of his Egyptian Sudanese armed escort. In order to attempt to detach Ras Menelik of Shoa from his loyalty to the King, he undertook to visit Menelik by the only route available to him, through the hostile country of the Danakil who destroyed the column.

The Sudanese Infantry of the Line was the mainstay in garrisoning this ill-defined, administratively difficult, Eastern Province. It was they who in 1871 had enabled Munzinger to extend Egyptian rule to the disputed frontier district of Keren which became for the time the military headquarters of the province. Seven veteran officers from the Mexican campaign can be identified in the battle roll: Faraj al-Zayni[22] battalion commander at Keren and six other officers, whose ranks at the time are not recorded: 'Abd al-Jabbar Bakhit,[23] 'Abdallah al-Faqi,[24] Faraj Wani, Hadid Farhat,[25] and Idris Na'im,[26] all of whom took a strenuous part in the occupation of the province. An exception was our chronicler 'Ali Jifun, now a lieutenant. He had been attached to the military post of Amideb on the Keren-Kasala road where he was exposed to desultory Ethiopian raids but was spared the Egyptian military disasters of 1875-76.[27]

Khedive Isma'il shared with General Gordon a capricious instinct in the selection of recruits to his service. He made bizarre appointments throughout his reign but, like Gordon, on rare occasions he could make a wise choice. Isma'il's most eccentric appointment, and in terms of human sacrifice one of the most expensive, was that of commander-in-chief of the expedition being mobilized during 1875 for the invasion of Ethiopia.

Søren Adolph Arendrup, age 41, a lieutenant in the Danish artillery, was in Egypt convalescing from tuberculosis when he met General C.P. Stone, the U.S. Chief of the Egyptian general staff. Stone offered him a post with rank of lieutenant-colonel and responsibility for weapons. Arendrup's service dossier reveals a career devoted to ballistics, latterly as control inspector at the Finspong gun factory in Sweden. Technically he was a very experienced acquisition by the munitions branch of the Egyptian army.[28] He had retired from the Danish army with rank of captain.

Arendrup's next step was his death warrant. He was a technical, not a combat, soldier. There is no evidence in his military dossier that he had even fought in the Schleswig-Holstein War of 1864 against Prussia and Austria or had ever been under fire. He had no experience of handling Egyptian troops under the stress of battle, especially against an unknown enemy. To lend him appropriate authority in the Egyptian army he was promoted colonel.

His force was moved from Suez to Musawwa‘ by sea and from Musawwa‘ (their supply base) they marched, painfully dragging their artillery, stores, and equipment up the mountain track to the Ethiopian border on the Tigrean plateau. Already within the enemy zone, Arendrup halted the column to be joined by four of the six companies of Sudanese troops from their two bases at Keren and Amideb commanded by an officer whom Arendrup was to refer to as "Commandant Farag Effendi." The united column then continued in the direction of the Tigrean capital, Axum. Not a single enemy had been seen.

Six days before battle was joined, Arendrup wrote an extraordinary dispatch to the Khedive's secretary which began: "Commandant Farag Effendi, thrice decorated in Mexico, does not inspire me with much confidence in his ability." Faraj, he went on, had committed a grave military misdemeanor. He had been ordered to make a night attack on an enemy force encamped at a known site. He had given Faraj precise instructions on the route to be followed. "My order was simple, all it required was courage." Faraj, Arendrup added, had ignored his instructions, followed a different route and thereby failed to engage the enemy.[29]

Arendrup summoned a court martial with himself, seemingly the senior officer, as president. The court sentenced Faraj to immediate suspension from his command and return to his base at Keren. The adjutant-major, whose name does not appear, arrived in the camp from Keren in the evening with the remaining two companies of the battalion and took over Faraj's command. On 17 November, within four days of the trial, the dead bodies of Colonel Arendrup and almost half his total force were lying unburied at Gundet after the virtual massacre of the column. Faraj al-Zayni had experienced an unconventional escape from the imminent danger of death. His men were less lucky.

To do justice to Colonel Arendrup, it is possible that he shared the widely held tactical fallacy that the single-shot, non-repeating, breech-loading rifle was superior to all primitive "native" weapons including the spear. This fallacious exaggeration cost the British dearly in the campaigns against the Zulu in South Africa and the Italians in their first battles against the Ethiopians. It was simply a matter of proportion of spears against each rifle. In an engagement in which each rifleman was attacked by one, or even two, spearmen, he had time to hold his ground; but if he were attacked by fifteen spears, a reasonable estimate of the numbers of Ethiopian spearmen in swift, yelling, charging mass on the day of the massacre, the rifle had no chance against the spear. The supremacy of the ballistic weapon over the massed charge of superior numbers of spearmen was not conclusively proved until 1898 when the Maxim machine gun ensured Kitchener's victory over the Mahdists at Omdurman.

The error in Faraj's rank at the court martial, which misrepresented him as a major, may have disadvantaged him at the trial. The error could have been the result of a simple clerical mistake by the person responsible for updating his dossier, if indeed a copy of the original dossier at the Egyptian War Office, Cairo, was available at the court martial. It could equally have been a falsification perpetrated behind Faraj's back by some personal enemy.

Prince 'Umar Tusun later realized that he had been led astray and corrected his own record by citing the official gazette, *al-Waqa'i' al-misriyya* No. 635 of 9 December 1873 announcing the promotion of Faraj Bey to the rank of colonel and his appointment as governor of the province of Taka two years before the promulgation of the sentence of Arendrup's court martial.[30] A suspicion lingers that there was a sinister force at work manipulating an exhausted and confused Arendrup with the intention of ruining the career of a field officer not only under his own command but senior to himself in length of service. We know from the pen of the supply and transport officer of the expedition, Lieutenant-Colonel Ahmad 'Urabi, the future Egyptian Nationalist leader, that ethnic Egyptian officers were bitterly disillusioned with the contemptuous treatment they received from their own Turco-Egyptian superior commanders. Their bitterness extended to the entire ruling dynasty with its supporters such as the Sudanese *Nizam* troops with their undeviating loyalty to the Khediviate. In the mountains of Ethiopia, and down at the base at Musawwa' the disaffected *fallahin* officers were powerless; but at least they could safely vent their rancor on one black officer in trouble.

Faraj's allegiance to his Khedive had nothing to do with the Egyptian Nationalist campaign for justice; his was a personal allegiance undiluted by ethical complications and restraints; it was total. And there was a precedent for his loyalty.

Nine years before, on the return of the Sudanese battalion from Mexico, Khedive Isma'il had promoted its commander, Major Muhammad Almas Efendi, to full colonel and accorded him the grade of bey. By 1876, Colonel Muhammad Bey had become Brigadier-General Muhammad Pasha, governor of the Dongola province in the Sudan.

In that year Khedive Isma'il began to suspect that Isma'il Pasha al-Siddīq, head of the Egyptian state finances and known to peasant tax-payers as *al-Mufattish,* the Inspector, was disclosing his master's private financial affairs to the European debt commissioners. The Khedive's anger against the all-knowing Inspector became an obsession. At his orders, the Inspector was secretly arrested at the Khedivial palace, brought before a secret court of exalted persons, bundled into a waiting steamer, and conveyed to the First Cataract. Here he was transferred to another steamer which brought him to the Second Cataract where he mounted a camel for the final stage to Dongola town. There he was quietly strangled by executioners who had accompanied him from Cairo with the active assistance of Muhammad Abu Hijil, the governor's administrative assistant, and the tacit connivance of the governor, Muhammad Almas Pasha. The governor had discharged an obligation to his benevolent Master the Khedive.[31]

Isma'il's weakness lay in his ignorance of modern army management. The astounding speed of the Prussian victory over the French in 1870 seems to have paralyzed his ability to realize that his own army organization was hopelessly out-of-date. Yet he could not apply himself to drastic change. In 1875 he had detached a trained soldier, Shahin Pasha Genc, from the War Office and sent him to the Northern Sudan as administrator of the Sudan Railway around the cataract at Wadi Halfa. In the same year he had appointed Muhammad Ratib Pasha, commander-in-chief of the Egyptian army, who, like Arendrup, had never fought a battle, to lead the second expeditionary force against the Ethiopians.

But he was faced by great difficulties beyond his power to resolve. To have attempted to apply even the most simplified adaptation of the Prussian model to his own forces, to abolish at one blow their historic monolithic command structure and replace it with something approaching a nineteenth-century American or European business machine, would have been an act of idiocy.

Isma'il seems to have had no clear idea of what he wanted. What he got was an instant, Egyptian general staff composed of American Civil War veterans of high average quality whose immediate task was to constitute a ready-made military staff for an impending war against an enemy they knew nothing about, with Turco-Egyptian fellow officers whose languages they did not understand and to whose ways of thought they were strangers.

At that time Isma'il's choice of white Americans for this assignment would have been received with approval. The United States was not among the principal creditors who were making life difficult for Isma'il nor had they any known territorial ambitions in North-East Africa. In their own recent civil war they had demonstrated amazing technical inventiveness in land and sea warfare, and they were excellent cartographers. They had available ex-officers eager to return to soldiering; and in the main, they proved a friendly community, easy to get on with.

There was however one objection, unnoticed at the time, to employing white Americans in the Muslim Middle East. Both they and the Turco-

Egyptian rulers of Egypt came from slave-states but with this difference: in 1865 the American slaves had been "freed" in the sense of segregated into a servile status. The Muslim ex-slave conscript troops, by the very act of their enlistment, had entered the lower ranks of the government. American slaves enlisted during the civil war were usually employed only as auxiliaries to free white troops for front-line service.[32]

The American staff officers were from the first confused on this issue. While the second Egyptian expedition was on its way to Ethiopia, Muhammad Ratib Pasha was overheard to regret that his War Office had limited him to one black Sudanese regiment. The Americans who heard his expression of regret at the small number of blacks allocated to his command were astonished that the old general should make so extraordinary a remark, which to most Americans was absurd. They did not realize that these Sudanese blacks formed the crack regiments of the Egyptian army.

The paralyzing effect of the confusion in the Egyptian field headquarters was painfully evident to the Commander-in-Chief, who himself had no practical experience of war, and none of working with Americans. His extremely worried American Chief of Staff, Brigadier-General W. W. Loring Pasha, in a letter written from the Egyptian field headquarters on 27 March 1876, to General Stone, head of the American Mission, begged him to have Ratib removed: "I have only to say for God's sake put some bold and able Arab in command—or there is no telling what may happen."

During the long drawn-out peace negotiations, which Isma'il himself prolonged (possibly in the hope of extracting some residual mitigation from the shameful catastrophe for himself and his army), he was informed that the Ethiopians were retaining their Sudanese military captives as slaves and were failing to return them as the peace treaty required. This stung Isma'il to the core. He instructed Ratib to explain to King John that those Sudanese were not slaves but soldiers of the Egyptian government and were his subjects. He ordered Ratib to request their return "with the Arabs."[33]

No authentic record of the number of Sudanese casualties, let alone the names and ranks of Sudanese veterans from the Mexican campaign, is thought to have survived from either expedition. The dead died anonymously. So complete had been the disorder reigning in both expeditions that posterity has had to be content with such diplomatic platitudes as those expressed by A. von Suzzara, Austrian consul-general in Egypt:

> . . .on the whole the Egyptian troops conducted themselves well particularly the Sudanese who, even in the most critical moments, lost nothing of their natural good humor.

5. A Brush with the Egyptian Nationalist Movement

The black troops of the Egyptian Army were of small concern to the White Egyptians in the towns and the peasants in the villages of Lower Egypt. For centuries they had been oppressed by the Mamluks and their descendants, a predatory land-owning, military and governing class.

We have found no instance of Sudanese troops as a body sharing the burning sense of injustice for the "native" Egyptians that was inspiring a number of senior Egyptian officers to abolish this oppressive society and replace it by a regime of justice. The disinterest evident among the black troops could have reflected their concept of loyalty to the Khedive which survived the dismissal of Isma'il in 1879 in favor of his son Tawfiq. Another alienating sentiment may have been a touch of color prejudice among the Egyptians against blacks taking airs, or Sudanese pride, the feeling of superiority of the military conscript, inwardly proud of his place in the framework of government, in the presence of outsiders, agricultural serfs. They may have remembered the poor showing of the *Fallahin* in the battles of Ethiopia without understanding the cause. Colonel Faraj Bey al-Zayni having narrowly escaped death in the Ethiopian campaign of 1875 on the frontier was now to fall foul of the Egyptian Nationalist establishment at the center.

In an atmosphere of growing public excitement the Arabic satirical journal *Abou Naddara (Abū Nazzāra)* piquantly anti-British and anti-Khedive Tawfiq, now edited in Paris and distributed clandestinely in Egypt, carried in its issue No. 5 of 24 June 1881, at p. 158, a scandalous story in the form of a dialogue in street Arabic of which the following is no more than a translated summary:

> An important member of the government got one of his friends to suggest to a Sudanese officer, by name Faraj Bey Zayni, to go to Tura (Sudanese regimental depot) to address the soldiers in the absence of their officers calling upon them to "Rise, all 4000 of you as one man, and kill your two white [nationalist therefore rebellious] officers and make me, the beloved of Efendina [our Khedive] your commander." The Sudanese, instead of agreeing with his appeal to them, tied him up and reported him to the War Office which promptly courtmartialed him with the result that he was banished to the White Nile. Abu Rayda, the editor's pseudonym for Mustafa Pasha Riyad [then president of the Council of Ministers] was compelled to sign the warrant because, if he hadn't, his part in the conspiracy would have been made public and that would have given him quite a headache.[34]

This allegation is repeated at greater length and in a less impudent, more pedestrian, style by Ahmad 'Urabi himself in his memoirs:

> Faraj Bey al-Zayni the Sudani, was one of the senior officers of the reserve regiment. Some of the non-commissioned officers of that regiment frequently went to visit him. Now when Yusuf Pasha Kamal, chief of the Khedivial administration, became aware of Faraj Bey's proximity to the Sudanese regiment and the fact that the non-commissioned officers were visiting him, he summoned him in April 1881 and suggested that he should urge those junior officers to rebel, and promised him that, if successful, he would be promoted colonel of that regiment. Accordingly Faraj Bey carried out the plot as directed. He invited the junior officers and corporals who came to visit him at his house to meet him by night in a wheat field at a distance from the camp, and he urged them to take the path of insubordination and rebellion.
>
> They however, as soon as they realized what he was asking of them, were quick to tie him up and send somebody to tell Colonel 'Abd al-'Al Bey Hilmi what was going on. The colonel with some of his officers went to the wheat field where they found Faraj Bey tied up. The colonel had him released from his bonds and took him to the regiment threatening him with imprisonment. He then sent a report to the War Office asking for his trial by courtmartial.
>
> On his own confession he was sentenced to be banished to the Sudan, his home. The Khedive however, wishing to compensate him for what he had failed to achieve in his (the Khedive's) service in Egypt, instructed the Governor-General of the Sudan. Ra'uf Pasha, to employ him in the Sudanese administration. And so it was that he achieved the rank of brigadier-general. Gordon Pasha, however, executed him for his treachery in helping the Dervishes during the siege of Khartoum.[35]

Ahmad 'Urabi Pasha's last sentence is incorrect. He confused *our* Faraj al-Zayni with one of the two pashas courtmartialed during the siege of Khartoum in 1884 and executed for treason. On that occasion Faraj Bey was not the prisoner but the president of the courtmartial in his capacity of commander-in-chief of the Egyptian forces defending the capital under the overall command of General Gordon.

Col. Faraj Bey's sworn loyalty was to the Khedive Tawfiq and his legitimate government, not to a disloyal Egyptian clique, as he would regard them, who were usurping the legitimate government. The young non-commissioned officers saw the matter differently. To them the legitimate government was the one that they experienced wielding authority and which derived that authority by an act of the Khedive. In their eyes Faraj Bey was the traitor, and they arrested him.

6. In the Mahdist Revolt: Destruction of the Egyptian Army in the Sudan, 1881-1885

A thinning band of aging survivors from the Sudanese defense of Veracruz were now to enter upon their last and bloodiest campaign: the early Mahdist victories culminating in the fall of Khartoum.

The small élite brotherhood from Mexico with its subsequent long experience of fighting in the Equatorial and Eastern commands, and in Dar Far, supplied, for all its small size, a remarkable crop of general and field officers. Their casualties were in proportion to their worth. The military aspect of the Mahdist rising in 1881 was unique in the history of the Sudan; it was planned and led by men of high soldierly instinct, and the circumstances were ripe for violent change.

The Egyptian occupying power, weakened by 'Urabi Pasha's rebellion and the British occupation in its own homeland of Lower Egypt, suffered defeat after defeat. Four attempts between 1881 and 1883 were made to capture Muhammad Ahmad al-Mahdi; all were defeated with heavy loss. In the second of the two disastrous raids on the Mahdi's stronghold on Jabal Qadir in the Nuba Mountains in 1882, the second in command of the Egyptian force, Lt.-Col. Muhammad Bey Sulayman,[36] was killed along with his negligent commanding officer and almost all their men. But it was the culminating siege of Khartoum which exacted the heaviest toll from the surviving Sudanese officers from Mexico.

This is not the place to discuss the reason for General Gordon's arrival in Khartoum in February 1884. Here we are concerned only with the conspicuous part played in the defense of the city by a handful of Sudanese senior officers who had served in Mexico. Gordon was Governor-General having both civil and military responsibilities. The senior officer responsible for the conduct of the land defense was his chief-of-staff, Brig.-Gen. Faraj Pasha al-Zayni, whom Gordon later, with the intensification of the siege, promoted major-general. Directly under Faraj Pasha were two colonels each of whom commanded about half the total length of the line of ramparts and trenches extending south and east of Khartoum from the right bank of the White Nile to the left bank of the Blue Nile covering the approaches to the village of Burri. They were Colonel Hasan Bey al-Bahnassawi[37] (5th regiment) on the western section and the "Mexican" veteran, Bakhit Bey Batraki[38] (1st regiment) on the eastern. Under these two regimental commanders were (west to east) the four battalion commanders, Lieutenant-Colonels 'Uthman Hishmat, Hasan Bey, Muhammad Ibrahim and the "Mexican" Surur Bey Bahjat.[39] The fourth "Mexican" veteran, the commander of the troops engaged in amphibious naval raids on both Niles was Brigadier-General Muhammad 'Ali Husayn Pasha with Muhammad Nuṣḥī Pasha in charge of the dockyard and fleet.

All four veterans from Mexico were killed in action during the siege or in the massacre which followed.

Brigadier-General Muhammad 'Ali Pasha Husayn[40]

Major 'Ali Khayr al-Din, an officer of the Egyptian army at the end of the old Egyptian regime in the Sudan, gave Prince 'Umar Tusun a list of distinguished Sudanese "who rose to the senior ranks of the Egyptian army, men of the stamp of Muhammad 'Ali Pasha, 'A Sudanese through and through,' who had come up through the ranks of the regular infantry."

"When Gordon took over the governorship-general early in 1884 he at once recognized Muhammad 'Ali's worth and repeatedly promoted him because, whatever duty Muhammad 'Ali was asked to do, he did it successfully." As the Mahdi's troops from Kordofan were approaching Khartoum, Gordon promoted him colonel for he must have been aware of Muhammad 'Ali's riverain origin and his lifelong familiarity with the Nile and its navigation. Gordon saw to it that his fellow-enthusiast in river warfare was given his head. As the Mahdists were closing in on the city, he led a number of raids using armor-plated steamers and barges packed tightly with landing parties whose main object was to seize food for the hungry city and destroy enemy siege works on the river.

The first such raid was made in five steamers with 5,000 men to attack a line of river forts built by the enemy commander Muhammad 'Uthman Abu Qarja on the left bank of the Blue Nile at al-Jirayf, 8 km upstream of Khartoum. In rustic Arabic, the round number 5,000 is not intended to be accepted literally but rather to indicate a crowded force to transport in one river steamer towing two or three small barges. By the same estimation, the number 40,000 indicates "beyond counting"—infinity. The operation took fewer than two days, the forts were captured with great slaughter and the enemy commander driven out.

The second raid, with the same ships and landing force, was sent to attack a Mahdist army commanded by the two sons of Shaykh al-'Ubayd wad Badr at Halfaya on the east bank of the Nile, 8 km downstream of Khartoum. In three hours from the initial landing, Muhammad 'Ali's men penetrated the enemy's defenses and drove them off with great loss, capturing their stores of grain. Gordon prepared a great welcome for his return to Khartoum and promoted him brigadier-general.

The destination of Muhammad 'Ali's third raid was Abu Haraz, 170 km up the Blue Nile. The inhabitants fled leaving behind a great quantity of grain, livestock and coffee which the Egyptians carried back to the beleaguered city.

Muhammad 'Ali Pasha's fourth and fatal raid was a disaster for him and for the defense of Khartoum.

He was sent with the five steamers and five barges carrying 5,000 troops and an even larger [sic] body of volunteers to dislodge a Mahdist force round al-'Aylafun. This force broke under fire and, with their commander, Shaykh al-Mudawwi 'Abd al-Rahman,[41] retreated inland to Umm Dhubban. Muhammad 'Ali sent spies to Umm Dhubban but these may have been Mahdist sympathizers as they reported falsely that Shaykh al-'Ubayd [wad Badr], the religious leader there, had a mere 1,000 men with him, so that the Pasha with an inadequate and exhausted force marched after the enemy who had prepared an ambush at a spot thick with trees. No sooner had the Egyptian raiders reached the middle of the wood than the enemy fell on them from every side, overwhelming and butchering them. Seeing that all was lost, the Pasha and his officers dismounted and sat on the ground awaiting death according to the military tradition of the famous Sudanese of history. Only a few of the Egyptian troops escaped.

The effect of the disaster on General Gordon was a severe loss to his prestige.

Colonel Bakhit Bey Batraki[42]

Bakhit Agha left Mexico a sergeant with warrant officer's status on the homeward voyage, and on arrival at Alexandria was promoted first lieutenant and thereafter served mainly in the Equatorial command. When the Mahdist conquest of Kordofan threatened the capital, he was transferred to Khartoum as second in command to Colonel Faraj Bey Muhammad al-Zayni. On Faraj Bey's promotion to major-general during the Mahdist siege of Khartoum, Bakhit Bey took over his chief's regimental command. In August 1884, Bakhit Bey led an armed ship convoy from Khartoum to a point on the Blue Nile, 18 km downstream of Sinnar where the force loaded a heavy cargo of grain for besieged Khartoum. Bakhit Bey, now a colonel, took command of the two battalions defending the eastern perimeter of the city covering Burri. He was killed in the *mêlée* during the Mahdist assault of the city, 26 January 1885. A witness swore that he died fighting.

Major-General Faraj Pasha Muhammad al-Zayni[43]

Gordon Pasha had arrived at Khartoum by steamer on 18 February 1884. He bore the British rank of major-general and the Egyptian rank of *mushir*, marshal. On the following day *The Times* of London received from Frank Power, its special correspondent in Khartoum, this extraordinary telegram and published it verbatim on the 20th. In it the British public was informed that Gordon had appointed "Afresh Bey Shilook, a negro who won the Legion of

Honor under Bazaine in Mexico," as his Chief-of-Staff and Commander-in-Chief of the land defenses of Khartoum.

During the long siege, Gordon wrote often in his journal of Faraj's strengths and weaknesses rather like an assiduous mother jotting her child's behavior in her diary. For instance:

> Oct. 26: Some time ago I gave Ferratch Pasha L.E. 100 a month and I afterwards made him a Ferik or General of Division for political reasons. He had the cheek to ask me to give him L.E. 150 and forage for eight horses! quite ignoring the state of the fodder exchequer. I said, "Wait." He was foolish enough to renew the application which I tore up.
>
> Oct. 29: Ferratch Pash tried again in a roundabout way to get the L.E. 150 a month forage. . .for four horses and had to content himself with L.E. 100 a month.
>
> Nov. 18: I will say Ferratch Pasha (however irritating he is in some ways) is always the gentleman, which, I am sorry to say, *I am not.*
>
> Nov. 23: [Gordon is nervous for Faraj Pasha's safety at the Omdurman fort and has a steamer waiting to take him off.]
>
> Dec. 13: Ferratch Pasha is really showing an amount of vigor I did not give him credit for.

Exactly what happened to Faraj Pasha in the chaos of the massacre is uncertain. Several versions were reported to Muhammad Nuṣḥī Pasha's committee of enquiry. According to one witness, Faraj Pasha and Surur Bey Bahjat, seeing that all was lost, took off their uniforms and went out of the rampart by the Masallamiyya gate to seek safety. The act of shedding their uniforms was more than a bid to save their lives; it was a gesture of ending their fealty to the Khediviate which was no longer able to support them. They were now free to transfer their loyalty to another master.

They were however arrested and handed over to the Mahdist command. According to another witness the Khalifa ʻAbdullahi and Ahmad Sulayman, amir of the Mahdist treasury,[44] conferred and decided that Faraj Pasha and Surur Bey should be killed and their bodies thrown on the graves of Saʻid Pasha Husayn al-Jimiʻabi and Hasan Pasha Ibrahim al-Shallali, the "two Pashas" whom Gordon had had shot for treachery.[45] This story was contradicted by Burdayni Bey.[46] A third witness at the enquiry, stated that Surur Bey was killed near the Masallamiyya gate where Faraj Pasha had been on duty at the time and that Faraj himself was killed by the amir Makin wad al-Nur[47] in revenge for the death of his own brother ʻAbdallah who had been killed by Faraj Pasha.

An important witness in the enemy's camp who later changed sides, the judge and amir Shaykh Muddawwi ʻAbd al-Rahman, testified that the Arabs forced their way through the mud on the White Nile bank. Thousands of yelling men with spears and swords got behind the defensive line and rushed eastward along the whole length of the parapet, which colonel Bakhit Batraki powerfully defended until he was cut down.[48]

> Faraj Pasha, who was at the Massallamiyya gate, saw that further resistance was useless and ordered his men to stop firing and surrender. He was made a prisoner and taken to the camp outside. Three days later, he was killed by one of his old servants in revenge for something he had done to him a long time ago. He was not killed by order of the Mahdi, and he did not betray the town or open the Masallamiyya gate until after Khartoum was actually in our [Mahdist] hands.

Kitchener's *Report on the Fall of Khartoum* was completed in August 1885. At the time, its findings were regarded as based on the soundest available evidence. In brief, on 23 January 1885, two days before the fall of the city, Gordon had a stormy meeting with Faraj Pasha in which he lost his temper and struck his chief-of-staff. Faraj Pasha felt so deeply insulted that he refused a reconciliation with Gordon. There were grounds for supposing that the Mahdi had, through his agents in the town, acquainted Gordon with his terms of surrender through Gordon's chief-of-staff, and this had caused Gordon's outburst. On the next day, the 24th, Gordon held a council of notables when the question of surrendering the town was discussed. Some advised acceptance of the Mahdi's terms; Gordon refused point blank. On the following night the Mahdist army overwhelmed the defenses of Khartoum, and the massacre began.

The report also recorded yet another, rather improbable, version of Faraj Pasha's death, a story that, three days after the fall of Khartoum, he was asked to reveal the place where the Egyptian government had hidden its treasure. This Faraj Pasha was unable to do because, by the end of the siege, the government had no treasure left to hide. The Pasha was then killed in the market place at Omdurman.

In the flood of literature which poured from British publishers in 1884-1885, tragedy and bathos seemed inseparable. It was a season when the confused notions of the British public on the subject of slavery were being wildly advertised and, at the fringes, exploited. One mercenary soul discovered that Faraj Pasha, as well as Mr. Gladstone, was Gordon's betrayer. A silk bookmarker was on sale in Britain during the height of national emotion at Gordon's death. The words on the bookmarker reflect the market's mood:

> General Gordon / hero of Khartoum / which city he / defended. . .when / it was betrayed by / Faragh Pasha / a black slave / who had been freed / and promoted to a / position of rank by / Gordon[49]

Lieutenant-Colonel Surur Bey Bahjat[50]

On the return of the battalion from Mexico, 2nd Lieutenant Surur Bahjat, like his brother officer Bakhit Batraki, was posted to the Equatorial command where in 1874-1876 he commanded the post of Sobat, latterly renamed Tawfiqiyya at the junction of the Sobat River and the White Nile. About 1882 he was transferred north under the threat of the Mahdist revolt and, with the rank of major, was given the command of the garrison of al-Jira on the river Setit, a tributary of the Atbara in the Eastern Sudan command. In April 1882, C.C. Giegler Pasha, deputy governor-general of the Sudan, ordered troops from the Kasala area to concentrate at Abu Haraz on the Blue Nile to defend the Jazira from Mahdist followers and in particular from the Sharif Ahmad Taha who was defeated. During the siege of Khartoum Major Surur Bahjat was promoted lieutenant colonel and given command of the 3rd battalion of the 1st regular infantry regiment formerly commanded by his old comrade, Bakhit Bey Batraki who manned the eastern defenses of the city at Burri. Lt.-Col. Surūr Bahjat was killed in the Mahdist assault of 26 January 1885.

The two remaining area command centers still in Egyptian army hands, Kasala and Sinnar, both less important politically then the capital and less burdened with food-consuming civilians, held out until the rains of 1885: Kasala until 30 July, Sinnar until 19 August.

The garrison at Sinnar had no identified veterans from Mexico among its ranks, but the contrary is true of Kasala. Here the story of the long, and at the outset dilatory, Mahdist siege of the citadel is pivotal to our story of the survivors of the Sudanese battalion. Our chronicler, now 2nd Lt. 'Ali Jifun, not only recounts in detail the harsh and dangerous life on the Ethiopian border where he served for at least ten years, but he records the names of two other soldiers who, when Kasala ultimately surrendered, joined him during the chaos of the moment, fled with him to Musawwa', took ship to Suez, arrived at the 'Abbāsiyya barracks in Cairo, and enlisted in the new Egyptian army. They were Sergeant-Majors Baraka Ahmad 'Ali[51] in the new Xth Sudanese battalion and 'Abdallah al-'Abd[52] in the still newer XIIth.

That hard frontier service, probably the most dangerous, if not the roughest in his long military career, brought out the best of 'Ali Jifun as a raconteur and, as so often happens with translations, the translator catches the enthusiasm of the teller and responds in kind.[53]

In the isolated South, Emin Pasha was fighting a rearguard campaign against a Mahdist invasion of the Bahr al-Ghazal province on its way toward Emin's headquarters at Lado on the Nile.

The success of the Mahdist offensive under the command of the amir Karamallah Kurqusawi in the Bahr al-Ghazal province during 1884 broke the morale of the Egyptian army, which fell back on Amadi. Its fall and the killing of its commander, Major Marjan 'Ali al-Danasuri in March 1885, caused Emin Pasha to reorganize two battalions of his regular infantry of which a copy of a nominal roll of officers survives (*Ta'rikh* II, 276-80). This furnishes ten names identical with those already appearing in the battalion nominal roll from the Mexican campaign 18 years before.

The coincidence of names suggests probability rather than certainty and should be accepted with caution.

Among the last retreating Egyptian troops to escape from the Sudan were the frontier garrisons from al-Qallabat and al-Jira who were evacuated through Ethiopia to Musawwa' by a treaty with King John. We have not yet identified veterans from the Sudanese battalion in Mexico in this operation.

There is no statistic or even estimate of the number of veterans from the Sudanese battalion who deserted to the Mahdist cause. Two field officers, both commissioned from No. 1 company in Mexico, took the step. Both served their new masters as honorably as they did their old.

The junior of the two, Lieutenant-Colonel Abu Bakr Bey al-Hajj Muhammad[54] had served in the campaign against the sons of al-Zubayr Pasha and had a long fighting record. Then came the Mahdist occupation of Kordofan province which isolated Dar Fur from all help. His own military commander, Colonel Rudolf Slatin Bey, had become a Muslim with no tangible result on the gloomy military situation in Dar Fur. The hope of rescue vanished after the crushing defeat and massacre of General Hicks's expedition to recover Kordofan. Slatin sent one of his senior officials, Muhammad Khalid Zuqal, a relation of the Mahdi, to treat for surrender. The Mahdi appointed Muhammad Khalid in Slatin's place. Abu Bakr had no choice; he changed sides with the rest.

After some years campaigning with the Mahdist armies, he was transferred to the frontier region of al-Qallabat as an amir under the supreme command of his maternal uncle, al-Nur Muhammad 'Anqara, another former Egyptian bey, to await an expected invasion of the Khalifa 'Abdallahi's dominions by an Ethiopian army led by King John.

Amir Abu Bakr was sent forward at the head of a force of 3,000 men to reconnoiter and keep contact with the enemy. His guide deserted by night and warned the enemy who attacked with overwhelming force. By a masterly withdrawal, Abu Bakr brought his force back to al-Qallabat. On 9 March 1889, the Ethiopians assaulted and breached the Mahdists' *zariba*. But the commanding amir, Zaki Tamal, had retained in the center of the *zariba* a reserve force of 2,300 men of whom 500 were under Abu Bakr's command. Zaki Tamal counterattacked whereupon the Ethiopians retreated. In the fighting that followed, the Mahdists won a massive victory and a great haul of booty. King John was killed.[55]

The senior in age and rank, Colonel Faraj 'Azazi Bey was not like Abu Bakr, a volunteer, but a former slave from Jabal Taqali, the home of so many senior officers of the regular black infantry. From Mexico he was posted to the Eastern Sudan area and was finally Officer Commanding Troops at Kasala. The Mahdi treated him with consideration and attached him to the amir 'Uthmān Jānū to whom he became commander of the reserve. It was said of him that he became so closely attached to 'Uthman that he called him, with play on his own name, "Faraj 'Uthmān" literally "'Uthmān's Comfort." His battle record as a Mahdist officer is impressive: five in Dar Fur, three in the Nile Valley: at Matamma,[56] 'Atbara and Karari [Omdurman] in 1896-1898.

Faraj 'Azazi survived his last battle. Instead of following his Mahdist commander, the Khalifa 'Abdullahi, and the battered remnant of his army into the desert to make another stand against the British and Egyptians, he decided to take refuge in Dar Fur where he had served the amir 'Uthman Jānū and had got to know the country. So, with four other fugitives including Sergeant Fadl al-Sīd Abū Jumā',[57] formerly of No. 3 company in Mexico, he fled from what they may have feared would have been the rough justice that the victors would visit upon deserters from the Egyptian army. The five men followed Sultan 'Ali Dinar in his hurry to gain his patrimony before any other rival could beat him on the road.

Unhappily for the fugitive deserter colonel-amīr, 'Alī Dīnār suspected his Mahdist refugees of plotting to overthrow him and had him and other former Mahdist notables killed. 'Umar Tusun's contributor ends his long letter with a pious comment:

> God endowed Faraj Bey 'Azazi with a combination of the reverence due to old age and the grace of youth, for although he had reached the age of decrepitude he still retained his upright carriage and greatness of mind and he played a praiseworthy part in the Mahdi's wars. If only he had surrendered to the Egyptian forces after the battle of Omdurman and asked for a pension! But praise be to him who said "No soul knows what it shall earn tomorrow, and no soul knows in what land it shall die."[58]

7. In the New Egyptian Army: The Last Survivors from Mexico

The new Egyptian army was created in 1883 after Khedive Muhammad Tawfiq, by the stroke of his pen and British pressure, dissolved the old Egyptian Army to which the Sudanese battalion in Mexico had belonged.

Only a few months previously the British army had entered Cairo and now controlled the government of Egypt.

The Sudanese battalions of the new Egyptian army were officered by British and Egyptians. Entry to the Egyptian army by British junior officers was by secondment from the home-based regiment. The 10-year period of secondment became the norm. Competition for entry was keen, and the criteria demanded by the British selection boards exacting. Somebody heard a rumor that "the dashing young cavalry officer" idealized by "Ouida" in her romantic novels represented a type summarily rejected by the selection boards on strict instructions from the War Office.

Ambiguities of military vocabulary were disposed of early. In 1886, the year in which 'Ali Jifun's Xth Sudanese left their base at al-'Abbasiyya for Sawakin, the order came that all ranks were to be "designated by the Turkish army ranks." That is, in Arabic script the Turkish form continued with Arabic pronunciation. British officers picked up a basis of Lower Egyptian spoken Arabic from Cairene teachers of the colloquial, or in the Cairo barracks evolved their own special argot, "Bimbashi Arabic," a simple colloquial Hobson-Jobson pronounced with conscientious exclusion of all un-English sounds, a patriotic discipline to which their school French had already accustomed them. Some of the newly-raised battalions were more zealous than others in preserving their intimate history. 'Ali Jifun's Xth battalion has left what is in effect a collective scrap book of battalion history with maps and plans, compiled by one of its commanders Lieutenant-Colonel W. H. Hunter Bey.[59]

By the end of 1887, the rest of the Xth battalion had already transferred to the Nile leaving 1st Lieutenant 'Ali Jifun's "depot details" at Sawakin to fight a battle.

The battle of Handub was at best a heroic mismanagement. Kitchener, then governor-general of the Red Sea Littoral, was severely wounded in the combat, the Egyptian force was badly mauled during the retreat to Sawakin and the object of the raid, to capture the Mahdist amir 'Uthman Digna, failed.[60]

Here is an unofficial account of the engagement written by an officer present in the action:

> At the beginning of the year [1888] news came into Suakin that Osman Digne had a large force at Handub and it was decided to attempt to capture him. Accordingly a small force composed of the following under El Lewa Kitchener Pacha moved out from Suakin on 17 January:
>
> 1 sq[uadron] cavalry
>
> 1 coy Xth Sudanese (from depot details)
>
> Some Sudanese refugees
>
> 300 Friendlies
>
> The veteran company of the Xth under 2lt. 'Ali Effendi Gafoon. Starting

at 1. a.m. the force halted at 4.00 a.m. The Friendlies and Xth Sudanese advanced, the cavalry and camel corps being held in reserve. The enemy were taken quite by surprise and bolted, but, quickly seeing how few in numbers were the intruders, they returned to the attack upon which the Friendlies bolted leaving the little party of the Xth Sudanese alone. These took up a position on a small hill to the south of the zariba where they were surrounded by the enemy but gallantly held their own.

By this time the news of the counter-attack had reached Kitchener Pasha, and he ordered up reserves. At the same time the buglers sounded the Xth call of assembly. Bimbashi McMurdo[61] who was present recalled, "It was a fine sight to see the old blacks to a man jump up from behind the rocks and come steadily down the hill towards us bringing their wounded comrades with them. The reserve were at the same time clearing the bush of Dervishes so as to open the way for the Xth."

It was not ten minutes before the little force joined hands and moved on to the open space closed [sic] to the Dervishes. Here Kitchener formed up the Xth and dismounted Camel Corps in line with the left flank protected by the country and the order to advance again on the zariba was given. All told we did not then muster 150 rifles.

The advance took place very steadily but men soon began dropping for there was a semi-circle of about 600 rifles letting drive. Shortly after the advance began Kitchener got badly hit and was taken to the rear, the command devolving on Hickman[62] and while he was superintending the advance, Kitchener's A.D.C. came up with an order to retire on Suakin.

It was during the retirement, and for the second time that day, that the old soldiers of the Xth showed their sterling steady qualities and it is a recognised fact by us few British officers who were present at the affair that, had it not been for the gallantry and steadiness of the Xth, we must have all been scuppered. As it was, the Xth with the rest of the little force, with ammunition practically finished, retreated, helping their wounded and carrying their dead for about two hours along the Suakin road with a semi-circle of about 1000 Dervishes harassing us. Mulazim Awal 'Ali Effendi Gafoon was badly wounded in the leg just after the retrograde movement commenced and I remember Sgt. Rahan [?Rihan] of the Xth taking command doing yeoman service collecting ammunition for his men and keeping off the Dervish rushes. . .We reached Suakin about 11.30 a.m. after a very nasty time of it and I can only repeat that it was mainly due to the fighting qualities and steadiness of the old soldiers of the Xth that we were not annihilated.

'Ali Jifun said that, with his wounded leg he could not have walked out to safety had not Major McMurdo, who was himself already wounded in the knee, taken him up on his horse and rode with him out of danger.[63]

At the end of 1888, 'Ali Jifun was promoted captain and transferred to No. XII battalion, which had been raised in Cairo and recently disembarked at Sawakin. Its new battalion commander, Colonel P. W. Machell Bey, must have been fascinated by the veteran captain's stories and realized their historical value.

On 20 December the old warrior was at it again, this time in an engagement at al-Jummaiza named after a tree near the defenses of Sawakin itself. His company helped to beat off a Mahdist attack, and he was awarded the Majidiyya decoration in the 5th class.

After more fighting in the delta of the flood-river Baraka at Tokar in 1891, Captain 'Ali Jifun's XII battalion now transferred to Wadi Halfa on the Nile, crossing the desert from the Egyptian port of Kosseir (al-Qusayr) to the Nile at Koft (Quft). Commandant Machell describes the march:

> With the exception of 'Ali Effendi Gifun, [sic] who has over 36 years service and whom I compelled to occasionally ride one of my horses, every company officer marched with his men throughout [Bugles and drums marched complete]. When they were not playing the men sang together dervish chants which carried them along in such a way that no one ever thought of fatigue.[64]

In 1896, the general advance against the Mahdist armies began and Kitchener, now commander-in-chief of the Egyptian army, promoted Captain 'Ali Jifun to Adjutant-Major, his promotion dating from 23 December 1897.

An Egyptian brother-officer, Hamdi Bey Sayf al-Nasr, provides a moving testimony to the old campaigner's last two years as an officer of the XIIth Sudanese.

> His men called him "Father of the Sudanese" for, although he was not yet the highest-ranking officer in the battalion, he was the oldest of the Egyptian and Sudanese officers. He would tell strange tales from the Mexican war and he was always chosen to preside over the Sudanese dances[65] and other festivities of the Sudanese.

'Ali Jifun's last mission was to his own people, the Shilluk, whose capital village in Turco-Egyptian times was Fashoda. Kitchener had no sooner crushed the Mahdist army before Omdurman than he set out with a small force in a flotilla of river steamers to confront the French mission which had come to claim the greater part of the Sudan as abandoned territory. Egyptian reoccupation of the Nile Valley would have been compromised if Commandant Marchand had persuaded the Shilluk King to make a treaty of alliance with the French.

The King denied that he had signed any such treaty. At the end of his statement H. W. Jackson o.c. Egyptian troops, Fashoda wrote: "Taken by me in the presence of the following witnesses: Ali Ahmed, Artillery, [Sagh qul aghasi] Ali Eff. Gafun[66] dated 10 October 1898."

'Ali Jifun's itinerary and timetable between Berber and Fashoda were not discovered. We know only that he was at Fashoda signing a document on 10 October and, bearing in mind his advanced age, he would probably have made the whole journey by river with a transhipment at Omdurman, the temporary Egyptian naval dockyard. Whatever the date of his return to the XIIth Sudanese base camp at Berber, his brother officers state that he died from an infection "toward the end of 1898."

"He was buried with full military honours," his brother officers wrote, "and we grieved at our loss of his noble character and his perfect manners."[67]

Notes

1. All the battalion personnel whose last post before embarking at Alexandria on 7/8 January 1863 was the Nile Barrage Fort were part of the 19th Regiment of the Line.
2. Sgt. Fadl al-Sīd Abū Jumā, cn. 3 coy
3. Arab., Qawālalī Muhammad 'Alī Bāshā, a literal rendering of Turk. Kavālalt Mehmed 'Alī Paşa.
4. al-Farīq Sir Samuel Baker Pasha, BD 68-69.
5. Lt. Faraj Ahmad Hāshim, cn. 2 coy
6. Lt. Marjān 'Alī al-Danasūrī, cn. 4 coy
7. Adj-Maj 'Abdallāh Sālim al-Faqī, cn. 4 coy
8. Adj-Maj 'Abdallāh al-Dinkāwī, cn. 1 coy
9. Capt. Marjān Sharīf, cn. 3 coy
10. Ernest, son of L. M. Linant de Bellefonds Pasha, then director of Public Works, Egypt, had volunteered to replace his brother, Auguste-Edouard, who had died of fever at Gondokoro in 1874.
11. Chaillé Long, C. *Central Africa* [etc], 1876, 74, 186, 191; BD 98-99; portrait in *Ta'rikh* I, 156.
12. H. Johnston, *The Nile Quest* (London: A Rivers, 1905), 239.
13. By error no conferment of the Legion of Honour to either officer is recorded in *Historique*, 281-282 under Liste des officiers décorés de la Légion d'Honneur [with extracts of decrees printed in the *Moniteur Officiel*].
14. Sgt. Tawakkul Muhammad, cn. 4 coy.
15. Emin's administration has attracted much attention of students of the continuing influence in modern Uganda and neighboring countries of colonies of "Nubi" settlers descended from the *nizam* troops in Emin's garrisons.

16. F. R.Wingate, ed., *Mahdiism in the Egyptian Sudan*, (London and N.Y., Macmillan 1891), 293.
17. Lt.-Col. H. G. Prout Bey, an American military engineer in the Egyptian service, was general governor of the Equatorial province, 1876-1878, when he was invalided and succeeded by Col. Ibrāhīm Fawzī Bey later Pasha. Zaki, 71; BD. 309-10.
18. al-Zubayr Pasha Rahma Mansur (1830-1913), a Ja'ali magnate who in 1873-1874 conquered Dar Fur with his private army, awaits a serious biographer. For a provisional sketch: BD. 390-91.
19. Sālih Bey Hijazi, cn. 2 coy, portrait in Tūsūn 1. Ignore BD. 328.
20. al-Nūr Bey Muhammad 'Anqara, BD. 297; Brig-Gen. Sa'id Pasha Husayn al-Jimi 'ābī. Both served the Egyptian government. The former joined the Mahdist cause and later accepted the Anglo-Egyptian regime. The latter chose the wrong moment to change sides (see note 45 below).
21. Munzinger Pasha, Johann Albert Werner, BD. 281-82.
22. Faraj al-Zaynī. See note 43 below.
23. 'Abd al-Jabbār Bakhīt, cn. 2 coy
24. 'Abdallāh Sālim al-Faqī, cn. 4 coy
25. Faraj Wanī and Hadīd Farhāt, cn. 1 coy
26. Idrīs Na'īm, cn. 2 coy
27. 'Ali Jifūn, 335-36.
28. P. N. Nieuwenhuis, *Dansk Biografisk Lexikon*, I, 313-314, København 1887; biographical military documents in the Royal Military Library, København.
29. Arendrup to Khayrī Pasha, 11 November 1875 (cited in Douin, III fasc B., 765).
30. Tūsūn, 137.
31. Sources for this incident include SNR (Khartoum, 1922, IV, 2, 106-7); L. Santoni, *Alto Egitto e Nubia* (Rome, 1905), 255-59; ibid., excerpt from Santoni's Ms. Diary, in P. Santi and R. Hill, *The Europeans in the Sudan* (Oxford: Oxford University Press, 1980), 236-37; R. C. Wilson, *Chapters from My Official Life* (1916), 81, 96.
32. See D. Taylor, *The Sable Arm: Black Troops in the Union Army, 1861-1865* (Kansas, 1956, reprint 1987).
33. Khayrī Pasha to Sirdār [Ratib Pasha], 29 April 1876 (Le Caire, Archives Abdine, Registre 28, pièce 364, cited in Douin III, 3 fasc B. 1196. The disparaging use of "Arab" for a savage and dirty nomad by Arabic-speaking townspeople and urban foreigners in the Sudan, has no strict racial connotation (cf. English street Arab) but may reflect an age-long antipathy between the desert and the sown, e.g. a survival of the bitter feeling of the settled pre-Arab peoples of the Nubian Nile Valley against the predatory nomad Arab invaders.
34. *Abū Naẓẓāra*, issue No. 158, 24 June 1881.
35. Ahmad 'Urābī Pasha, *Kashf al-sitār 'an sirr al-aẓsrār* (Cairo, n.d).
36. Muhammad Sulaymān Bey, cn. 2 coy
37. Col. Hasan Bey Bahnassāwī was in command of the 5th regiment at the extreme western portion of the defenses of Khartoum where the Mahdists

broke through on the night of 25-26 January 1885. He was spared, escaped and, after an adventurous journey, reached Cairo.

38. Bakhīt Bey Batrākī. See note 42.
39. Surūr Bey Bahjat. See note 50.
40. Brig-Gen. Muhammad 'Ali Pasha Husayn. cn. 3 coy
41. Mudawwī 'Abd al-Rahmān. BD. 243 (where Mudawwī mis-spelled).
42. Col. Bakhīt Bey Batrākī. cn. 2 coy, BD. 70.
43. Maj. Gen. Faraj Pasha Muhammad al-Zaynī, cn. 3 coy; ignore BD. 124-25.
44. *Bayt al-māl*, the Mahdist treasury.
45. Brig.-Gen. Sa'īd Pasha Husayn al-Jimī'ābī (BD. 325) and Brig.-Gen. Hasan Pasha Ibrahim al-Shallali (BD. 155-56) were court-martialed and shot for betraying their own troops to the enemy during an Egyptian sortie from Khartoum against a Mahdist force at Halfāyyat al-Mulūk, an outer northern suburb. The troops arrested both officers and brought them back to Khartoum and explained their treachery. A court martial of which the president was Gordon's chief-of-staff, Maj.-Gen. Faraj Pasha al-Zaynī, found both men guilty of treason. See *The Times*, 31 March and 1 April 1884 for an account of the battle.
46. Burdaynī Bey, a substantial Khartoum merchant who, during the siege, greatly assisted the provisioning of the city.
47. Makīn wad al-Nūr, BD. 228; his brother 'Abdallāh, BD. 7.
48. Bakhīt Batrākī, see note 42 above.
49. Copied by courtesy of Phillips International Fine Art Auctioneers, Oxford.
50. Lt.-Col. Surūr Bey Bahjat cn. 3 coy
51. sm. Baraka Ahmad 'Ali, cn. 2 coy
52. sm. 'Abdallāh al-'Abd. cn. 4 coy
53. 'Ali Jifūn, 330-37; cn. 2 coy
54. Lt.-Col. Abū Bakr al-Hājj Muhammad, cn. 1 coy
55. For Amīr al-Zakī Tamal's organization of the Mahdist defense of al-Qallābāt see Muhammad Sa'īd Qaddāl, *al-Mahdiyya wa'l-Habasha. . .* Khartoum, University Press, 1973, 112. The "zarība" (a permanent fortress), drawn, p. 167.
56. The massacre of the Ja'aliyīn at al-Matamma, 1897, by order of the Mahdist commander, Mahmūd wad Ahmad.
57. Sgt. Faḍī al-Sīd Abū Jumā', cn. 3 coy, *Taqwīm* 662 and Tūsūn 66 have Jum'a.
58. *Koran* Sūra 31, verse 34.
59. Lt.-Col. W. H. Hunter Bey, BD. 168.
60. 'Uthman ibn Abi Bakr Diqna, see H. C. Jackson, *Osman Digna*, 1926; BD. 367-68.
61. After the formation of the Anglo-Egyptian Condominium of the Sudan, A. M. McMurdo became Director of the Anti-Slavery Department with headquarters in Cairo and surveillance posts in the Sudan. He was continually at odds with the Sudan government over anti-slavery policy which came to a head in 1911 when he was appointed to another post and his department

merged with the Sudan Police. For the background to the controversy, see M. W. Daly, *Empire on the Nile, the Anglo-Egyptian Sudan, 1898-1934*, (Cambridge, 1986), 231-39.

62. T. E. Hickman Bey, later brig.-gen., BD. 164.
63. 'Ali Jifūn, 491.
64. Machell, com[mandant] XII Sudanese, to Staff Officer, [Wādī] Halfā, 13 April 1893 (SAD, Wingate papers, 255/1/90). For "Dervish chants" see D. Hay Thorburn, "Sudanese Soldiers' Songs," *Jour. African Soc.* (London) 24 (1925): 314-21.
65. Arab singular *dallūka*, meaning originally drum, inseparable from the traditional Sudanese dance.
66. Our thanks to Dr. Douglas Johnson for making us aware of the following document: Manuscript rpt. on p. 95 of the Sudan Intelligence Report NO. 60 (25 May to 31 Dec. 1898), Appendix 58: Summary of Intelligence Diary, Fashoda District, 21 Sept. to 9 Oct. 1898, signed by o.c. Egyptian troops, Fashoda, H. W. Jackson, 10 Oct. An appendix to that summary is entitled "Statements of Shilluks regarding arrival of Marchand Mission at Fashoda" in which the King of the Shilluk is cited as denying having made a treaty of alliance with the French. At the end of this statement Jackson wrote: "Taken by me in the presence of the following witnesses: . . .Sagh [qūl aghāsi] Ali Eff Gafun [sic]." His promotion to major was not announced at his bn. base camp at Berber until 14 October.
67. Tūsūn, 174-175, from the story of the life of the late Bikbashi 'Ali Efendi Jifun by officers of the Egyptian army.

Appendix 1

The Contrôle Nominatif (Battalion Nominal Roll) with Brief Records of Service

The attempt which follows, to construct an authentic biographical record of the Sudanese battalion, is derived from four sources:

1. Amīn Sāmī Pāshā's *Taqwīm al-Nīl,* a collection of Egyptian documents derived from *al-waqā'i'al-miṣriyya* (the official gazette) and other documents which the editor judged to be of permanent public interest.
2. The printed lists in Prince 'Umar Ṭūsūn's history of the battalion in Mexico, *Buṭūlat al-orṭa al-sūdāniyya al-miṣriyya fī ḥarb al-Maksīk* [Exploits (literally heroism) of the Egyptian Sudanese battalion in the Mexican War], a work derived partly from No. 1 above but with corrections where the author suspects misprints.
3. Conflation of the French periodical nominal rolls of the battalion in Mexico, preserved in S.H.A.T. under reference G7, box 124.
4. Other biographical sources, mostly disappointing, for the subsequent careers of veterans from the Mexican campaign.

It appeared evident to us that some soldiers overlooked or suppressed their acquired names and substituted different names, reverted to their native names, or adopted nicknames. The French or Francophone "Algérien" military clerk in charge of the roll would register whichever name a soldier gave him, writing it in roman characters as required by military regulations, not as it sounded to the Sudanese soldier but as it sounded to the clerk. The roll therefore abounds in exotic spellings of what were originally Arabic or

African names which we, with guidance from Sudanese, American, and European colleagues, have tried, not always with success, to identify. Our endeavors to reconcile the sources have resulted in an arithmetical contradiction. The total strength officially recorded by the French as having embarked at Alexandria in January 1863 was 447, but the names recorded in the periodical battalion rolls from Mexico attain a variable total, a surplus of no fewer than 74 names which are marked X in the nominal roll below.

We were wrong. As the late Professor Stevenson explained: Nuba and Southerners often have several names originating from various relations and friends, whose names they use freely as alternatives without worrying about contradiction or ambiguity. So, what with his official name, camp names, nicknames, and the practice of warriors the world over (of declaring an alternative name for the purpose of drawing extra rations or for some other profitable end) it is not surprising that there is a surplus of names on the battalion roll.

Unconcern about names was not confined to Africa. The Sudanese former domestic slave enlisted in the Piedmontese Bersagliere Corps in 1848 under the name Michele Amatore. His Italian comrades insisted on calling him Luigi. He himself answered happily to both Michele and Luigi, which puzzled the civil court in which he (with others) was a defendant.[1] Had Michele joined a Scottish regiment his fellow Scots would probably have called him Jock.

Battalion Commanders

Jabāratallāh Muḥammad Efendi, maj., ethnic origin unknown, said to have been a veteran of the Syrian campaigns of Muḥammad 'Alī Pāsha which ended in 1841. Died at Veracruz of yellow fever, 29 May 1863.

Muḥammad Almās Bey, col. (later brig.-gen. and pāshā), Dinka, enlisted in the Egyptian Army, 1844, and embarked with the bn. at Alexandria with rank of capt. and bn. second-in-command. Promoted adj.-maj., 11 March 1863; further promoted acting maj. and o.c. bn. on death of Maj. Jabāratallāh Muḥammad. His acting rank was made substantive by the Egyptian *Dīwān al-Khidīwī* on 29 September 1865 and notified in the field by arrêté of 6 February 1866; Legion of Honour (chevalier) by arrêté of 20 April 1864, citation: "commanded the bn. with energy, intelligence and devotion." Received from the Emperor Maximilian the Imperial Mexican Order of Notre Dame de la Guadeloupe, 1864. At the review in Paris 9 May 1867 Emperor Napoleon III conferred on him promotion in the Legion of Honour to the class of officier. At an investiture in Alexandria on 28 May 1867 Khedive Ismā'īl promoted him col. and conferred on him the grade of bey. Posted to the Sudan as o.c. 2nd Infantry Regt., 1869, promoted brig.-gen. and pasha (4th grade), and appointed governor of Dongola province, 1874-1875 and again 1875-1879 when—for causes officially unknown—he was removed from office and relegated to his military duties by Gov.-Gen. al-Farīq C.G. Gordon Pāshā. Appointed governor of Khartoum by Gordon Pāshā's successor, Brig.-Gen. Muḥammad Ra'ūf Pāsha, c. 1880, he died in the capital after little over two lunar months in office. He was buried beside the tombs of two former governors-general, Aḥmad Pāshā Shāmli ("Abu Widān") and Mūsā Pāshā Ḥamdī. (Plate 16)[2]

Bn. Chief Translator-Interpreter

Aḥmad 'Ibayḍ Efendi, civilian, ethnic origin unknown, probably of Lower Egyptian domicile, accorded honorary rank with pay and allowances of adj.-maj., 1863; Legion of Honour (chevalier), 1867.[3]

Seconded to the Sudanese Battalion at Various Times for Administrative Duties

Anglade, Jean-Baptiste, pte 1 cl., attached to bn staff, 1863.
Bardey, Évrard, sgt., attached to bn staff, 1863.
Baron, Gabrie-François Xavier Aimé, sub-lt, administrative officer, 1863.
Borghella, sub-lt, bn accountant, died 1863 (see Colas below).
Brincourt, sub-lt.
Bruyneel, Charles, pte. clerk on bn staff.
Colas, Joseph-Félix, administrative adjudant, transferred from the camping service to succeed Borghella, 1863.
Despierre, Claude, staff sgt, attached 1863.
Gonon, Victor-Constant, pte, Gaudeloupe Engineers, attached 1863.
Grincourt, Aimé-Honoré, sub-lt, administrative officer, attached 1863.
Lavenir, Jules, staff sgt. attached 1863.
Mangin and Charpplain, adjudants, 2nd Intendance, 1863.[4]
Maupin, sub-lt.
Ménardière, Stéphen Stanislas, pte, attached to bn. staff, 1863.
Patin, sub-lt.
Solle, Hippolyte, staff sgt., 1863.
Voirin, Louis-Ernest, cpl. clerk, bn staff, -1867.

Seconded to the Bn from III Tirailleurs Algériens as Interpreters, 1863

'Abd al-Qādir b. Ḥammu, sgt.
Aḥmad b. Amara (?'Umara), rifleman 1 cl.
'Alī b. 'Arabī, rifleman 2 cl. Died in hsp. Veracruz, 18 July 1863.
'Amr b. Muḥammad, interpreter 2 cl., on staff.

'Amr b. Suwar, interpreter 1 cl., on staff.
al-'Arabī, sgt., interpreter, on staff.
Abū'l-Qāsim Muḥammad, sgt. 1863; 1 lt 1863; entered hsp., Veracruz 30 July 1863.
Khenil b. 'Alī Tir, interpreter 1 cl. Died at La Soledad, 19 July 1863.
Muḥammad b. Aḥmadī, sgt. interpreter on bn. staff. Awarded M.M. (arrêté of 20 April 1867), citation: "Very brave in action; he carried out efficiently his duties as interpreter with the Egyptian black bn."
Muḥammad b. ?Ammach/?Ammaih, cpl. interpreter.
Muḥammad b. Doho, rifleman interpreter 1 cl.
Muḥammad b. Ghebar [? Jabbār/? Kibr], sgt. interpreter.
Muḥammad b. 'Īṣāwī, rifleman interpreter.
Muḥammad al-Saghīr b. Ḥamad, rifleman interpreter.
Muḥammad al-Saqr, rifleman interpreter, bn. hq.
Sa'īd b. Amar (?'Amr/?'Umar), rifleman interpreter, died in hsp., Veracruz 12 July 1863.
Salāh/Sālih Gharbī, rifleman interpreter.
al-Ṭayyib b. Abū'l-Qāsim, rifleman interpreter, died in hsp. Veracruz, 29 June 1863.

The Battalion and the Company

The battalion was the impersonal administrative center which rarely impinged upon a soldier's life. The company on the contrary embodied the human side of the soldier's world of marching, battle, friendship, mutual help and, for the veteran, fond memories of campaigns and glory.

No. 1 Company

Officers

Faraj 'Azāzī (later col., bey and Mahdist officer) a native of Jabal Taqalī in the Nuba Mts, stolen as a child by slave raiders who sold him in Egypt; enlisted, 1849, he is said to have been commissioned 1854; 1 lt. 11 March 1863; Legion of Honour (chevalier) by arrêté of 20 April 1867, citation: "a good officer giving a good example by his own bravery"; awarded the Imperial Mexican Decoration of Notre Dame de la Guadeloupe, 1864; gazetted adj.-maj. 28 May 1867. On his return from Mexico successively promoted maj. and lt.-col. Posted to the Eastern Sudan he was appointed to command the Kasala garrison with rank of col.; the spread of the Mahdist rising to the area posed threat to the Egyptian forces; after actions with the enemy at Sabdarāt and Qūl-sīt[5] he surrendered along with the governor, Aḥmad ʻIffāt Pāsha and, though Aḥmad Pāshā was murdered, he himself was kindly received by the Mahdi at Omdurman and appointed to the staff of the Taʻīshī amīr ʻUthmān Adam Jānū to whom he finally became commander of the reserve. He fought in many battles both in Dār Fūr and in the final battles of the ʻAtbara and Kararī, 1898. After Kararī he fled westward to Dār Fūr in the entourage of Sultan ʻAlī Dīnār who had him and others killed on suspicion of treachery shortly after their arrival at al-Fāshir toward the end of A.H. 1316 [spring 1899].[6]

Faḍlallāh Ḥabīb, stated to have enlisted 1848;[7] s.m. 1863; Legion of Honour (chevalier) by arrêté of 26 April 1864, conferred in person by Emperor Napoléon III in Paris on 9 May 1867, citation: "a first-class soldier, most meritorious"; 2 lt. 10 September 1864, confirmed by the *Dīwān al-Khidīwī*, Egyptian government, 29 September 1865; capt. 1867; he was later posted to the Eastern Command at Kasala and took part in the defence of the area against the Mahdists; he was killed along with Adj.-Maj. Ḥadīd Farhāt in battle at Qulūsīt.[8]

Ḥusayn Aḥmad, enlisted 1854; embarked at Alexandria as 1 lt., 1863; provisionally promoted capt. 11 March 1863, later confirmed; mentioned in dispatches for leadership in the assault on the fort at Conejo, 9 April 1864; Legion of Honour (chevalier) by arrêté of 20 April 1864, citation: "always ready to march into action; commands his men with vigour"; gazetted maj. 28 May 1867.[9]

Abū Bakr al-Ḥājj Muḥammad (later lt. col., bey and Mahdist officer) of Dongolāwī (Bidayrī) origin, from Abkar near al-Dabba; sgt. 1863; 2 lt. 1867; later, as a maj., he commanded a bn. of regular infantry in Khartoum when his unit moved to the Bahr al-Ghazāl under the overall command of R. Gessi Pāshā, governor of the province; he took part in Gessi's campaign against the sons of the exiled ul-Zubayr Pāshā Raḥma and saw active service at Shakka, Dāra, Kabkabiyya and Qūlqūl. His promotion to lt.-col. and bey followed. The surrender of Col. R. Slatin bey, general governor of Dār Fūr to the forces of Muḥammad Aḥmad al-Mahdī made further resistance impossible so he too surrendered to the Mahdist amīr Muḥammad Khālid Zuqal (Bey), a former Egyptian civil servant, whom the Mahdi had appointed to succeed Slatin. After service in the Mahdist army against King John in 1889 he died about A.H. 1309 [A.D. 1891-1892].[10]

ʻAbdallāh al-Sūdānī/ʻAbdallāh al-Dinsāwī (i.e. Dinkāwī) 1863; M.M. 1865, citation: "most brave"; s.m. 1867; 1 lt. 1867; he later served with Baker Pāshā's expedition to the Equatorial regions, 1869-1873 and during Baker's final advance to Bunyoro, 1872, he remained in command of the

Egyptian fort and post at Fatiko with rank of adj.-maj. He was then appointed governor of Rajjāf.[11]

Faraj Wanī, cpl. 1863; M.M. 1867; w.o. 1867; after his return from Mexico he was commissioned and served at Zayla', Tajūra, Muṣawwa' and Keren and attained the rank of adj.-maj.; he served in the Kasala military area during the Mahdist offensive of 1884-5 when he took part in the battles of al-Jammām, al-'Ushūr and Qulūsīt in the last of which he was killed. Portrait in Plate 17.[12]

Hadīd Farhāt, pte. 1863; sgt. 1864; in 1865 awarded the M.M. for conspicuous service at the assault of the entrenched camp of Conejo, July 1864, and for two further actions in 1865; 2 lt. 1867. His military career was spent thereafter in the Eastern Command in the Sudan, serving in garrison duty at Zayla'. Muṣawwa' and Keren when he was promoted adj.-maj. During the defence of Kasala against the Mahdist forces, 1884-5, he took part in engagements at al-Jammām, al-'Ushūr and finally with Capt. Faḍlallāh Ḥabīb at Qulūsīt where both officers were killed.[13]

Bakhīt Aḥmad al-Miṣrī, pte 1863; pte. 1 cl. 1863; sgt. 1867 when awarded the M.M.; 2 lt. 1867.[14]

Ḥasan Aḥmad, pte, 1863; sgt. 1867; 2 lt. 1867.[15]

Marjān Muḥammad al-Jamāl, pte. 1863; pte. 1 cl. 1863; discharged from hsp., Veracruz, 27 July 1866; sgt. 1867; 2 lt. 1867.[16]

Marjān Sulaymān, pte. 1863; pte. 1 cl. 1863; sgt. 1867; 2 lt. 1867.[17]

Mas'ūd Tā'ūs, cpl. ?1863; sgt. 1867; 2 lt. 1867.[18]

Other Ranks

'Abdallāh Aḥmad, pte. 1863; cpl. 1863; died in hsp., La Soledad. 21 February. 1865.

'Abdallāh Aḥmar, pte., 1863; died in hsp., Veracruz, 25 July 1863.

'Abdallāh 'Alī, pte. 1863; cpl. 1863; disappeared during battle of Cocuite, 22 January 1865; later returned to camp and on 22 February 1865 demoted to pte.; tried by court martial, Veracruz on a charge of desertion; committed to prison 12 May 1865; in hsp. 1-9 June 1865; acquitted by court martial, 17 June 1865.[19]

'Abdallāh Dāyīm, pte. (bugler or drummer) 183; sgt. 1865.[20]

'Abdallāh Kunjārī, from the militant branch of the Fur, pte. 1863; killed in action at Cocuite, 22 January 1865.

'Abdallāh Muḥammad, pte., 1863; killed in action at Callejon de la Laja, 2 March 1865.

'Abd al-Farrāj Abiss. pte.; died in hsp., Veracruz, 16 April 1863.[21]

'Abd al-Farrāj Marjān, pte. (bugler or drummer), 1863-7. X

'Abd al-Fārūq Aḥmad, pte. 1863; died in hsp., Veracruz, 23 March 1863.

'Abd al-Khayr Khamīs, pte. 1863; sgt. 1867.
'Abd al-Nabī 'Abd al-Karīm, bugler, 1863-7; pte. 1863; pte. 1 cl. 1863; sgt. 1867.
'Abd al-Naḍḍāra Marjān, pte. 1863; sgt. 1867.[22]
'Abd al-Sayyid 'Abd al-'Azīz, pte. 1863; killed in ambush at La Tejeria, 5 September 1866.[23]
'Abd al-Tawrāh Marjān, pte. 1863.
Aḥmad 'Abdallāh, pte. 1863; sgt. 1867; in hsp., Veracruz, 29 November 1866.
Aḥmad Adam, pte. 1863; pte. 1 cl. 1863.
Aḥmad 'Alī, pte. 1863.[24]
Aḥmad Muḥammad, pte. 1863; died in hsp. Veracruz, 12 September 1863.
'Alī Ibrāhīm (1), pte. 1863; sgt. 1867.
'Alī Ibrāhīm (2), pte. 1863; pte. 1 cl., 1863; sm. 1867.
'Alī Idrīs, pte. 1863; pte. 1 cl. 1863; seriously wounded at Callejon de la Laja, 2 March 1865; M.M. 1865; sm. 1867.
'Alī Mahala, pte. 1863; pte. 1 cl. 1863; sm. 1867.
'Alī Sa'īd, pte. 1863; in hsp., Veracruz, January 1867.
'Alī Sulaymān, cpl. 1863; seriously wounded at Las Palmas, 5 October 1866 when he "distinguished himself by his ardor and energy" for which he was awarded the M.M. by arrêté of 6 January 1967; w.o. 1867.
'Alī Yūsuf, pte. 1863; sgt. 1967.
Amān 'Abdhu Aghā pte. 1863; sgt. 1867.
Amān al-Ḥabash, pte. 1863; died in hsp. Veracruz, after four admissions, 19 November 1863.[25]
Amīn 'Izzat (1), qmc. 1866; admitted to hsp., Veracruz, 2 November 1866; died 24 November 1866.
Amīn 'Izzat (2), pte. 1863; cpl. 1867; w.o. 1867.
Anjalū Ḥabīballāh, pte. 1863; took part in the disaster at Callejon de la Laja, 1865, and was awarded the M.M.; sgt. 1867.[26]
Aqīb/'Aqib Adam, pte. 1863; died in hsp., Veracruz, 5 November 1864.
Arbāb 'Abd al-Jalīl, pte. 1863; sgt. 1867.
Bakhīt 'Aḥmad (1), pte. 1863; pte. 1 1863; sm. 1867.
Bakhīt Aḥmad (2), pte. 1863; sgt. 1867.
Bakhīt Badrān/Badr, pte. 1863; transferred from No. 2 coy; pte. 1 cl. 1863; M. M. 1864, citation; "He has shown the greatest bravery" when on 2 October 1863 he led a detachment of six Sudanese privates who formed part of the travelling escort on a train derailed by the enemy who were repulsed after heavy fighting; cpl. 1867; w.o. 1867.[27]
Bakhīt Faḍlallāh, pte. 1863; sgt. 1867.
Bahīt Khamīs, pte. 1863; sgt. 1867.
Bakhīt Muḥammad, pte. 1863; admitted to hsp., Veracruz, 27 January - 13 February 1866; sgt. 1867.

Bilāl Ibrāhīm (*alias* Khalīl Ayyād), pte. 1863; died in hsp. Veracruz, 9 September 1864.

Bilāl Muḥammad (1) pte. 1863; killed in action while lifting the mortally wounded Commandant Ligier into a train ambushed on 2 October 1863.

Bilal Muḥammad (2) pte. 1863; sgt. 1867.

Bishāra Muḥammad, pte. 1863; sgt. 1867.

Brest [?Barac] Aḥmad, pte. 1863; absent from roll-call, 4 September 1865; posted as a deserter 15 September; preventive detention 22 November 1865 - 23 January 1866; freed 23 January 1866 by superior order, on appeal.[28]

Eimara [?'Umara] Marmī, pte. 1863; killed in battle of Callejon de la Laja, 2 March 1865.

Faḍlallāh Aḥmad, pte. 1863; killed in battle of Callejon de la Laja, 2 March 1865.

Faraj Sālim al-Faqī, pte. 1863, sgt. 1867.[29]

Faraj Ṣidkī, drummer 1863; cpl. 1867; sgt. 1867.

Fatḥallāh 'Abdallāh, pte. 1863; sgt. 1867.

Ḥadīd Farhāt (see under "Officers" above). An error in the rolls may have created another man of the same name said to have died 5 January 1866.[30]

Ḥamad 'Alī, pte. 1863; sgt. 1867.

Ḥasan Sayyid, al-Hājj, pte. 1863; pte. 1 cl. 1863; csm. 1867.

Ḥasīballāh Muḥammad. Transferred to No. 2 coy.

Ḥusayn Aḥmad, cpl. 1863; sgt. 1865; admitted to hsp., Veracruz, 5 October 1866; died 12 October 1866.

Ibrāhīm 'Abd al-Raḥmān, pte. 1863; promoted pte. 1 cl. 1863 for his part in defending a train ambushed on 2 October 1863; sm. 1867.

Ibrāhīm Ramaḍān, pte. 1863; sgt. 1867.

Ibrāhīm Shīḥa, pte. 1863; pte. 1 cl. 1863; sm. 1867.[31]

Idrīs Muḥammad Sandalūba, pte. 1863; cpl. 1863; reduced to pte. 10 November 1865; taken prisoner at Le Tejeria during an enemy raid, 5 September 1866; released after the evacuation of the bn. from Mexico, he reached Alexandria 2 September 1867.[32]

Ittum Sūdān, pte. 1863; pte. 1 cl. 1863; M.M. 1864, citation: "a very brave soldier, disciplined and devoted"; died of fever at Minatitlan, 10 March, 1864.[33]

Jābir Adam, pte. 1863; 1 cl. 1863; sm. 1867.

Jabr Ḥammād, pte. 1863; cpl. 1867; w.o. 1867.

Jāhallāh 'Abdallāh, pte 1863; pte. 1. 1863; sm. 1867.

Jāmi' Muḥammad, pte. 1863; sgt. 1867; once wounded, M.M. 1867.

Juma' 'Abdallāh, pte. 1863; pte. 1 cl. 1863. X

Khalīfa Sūdān, pte. 1863; sgt. 1867.

Khalīl Ayyād. *See* Bilāl Ibrāhīm (*alias* Khalīl Ayyād).

Khamīs Muḥammad, pte. 1863; sgt. 1867.

Khayr ʻAbdallāh, pte. (bugler or drummer) 1763; sgt. 1867.
Khayr ʻAbd al-Fattāḥ, cpl. 1863; killed in the battle of Callejon de la Laja, 2 March 1865.
Khayrallāh Muḥammad, pte. 1863; sgt. 1867.
Khayr Ḥamad, pte. 1863; cpl. 1867. X
Kōdī al-Fīl, Dinka by origin, pte. 1863; sgt. 1867.[34]
Kūkū Bashīr, pte. 1863; killed in action at El Palmar, 24 January 1865.[35]
Kūkū Muḥammad Saghayrūn, pte. 1863; found not guilty in a case of murder at Medellin, tried by court martial at Veracruz, 28 and 29 September 1863. X
Kūkū Sindala/Sindaleb/Sandalūba, pte. 1863; admitted to hsp., Veracruz, 1864; sgt. 1867.[36]
Kūkū Sūdān, pte. 1863; sgt. 1867.
Kūkū Sūdān al-Kabbāshī, pte. 1863; pte. 1 cl. 1863; mentioned in dispatches for his part in the defence of Tlacotalpan on 14 July 1864 when seriously wounded, having already won distinction in the fighting at Las Palmas, he was awarded the M.M. (clasp 1867) and promoted sgt. 20 March 1865; sm. 1867.[37]
Mabrūk Nasīm pte. 1863 (bugler or drummer); sgt. 1867.
Mahbūb Abu'l-Bakhīt, pte. 1863; killed in the battle of El Palmar, 24 January 1865.
Marjān Bakhīt, pte. 1863. X
Marjān Kūrmuk/Kūrmukra, pte. 1863; cpl. 1867; w.o. 1867.[38]
Marjān Maṭar, pte. 1863; cpl. 1863; seriously wounded while pursuing the enemy at Tlalixcoyan; took part in the defeat at Callejon de la Laja, 1865, awarded M.M.; deserted on 22 September 1865 and, on his return to duty, was deprived of his rank and reduced to pte.
Marjān Rāfiʻ, pte. 1863; wounded in the battle of Callejon de la Laja 2 March 1865; M.M. 1867.
Marjān Yūsuf Ḥusām al-Dīn, pte. 1863; pte. 1 cl. 1863; cpl. 1867; M.M. (one wound) 1867; w.o. 1867.
Marzouth [?Marzūk] Muḥammad Mahlad [?Makhlad], pte. 1863; pte. 1 cl. 1863; cpl. 1865; died in hsp. La Soledad, 9 November 1865.
Muḥammad ʻAbd al-Raḥmān, pte. 1863; sgt. 1867.
Muḥammad ʻAbduh, pte. 1863; pte. 1 cl. 1863; csm. 1867.
Muḥammad Aḥmad, pte. 1863; sgt. 1867.[39]
Muḥammad ʻAlī ʻAbd al-Karīm, pte. 1863; promoted pte. 1 cl. for his part in defending an ambushed train on 2 October 1863; M.M. 1867, one wound; sgt. 1867.[40]
Muḥammad Ḥāmid, pte. 1863; sgt. 1867.
Muḥammad Khamīs, pte. 1863. X
Muḥammad Mūsā, pte. 1863; sgt. 1867.

Muḥammad Simbil, pte. 1863; transferred to the mounted detachment; wounded in enemy raid at La Tejeria, admitted to hsp., Veracruz, 6 September 1866, died 16 September from his wounds.[41]

Muḥammad Sulaymān, pte. 1863; cpl. 10 January 1863; awarded M.M. for his part in counter-attacking the enemy who had derailed a train (arrété of 3 January 1866), citation: "two wounds, one serious. He has never been absent from any of the battalion's actions and has at all times exhibited the most outstanding bravery"; w.o. 1867.

Muḥammad Yūnus, pte.; died at sea on board *La Seine*, 4 February 1863.

Mursāl Adam, pte. 1863; sgt. 1867.

Mursāl Muḥammad, pte. 1863; killed in battle of Callejon de la Laja, 2 March 1865.

Mursāl Muḥammad Sirr al-Din, pte. 1863; sgt. 1867.

Mursāl Rajab, pte. 1863; pte. 1 cl. 1863; w.o. 1867.[42]

Mursāl Sūdān, pte. 1863; sgt. 1867.

Nāfi' Raḥmed [?Raḥma/?Aḥmad]; pte. 1863; died in hsp., Veracruz, 7 July 1863.[43]

Nāfi' Sūdān, pte. 1863; 1 cl. 1863; M.M. (arrêté of 20 April 1867), citation: "a brave and devoted soldier"; sm. 1867

Na'īm Khādimallāh, pte. 1863; died at sea on board *La Seine*, 4 February 1863.

al-Nūr Jum'a, pte. 1863, died in hsp., Veracruz, 20 March 1863.

al-Nūr Kūmī, pte. 1863; sgt. 1867.[44]

Raḥma Adam, pte. 1863; sgt. 1867.

Raḥma Muḥammad, pte. 1863; died in hsp., Veracruz, 25 February 1863.

Raḥmed [?Raḥma/?Aḥmad] Naṣr al-Dīn, pte. 1865; died in hsp., Veracruz, 14 May 1866.

Ramadān Kūkū, pte. 1863; pte. 1 cl. 1863; lost an eye in action at Tlalixcoyan ? April 1864; M.M. 1865; sm. 1867.[45]

Rast [?Rizq] Aḥmad, pte. 1863. X[46]

Rizq Sa'īd, pte. 1863; sgt. 1867.

Sa'īd al-Abachi [Ḥabashī], pte. 1863; in hsp., Veracruz, 18 January 1867.

Sa'īd al-Ḍaw, pte. 1863; pte. 1 cl. 1863; sm. 1867.

Sa'īd al-Ḥājj 'Abduh, pte. 1863. X

Sa'īd al-Jaysh, pte. 1863; sgt. 1867.

Sa'īd Muḥammad, pte. 1863; early in 1865 sentenced to prison, San Juan de Ulua, for intention to desert; pardoned and returned to unit, 9 March 1865.[47]

Sa'īd Muḥammad Zarbūl, pte. 1863; pte. 1 cl. 1863; died in hsp., Veracruz, 24 April 1865.

Salim [?Sālim/?Salīm] Sa'īd, pte. 1863; on 30 September 1863 sentenced by court martial, Veracruz, to five years' hard labor (accessory to murder at Medellin), sentence later remitted.[48]

Sulaymān Adam, pte. 1863; sgt. 1867.
Sultān 'Abdallāh, pte. 1863; pte. 1 cl. 1863; cpl. 1866; w.o. 1867.
Surūr Ḥasan, pte. 1863; sgt. 1867.[49]
Surūr Muṣṭafā, pte. 1863; admitted to hsp., Veracruz, but died in delirium on his way there from La Soledad.
Tabinī Adam, pte. 1863; died in hsp., Veracruz, 23 January 1867.[50]
'Umar Muḥammad Camaroui [?Qamrāwī], pte. 1863; sgt. 1867.[51]
'Uthmān Abū Bakr, sgt. 1863; killed in action at Callejon de la Laja, 2 March 1865.
Wādī al-Sharīf, pte. 1863; pte. 1. cl. 1863; sm. 1867.
Yāsīn Kūnda, pte. 1863; died in hsp. Veracruz, 12 October 1863.[52]
Zā'id Qazqaz, pte. 1863; sgt. 1867.[53]
al-Zubayr Aḥmad, pte. 1863; on 30 September 1863 sentenced by a court martial at Veracruz to 5 years hard labor for being accessory to murder at Medellin, April 1863.

No. 2 Company

Officers

Muḥammad Sulaymān (later lt.-col. and bey), a Shāīqī of the Surūrāb branch, he had enlisted in 1846 and had already served in two campaigns before his departure for Mexico; sm. 1863; 1 lt. 11 March 1863; Legion of Honour (chevalier) by arrêté of 27 February 1865, citation: "sets the finest example to his men and gets the best out of them"; promoted capt., approved by the *Dīwān al-Khidīwī*, 29 September 1865 with effect from 10 February 1866, as replacement to Muḥammad Almās who was appointed o.c. battalion; promoted maj. at the Paris review of 9 May 1867. On his return to the Sudan, he saw much service in the recently conquered sultanate of Dār Fūr; he was promoted lt.-col. and given command of a bn. stationed at Dāra; by 1879 he was commanding at Kūlkūl/Qūlqūl; in the summer of 1882 the growing threat by Muḥammad Aḥmad the Mahdi to the stability of the Egyptian administration in the Sudan moved C.C. Giegler Pāshā, acting governor-general, to mobilize a considerable force[54] to destroy the Mahdi's stronghold on Jabal Qadīr in the Nuba Mountains; the command was given to Brig.-Gen. Yūsuf Pāshā Ḥasan al-Shallālī with Muḥammad Bey Sulaymān as his second-in-command; the entire force consisting of 2050 men and four guns was almost annihilated near the Mahdi's camp; according to a survivor Muḥammad Bey was last seen firing a Gatling gun.[55]
Bakhīt Bey Batrākī appears to have been a soldier of some standing as he was made sm. on 12 January 1863 during the voyage to Mexico and

awarded the M.M. 1867 with promotion to 1 lt. on his return to Egypt, 28 May 1867, he served mainly in the Equatorial command where he rose to the rank of lt.-col. In 1876 appointed governor of Makraka only to be suspended in 1878 and reinstated about 1880 by General Governor Emin Bey; in 1882 transferred to Khartoum as second in command of a Sudanese bn. under another officer from the Mexican campaign, Faraj Bey Muḥammad al-Zaynī. On Faraj Bey's promotion to brig. gen. during the siege of the city by the Mahdist forces, Bakhīt Bey, with the rank of col., took command of two battalions on the eastern perimeter covering Burrī; he was killed during the Mahdist assault on the city, 26 January 1886.[56]

'Abd al-Jabbār Bakhīt, cpl. 1863; w.o. 1867; on his return from Mexico he was promoted 1 lt. and took part in the Egyptian occupation of Harar under the command of Muḥammad Ra'ūf Pāshā, 1875-8; he then served in the Eastern Sudan at Keren and Muṣawwa'; he was taken prisoner by the Mahdists on the fall of Kasala, 1885, and lay low until 1890 when he made his way to Egypt to take his pension and left shortly afterwards for the new Italian colony of Eritrea where Sudanese were being recruited for the local forces; nothing is known of his activities there; in 1901, he traveled to Khartoum and in 1902 died at Karkoj.[57]

Khalīl Fannī, enlisted 1853; qms. 1863; 2 lt. 11 March 1863; awarded the Imperial Mexican decoration of Note Dame de la Guadaloupe, 1865; promotion to 1 lt. approved by the *dīwān al-khidīwī*, 29 September 1865, effective 6 February 1866; four months' sick leave in Alexandria granted, 6 June 1866,[58] embarked at Veracruz. 13 June 1866; adj.-maj. 1867.[59]

Idrīs Na'īm, pte. 1863; pte. 1 cl. 1863; wounded at El Palmar, 21 January 1865, in which he particularly distinguished himself; M.M. 1866; Imperial Mexican Silver Medal of the Mérite Militaire, 1867; sm. 1867; promoted early to capt. His career after his return from Mexico is poorly documented; he was on garrison duty at Muṣawwa', Hara Zayla', Tajūra and Keren and later saw continuous active service during the Mahdist wars, but detail is lacking. He died in retirement in Khartoum, 1902; portrait in Ṭūsūn.[60] (Plate 17).

'Alī Jifūn, Shilluk by tribe, born at Fashoda about A.D. 1836 and named Lual Dit, captured as a youth by the Baqqāra and handed over by them as tribute to the governor of Kordofan province for military service. Enlisted in the *nizām* infantry about 1859 he took part in a government attack on Jabal Taqali. Later transferred to the army depot at the Nile Barrage north of Cairo, joined the battalion which sailed from Alexandria on 8 January 1863 for Mexico; in hospital at Veracruz, 24 February - 7 April 1863. Transferred late in 1865 as a trooper in the Sudanese mounted detachment engaged in patrolling the railway and carrying dispatches, he was promoted sgt. and sm., 1865. At a review held in Paris on 9 May 1867 in the presence of the French Emperor he was awarded the French M.M.

On his return to the Sudan he was posted to the Eastern Command based on Kasala where he served many years in continuous small engagements against Ethiopian raiders and Sudanese tax evaders; from 1881 to 1885, the triumphant Mahdist movement reduced the Egyptian fortresses one by one. Kasala, besieged for many months, surrendered on 30 July 1885 when 'Alī Jifūn and other troops of the Kasala garrison escaped in the confusion and made their way to Muṣawwa' whence they sailed to Egypt and enlisted in the new Egyptian army formed in 1883. Commissioned 2 lt., 10th Sudanese bn., 1886; at Sawākin in 1887 in command of a depot detachment of old soldiers; in January 1888 wounded in Kitchener's raid on Handūb in an attempt to capture the Amīr 'Uthmān Diqna. In December 1888, his bn. repulsed a Mahdist attack on al-Jummayza nearer Sawākin for which he was mentioned in dispatches; promoted 1 lt. he received the Majidiyya decoration, 5th class, 1888; on his transfer to the XIIth Sudanese bn. 1889 he was promoted capt.; took part in capture of Tokar, 1891; with his bn. crossed the Nubian desert from al-Quṣayr to the Nile on transfer of the bn. to Wādī Ḥalfā; promoted adj.-maj. 1897; during the period of the advance of his bn. against the Mahdist forces through Dongola to Berber he continued to be o.c. base camp, XIIth Sudanese bn. Here he was promoted maj. 14 October 1898. A brother officer, (Ṭūsūn, 125) wrote that he died of an infection at Berber in late 1898.

'Alī Jifūn's name presents complications. *Taqwīm* records his name on the Egyptian army roll as Jifūn Dira'al-Fīl while Ṭūsūn has Jufūla Dira'al-Fīl; cn. provides the first intimation that, while in Mexico, he assumed the additional name 'Alī. His name does not appear on the list of troops awarded the French M.M. either in *Le Moniteur Officiel* or in *Historique*. Ṭūsūn 59, 124-125; SAD, Wingate Papers 255/1/190. For duty at Fashoda in connection with the Marchand mission, September-October 1898, see above Chapter 11(6), *passim*.[61]

al-Ḍaw Muḥammad, enlisted 1850 and at the time of embarkation at Alexandria had served in five campaigns and had attained the rank of sgt.; commissioned 2 lt. 11 March 1863 he continued to render exemplary service and received the cross of the Legion of Honour (chevalier) by arrêté of 20 April 1867, citation; "dedicated and energetic"; gazetted capt. 1867.[62]

Faraj Aḥmad Hāshim, Somali from the Red Sea region, pte. [?1863]; sgt. 1866; admitted to hsp., Veracruz May 1866; 15 days' prison, July 1866; 2 lt. 1867; on his return to Egypt he was posted to Sir Samuel Baker Pāshā's expedition to the Equatorial regions as an officer with rank of 1 lt. in Baker's bodyguard; Baker wrote well of him.[63]

'Abdallāh Ḥusayn Basha, al-Hājj, cpl. 1863; awarded M.M. for his conduct at Tlacotalpan on 14 July 1864 when, although seriously wounded, he evinced "courage and ferocity" and is said to have been observed, during a bayonet charge, running a Mexican through and then lifting him at arm's length on his bayonet (arrêté of 22 February 1865); transferred from 3 coy; sgt. 14 March 1866; in hsp. Veracruz, 21 May - 6 June 1866; 2 lt. 1867.[64]

Bashīr Muḥammad Qubṭān, cpl. 1863; sgt. 1867; 2 lt. 1867.[65]

Faraj Badawī, sgt. 1863; 2 lt. 1867.[66]

Other Ranks

'Abdallāh al-Bakāwī, pte. 1 cl. 1863; admitted to hsp., Veracruz 28 January 1866, discharged 15 April, re-admitted 28 April, died 11 June 1866.[67]

'Abdallāh al-Basṭawīsī, pte. 1863; sgt. 1867.

'Abdallāh Ḥasanayn, pte. 1863; sgt. 1867.

'Abdallāh al-Kabani pte. 1863. X[68]

'Abdallāh Maḥammad, pte. 1863. X

'Abdallāh Sūdān, pte. 1863; pte. 1 cl. 1863; wounded in battle of El Palmar, 21 June 1865, M.M. 1866; sm. 1867.

'Abd al-Khalīl Yūsuf, enlisted 1851; cpl. 1863; awarded M.M. by arrêté 20 April 1864, citation: "a good example to his entire company" sgt. ?1864; admitted to hsp. Veracruz, 9 August 1866; died 13 August 1866.[69]

'Abd al Khayr Idrīs, pte. 1863; cpl. 1863; w.o. 1867.

'Abd al-Mawlā Aḥmad Sūdān, pte. 1863; later cpl; w.o. 1867.

'Abd al-Nabāt/'Abd al-Banāt Raḥma, pte. 1863; sg. 1867.[70]

'Abd al-Raḥmān Muḥammad, pte. 1863; sgt. 1867.

'Abd al-Rijāl 'Abdallāh, pte. 1863; pte. 1 cl. 1867; sm. 1867.[71]

Abū 'Anin/Abū Ḥamza Bakhīt, pte. 1863; cpl. 1863; w.o. 1867.[72]

Aḥmad 'Abdallāh, pte. 1863. X.

Aḥmad Adam, pte. 1863; cpl. 1863. X

'Alī 'Abdallāh, pte. 1863; cpl. 1863. X

'Alī Hijāwī, pte. 1863; sgt. 1867.

Amīn al-Zayn, qmc. 1864 when he was posted as a deserter and deprived of his rank.

Anbar Ṣubhi/Ṣubqī, pte., 1863; qmc. 1863; demoted to pte. and transferred from 1 coy., 16 November 1865; sgt. 1867.[73]

Angālū Kūkū, pte. 1863; sgt. 1867.[74]

Arbāb 'Abdallāh, pte. 1863; admitted hsp. Veracruz, 2 December 1863; died 3 April 1864.

Arbāb Bartāwī, pte. 1863; died in hsp. Veracruz, 1 October 1863.[75]

Bakhīt 'Abdallāh, pte. 1863; sgt. 1867.

Bakhīt 'Amīr, pte. 1863; pte. 1 cl. 1867; sm. 1867.

Bakhīt Badr. transferred to No. 1 coy, 1863.
Bakhīt Muḥammad, pte. 1863; sgt. 1867.
Bakū Faḍūl, pte. 1863; died in hsp., Veracruz, 2 October 1863.[76]
Baraka 'Abdallāh, pte. 1863; sgt. 1867.
Baraka Aḥmad 'Alī, pte. 1863; pte. 1 cl. 1864; sm. 1867.[77]
Baraka Sa'īd, pte. 1863; bugler or drummer; sgt. 1867.
Bilāl Sūdān, pte. 1863; sgt. 1867.
Da'ān Ma'ūfī, pte. 1863; pte. 1 cl. 1863; sgt. 1867.
Faḍlallāh 'Alī Farah, pte. 1863; pte. 1863; bugler or drummer. X
Faḍlallāh al-Daw, pte. 1863; pte. 1cl. 1863; sm. 1867.
Faḍdlallāh Faḍlallāh, pte. 1863; sgt. 1867.
Faḍl al-Mawlā al-Gharbāwī, pte. ?1863; w.o. 1867.
Faḍl al-Nabī 'Abd al-Mahmūd, pte. 1863; sgt. 1867.
Faḍl Rukūmī, pte. 1863; sgt. 1867.[78]
Farajallāh Ḥamdān, pte. 1863; pte. 1 cl. 1863; sm. 1867.
Faraj Sa'īd, pte. 1863; died in hsp., Veracruz, 5 January 1864.
Faraj Sīd Aḥmad, pte. 1863; sgt. 1867.[79]
Faraj Yūsuf al-Sīd, pte. 1863; cpl. 1863; w.o. 1867.[80]
Faransī Sa'īd, pte. 1862; sgt. 1867.
Ḥamad Naṣr al-Dīn, pte. 1863; pte. 1 cl. 1863. X
Ḥāmid Adām, pte. 1863 cpl. later; w.o. 1867.
Ḥāmid Ḥāwī, pte. 1863; sgt. 1867.
Ḥasīballāh Muḥammad, cpl. 1863; sgt. 1863; died in his quarters 30 October 1864; a sgt. of this name was demoted to pte. and transferred from 1 coy in 1863 or 1864.
Ḥasan Muḥammad, pte. 1863; died in hsp., Veracruz, 5 March 1863.
Ḥasanayn 'Alī, pte. 1863; pte. 1 cl. 1867; sm. 1867.
Ḥusayn 'Alī, pte. 1863; died in hsp. Veracruz, 17 March 1863.
Idrīs'Abdallāh, sgt. 1863; died in hsp., Veracruz, 19 March 1863.
Jaddayn Aḥmad, pte. 1863; pte. 1 cl. 1863; right shoulder dislocated in action at Cocuite, 1865; M.M. 1865; sm. 1867. On return from Mexico posted to the Equatorial province where in 1885 he appears as a 1 lt, 1st bn. commanded by Maj. Rīhān Ibrāhīm in campaign against Mahdist forces under the amīr Karamallāh Kurkusāwī; o.c. military post Rajjāf, 1887.[81]
Jawhar 'Alī, pte. 1863; sgt. 1867.
Jawhar Tal'at, pte. 1863; died at sea on board *La Seine*, 18 January 1863.
Jawhar 'Umar, pte. 1863; sgt. 1867.
Jifūn Dira 'al-Fil/Jufūla dira 'al-Fil. See officers, No. 2 Compny, under 'Ali Jifūn.[82]
Jum'a 'Abd al-Bakhīt, pte. 1863; sgt. 1867.
Jum'a Ibrāhīm, pte. 1863; sgt. 1867.
Jum'a Muḥammad, pte. 1863.

Kāfī al-Nūfī, pte. 1863; wounded at Cocuite, 23 January 1865; sgt., M.M., 1867.[83]

Khamīs Duqal, pte. 1863.[84]

Khamīs Sa'īd, pte. 1863; sgt. 1867.

Khayrallāh Aḥmad, pte. 1863; pte. 1 cl. 1863; killed in action at Callejon de la Laja, 2 March 1875.

Khayrallāh Dā'ūd (1), pte. 1863; posted as a deserter, 29 January 1865. X

Khayrallāh Dā'ūd (2), pte. 1863; sgt. 1867.[85] X

Khayrallāh Sa'īd, pte. 1863; died in hsp., Veracruz, 20 March 1863.

Khayr Ibrāhīm al-Hanāwī/al-Hinnāwī, pte. 1863; sgt. 1866. X

Kūkū 'Abd al-Raḥmān, pte. 1863; sgt. 1867.[86]

Kūkū Bashīr,pte. 1863; killed in action at El Palmar, 24 January 1865.

Kūkū Kūrī, pte. 1863; sgt. 1867.

Kūlī [?Qūlī] Atonni, pte. 1863.[87]

Kūnda 'Umar, pte. 1863; sentenced on 30 September to 5 years hard labor as an accessory to murder at Medellin; returned to unit on evacuation of the bn. from Veracruz, 1867.[88]

Kurshi [?al-Qūrayshī] Sa'īd, pte. 1863. X

Maḥbūb 'Abd al-Bakhīt, pte. 1863. X

Maḥjūb Muḥammad al-Ḥabīb, qmc, thrice admitted to hsp., Veracruz, 1866-7; w.o. 1867.

Maḥmūd Manṣūr, pte. 1863; M.M. (arrêté of 20 April 1867, citation "devoted and fearless"); sgt. 1867.[89]

Malas Armīn, pte. 1863; sgt. 1867.[90]

Marjān Musbāh, pte. 1863; sgt. 1867. l.

Marjān Sūdān, pte. 1863; died in hsp., Veracruz, 26 March 1863.

Marjān Sūdān Bellard [?bi'l-Arḍ], pte. 1863; arrested 9 May 1863, on a charge of murder at Medellin; sentenced to death on 30 September 1863 by a court martial at Veracruz; sentence reduced by Imperial decision of 24 June 1864 to 20 years (later to five years) hard labor; penalty apparently ignored on evacuation from Mexico, 1867, when no further criminal action appears to have been taken against him. X

Marjān Sulaymān, pte. 1863; though committed to prison at San Juan de Ulua, Veracruz, on 6 July 1863, his promotion to pte. 1 cl. with effect from 16 September 1863 was ordered to stand; sm. 1867.

Marjān 'Umar, pte. 1863; sgt. 1867.

Muḥammad al-Ḥājj, pte. 1863; pte. 1 cl. 1863; M.M. 1865; sm. 1867.

Muḥammad Manṣūr, pte. 1863; sgt. 1867.

Muḥammad Ramaḍān, pte. 1863; sgt. 1867.

Muḥammad al-Riqq, pte. 1863; very seriously wounded in action at El Palmar 14 January 1865; M.M. 1865; pte. 1 cl. 1867. X

Muḥammad Sulaymān Ma'tūq, pte. 1863; sgt. 1867.

Mursāl Hamḍān, pte. 1863; sgt. 1867.
Mursāl Ḥammād, pte. 1863; sgt. 1867.
Mursāl Muḥammad; pte. 1863; bugler or drummer from March 1863. X
Mursāl Sūdān, pte. 1863; sgt. 1867.[91]
Mursāl walad Dūh, pte. 1863; sgt. 1867.
al-Nabī 'Abd al-Maḥmūd, pte. 1863. X
Nāfi Ibrāhīm, pte. 1863; sentenced to two months imprisonment at San Juan de Ulua, Veracruz, 1866. X
Nasīm Nafa'ī; drummer 1863; sgt. 1867. X
Nasīm Sulaymān, drummer or bugler; sgt., 1867.[92]
Nāṣir Arbāsh, pte. 1863. X
Nīya Nanda, pte. 1863; pte. 1 cl. 1863; sm. 1867.[93]
Niyālāwī, pte. 1863; sgt. 1867.[94]
Raḥma Aḥmad Adam, pte. 1863; sgt. 1867.
Raḥma 'Alī, pte. 1863; sgt. 1867.
Ramaḍān Dār Fūr, pte. 1863; died in hsp., Veracruz, 6 April 1864.
Rīhān Mikhā'īl/Rīhān Mahouad [?Mu'awad] pte. 1863; on 30 September 1863 a court martial sitting at Veracruz sentenced him to five years hard labor as accessory to murder at Medellin.[95]
Rizqallāh Sūdān, pte. 1863; confined to hsp., Veracruz, 16-27 February 1863; sgt. 1867.
Sa'd Bakhīt pte. 1863; deserted from his unit at El Appa, 27 March 1866. X
Sa'īd Faḍlallāh pte. 1863; bugler 1863-7; sgt. 1867.
Sa'īd Gharbāwī, pte. 1863; died in hsp., Veracruz, 2 May 1863.
Sa'īd 'Īṣā, pte. 1863; 1 cl. 1863; sm. 1867. X
Sa'īd Kurdukatla, pte. 1863; pte. 1 cl. 1863; sm. 1867.[96]
Shams Aḥmad, pte. 1863; pte. 1 cl. 1863; sgt. 1867.
Sīd Aḥmad al-Ḥājj, pte. 1863; pte. 1 cl. 1863; M.M. for gallantry in assault on the fort at Conejo, 1864; sm. 1867.
Sūdān 'Abdallāh, pte. 1863. X
Sulaymān Ibrāhīm Hilāl; pte. 1863; pte. 1 cl. 1863; sm. 1867.
Tīa Leonah.[97]
Tīa Tanda.[98] X
Zā'id Karkar, pte. 1863. X[99]
Zā'id Sūdān, pte. 1863; sgt. 1867.

No. 3 Company

Officers

Faraj Muḥammad al-Zaynī (later maj.-gen. and pāshā), born about 1832 by tribe a Taqalāwī from the Nuba Mts. he is said to have been stolen from his parents by slave raiders and sold in Egypt to a kindly master who had him educated and taught Turkish and French. In 1852, he enlisted and had already served in four campaigns and risen to the rank of sgt. before he left Egypt with the Sudanese bn. for Mexico; commissioned 1 lt. on 11 March 1863 he was present at the assault on Conejo on 9 April 1864; he was decorated with the Legion of Honour (chevalier) by arrêté of 17 May 1865, citation: ". . .distinguished himself on all occasions particularly in the fighting at Cocuite and Las Palmas, 1864"; he continued to command No. 3 coy but retained his rank of lt. until the bn. received double promotion on their return to Egypt in May 1867 when he became adj.-maj. overnight.

His record of service from 1867 until his death in the massacre of Khartoum in 1885 is unreliable. In 1873 he was appointed to command the Kasala military area with rank of colonel having in the previous year commanded the black battalion which occupied Keren in the district of Sinhayt/Senhit, claimed by the Ethiopians, as part of an aggressive strategy of A.E.W. Munzinger Pāshā, general governor of the Egyptian province of the Eastern Sudan. In November 1875, he, with his reinforced battalion, joined the expedition commanded by the Danish officer, Søren Aldolph Arendrup, against the Ethiopians. On the eve of the battle in which Arendrup and half of his force were killed Arendrup charged Faraj Bey with military misdemeanour and sent him back in disgrace to Keren under the impression that Faraj Bey was a maj. rather than a col. senior in service to himself. The proceedings lend suspicion of a conspiracy against him by disgruntled Egyptian Nationalist officers disillusioned with the conduct of the war. In May 1879 he was appointed town governor (*muḥāfiz*) of Berbera. This was his last post in active service. In 1881 he was on the reserve list as second-in-command of a reserve regiment under Col. (afterwards Pāsha) 'Abd al-'Āl ibn Abī Ḥashīsh Bey who would shortly be one of the triumvirate of Nationalist generals headed by Āḥmad 'Urābī Pāshā, whom Europeans were to know as "Arabi Pasha." The depot of this regiment was at al-Ṭura. Apparently after some verbal indiscretion on his part, see Chapter 11 (5), he was court martialed and sentenced to reduction to the rank of maj. and banishment to the Sudan. The Khedive Tawfiq however took no action on the sentence and instead posted Faraj Bey to Muṣawwa' with his original rank of col. unaffected. After the suppression of the Nationalist government and during the governorship-general of 'Abd al-Qādir Pāshā Ḥilmī in the Sudan (c. 1883) Faraj Bey was appointed in command of the 1st Sudanese regt. at Khartoum where he was stationed when C.G. Gordon Pāshā arrived in 1884. For the remainder of his service, see Chapter 11(6).[100]

Muḥammad 'Alī Ḥusayn (later brig.-gen. and pāshā), born at Khartoum of Kanzī stock, he enrolled as a volunteer in 1852 and was a sgt. when the battalion embarked at Alexandria in 1863; commissioned 1 lt. 11 March 1863 by which time he had already served in three campaigns in the Sudan; wounded at the battle of Callejon de la Laja, 2 March 1865, he distinguished himself in several engagement and by arrêté of 17 May 1865 was decorated with the Legion of Honour (chevalier) when he was cited "of noteworthy courage"; at the review of the bn. in Paris on 9 May 1867 he was promoted capt.

On his return to service in the Sudan he rose to the rank of col. and commanded the 1st Sudanese Regt. in Khartoum when in 1884 the Mahdist forces laid siege to the capital. During the siege he led a number of raids with armed river craft to bring back food and livestock to the besieged city; these cunningly conducted river raids were made to Ḥalfāyyat al-Mulūk immediately downstream of Khartoum and up the Blue Nile as far as Abu Ḥarāz; on his last raid he was killed in an ambush at Umm Dubbān (Dhu'bān) near al-'Aylafūn.[101]

Surūr Bahjat (later lt.-col. and bey), transferred from 4 coy; cpl. 1863; qms. 1865; M.M. 1865; 2 lt. 1867. On the return of the bn. to Alexandria he was posted to the Equatorial Province where, in 1874-1876, he commanded the post of Sobat later named Tawfīqiyya. By 1882 he had again been transferred north and as a maj. was commanding the garrison at al-Jīra on the R. Setit when troops from the Eastern Sudan command were ordered by the acting governor-general, C.C. Giegler Pāshā, to concentrate at Abū Ḥarāz on the Blue Nile to defend the Jazīra from Mahdist followers and in particular the Sharīf Aḥmad Ṭaha who was defeated. During the Mahdist siege of Khartoum promoted lt.-col. and given command of 3rd bn. 1st regt. Killed in the Mahdist assault on Khartoum on 26 January 1885.[102]

Surūr Bey Bahjat has been confused with an Adj.-Maj. Surūr Efendi Bahjat who was reported taken prisoner by the Mahdists during their assault on Bara in Kordofan on 5 January 1883 and left no trace.[103]

Marjān Sharīf, cpl. 1863; sgt. 1867; 2 lt. 1867; on his return to Egypt he was attached to Sir Samuel Baker's expeditionary force of 1869-73 to the Equatorial region as an officer in Baker's special detachment with the rank of capt. Baker commended his gallant conduct in an assault on a Bari stockade at Bilinyang on 31 August 1871. After Baker's departure for Egypt he transferred to the permanent Egyptian garrison of the newly-acquired Equatorial province; he and his commander, Ernest Linant de Bellfonds, were both killed in a fight with the Bari in 1875.[104]

'Abd al-Rāḍī Sūdān/al-Sūdānī, sgt. 1863; awarded M.M. and promoted sm. 1865; 1 lt. 1867.[105]

Sulaymān 'Alī al-Khaḍarī, sgt. 1863; 2 lt. 1867.[106]

Other Ranks

'Abdallāh Aḥmad, bugler, 1863.
'Abdallāh Ḥusayn (1), pte. 1863 transferred to No. 2 coy and commissioned, 1867.
'Abdallāh Ḥusayn (2), pte. 1863, deserted 1 November 1865, surrendered to an Egyptian patrol, 5 February 1866 when committed to prison, San Juan de Ulua, Veracruz.[107]
'Abdallāh Idrīs, pte. 1863; sgt. 1867.
'Abdallāh Shabaïk [? Shubayk], pte. 1863; pte. 1 cl. 1863; died of natural causes in his quarters, 8 April 1865.
'Abdallāh Sūdān Ḥamdān, pte. 1863; sgt. 1867.
'Abd al-Khayr Bakhīt, pte. 1863; sgt. 1867.
'Abd al-Khayr Ḥasan, pte. 1863; died in hsp., Veracruz, 14 December 1865.
'Abd al-Mawlā Jum'a, pte. 1863; sgt. 1867.
'Abd al-Nabī abū'l [?-Qāsim], pte. 1863. X[108]
'Abd al-Nabī Abū Rāsikh, pte. 1863; pte. 1 cl. 1863; sm. 1867. X[109]
'Abd al-Nabī Abū Ya's, pte. 1863; pte. 1 cl. 1863; sm. 1867.[110]
'Abd al-Sayyid Yaḥyā, pte. 1863; posted as a deserter, 24 Februry 1865.
'Abd al-Sayyid Zā'id, pte. 1863; died at sea aboard *La Seine*, 24 February 1863.
Abū Bakr Sūdan, pte. 1863; sgt. 1867.
Adam 'Abd al-Sīd, pte. 1863; sgt. 1867.
Adam al-Faqī, pte. 1863; sgt. 1867.
Adam Ḥusayn, pte. (bugler or drummer), 1863; sgt. 1867.
Adam Ḥamdān, pte. 1863; pte. 1 cl. 1863; sm. 1867.
Amīn 'Izzat, pte. 1863; died in hsp., Veracruz, 19 January 1864.
Anānū Abū Suriyya, pte. 1863; sgt. 1867.[111]
Angalū Sūdān, pte. 1863; received a serious wound while removing a barricade at Collejon de la Laja, 2 March 1865 awarded M.M. and promoted pte. 1 cl., both 1865; sm. 1867.[112]
Ankalū Abū Srebeh [= Surayba], pte. 1863. X[113]
Atem Farajallāh, pte. 1863.[114]
Bahr al-Nīl 'Abd al-Raḥmān, pte. 1863; sgt., M.M., 1867.
Bakhīt Baraka, pte (bugler or drummer), 1863; wounded in defense of Medellin, 25-26 July 1866; M.M. (arrêté of 20 April 1867); sgt. 1867.
Bakhīt Ibrāhīm al-Shirbīnī, pte. 1863; pte. 1 cl. 1863; seriously wounded in defence of Medellin, 25-26 July 1866; M.M. (arrêté of 8 November 1866); sm. 1867.[115]
Bakhīt Muḥammad Sulaymān, pte. 1863; pte. 1 cl. 1866; one wound, several times recommended for M.M., finally awarded 1867 (arrêté of 20 April 1867) sm. 1867.
Bakr Mikhā'īl, pte. 1863. X

Baraka 'Abd al-Raḥmān, pte. 1863; admitted to hsp., Veracruz 22 December 1864; died 9 February 1865.
Bashīr Naḥāyīl [?Nyayel], pte. 1863; sgt. 1867.[116]
Bilāl Muḥammad, pte. 1863; transferred from No. 4 coy 1863; w.o. 1867.
Dāldūm 'Alī, pte. 1863; died in hsp., Veracruz 14 March 1863.[117]
Darūr Ibrāhīm Abū Uffa. X[118]
Faḍlallāh 'Alī Faraj; pte. 1863; pte. 1 cl., 1966; sgt. 1867.
Faḍlallāh Muḥammad, pte. 1863; pte. 1 cl. 1863; sm. 1867.
Faḍlallāh Rīyān, pte. 1863; sgt. 1867.
Faḍlallāh Ziyāda, pte. 1863. X
Faḍl Jum'a, pte. 1863; sgt. 1867.[119]
Faḍl al-Sīd Abū Jumā' pte. 1863; sgt. 1867.[120]
Faqīr Sūdān, pte. 1863. X
Faraj Kūrī, pte. 1863; sgt. 1867.[121]
Faraj Muhammad Kanahān [?Kan'ān]; cpl. 1863; killed in the defense of Tlacotalpan, 14 July 1864.
Faraj Sīd Aḥmad 'Amrān, pte. 1863; admitted to hsp., Veracruz, 14 December 1863; died 12 April 1864.
Ḥabīb al-'Abd, pte. 1863; died in hsp., Veracruz, 24 March 1863.
Ḥalīm Farajallāh, pte. 1863.
Ḥamad 'Abd al-Salām, pte. 1863; sgt. 1867.
Ḥamad Adam, pte. 1863; pte. 1 cl. 1863; died in hsp., La Soledad, 21 September 1865.
Heidman [? 'Uthmān] Kaguera [?Kagera] pte. 1863; died in hsp., Veracruz, 24 March 1863.
Ibrāhīm al-Lamīn, pte. 1 cl. 1863; sgt. 1867.[122]
Ibrāhīm al-Maḥjar, pte. 1863; pte. 1 cl. 1863; M.M. 1867; sm. 1867.[123]
'ḍ Rādī al-Sūdān. *See* 'Abd al-Rādī Sūdān, note 105 above.
Idrīs 'Īṣa, pte. 1863; cpl. 1867; w.o. 1867.
Jabr Jābir. See Khabīr Jābir below.
Jād al-Lādū, pte. 1863; died in hsp., Veracruz, 15 August 1866.[124]
Jawhar Sulaymān Wahba, pte. 1863; pte. 1 cl. during the campaign; sm. 1867.
Jibrīl Muḥammad, pte. 1863; sgt. 1867.
Jum'a Faṭūr, pte. 1863; died in hsp., Veracruz, 15 October 1863.
Khabīr Jābir, pte. 1863; pte. 1 cl. 1863; sm. 1867.[125]
Khamīs 'Abd al-Mawlā, pte. 1863; sgt. 1867.
Khayrallāh Sa'īd, pte. 1863; died in hsp., Veracruz, 20 March 1863.
Khayr Ibrāhīm al-Ḥanāwī, pte. 1863; sgt. 1867.
Khayr Muhammad Shakūr/Mashkūr, pte. 1863; pte. 1 cl. 1863; wounded at Tlacotalpan and Las Palmas, awarded M.M. (arrêté of 8 November 1866); sm. 1867.[126]
Kūkū Adam Kabbāsha, pte. 1863 pte. 1 cl. 1863; later cpl; w.o. 1867.[127]

Kūkū Aḥmad pte. 1863; pte. 1 cl. 1863; disappeared 25 April 1865, posted as a deserter 26 April, reported voluntarily 14 May, admitted to hsp., Veracruz, 15 May, absconded from hsp., 26 May; posted as a deserter 27 May, arrested by "la cavalerie indigène" 3 July, readmitted to hsp., Veracruz, 5 July died 13 August 1865.

Kūkū Faydūn [?Qaydūn/?Qaydūm], pte. 1863; pte. 1 cl. 1863; sm. 1867.[128]

Kūkū Tīa, pte. 1863; admitted to hsp., Veracruz, 30 December 1865; died 5 January 1866.

Kūr Torr, pte. 1863; transferred from No. 1 coy 12 March 1863.[129]

Mabrūk Muḥammad, bugler 1863; sgt. 1867.

Mabrūk Sīd Aḥmad al-Sharīf, pte 1863; sgt. 1867.

Marjān Ismā'īl, pte. 1863; sgt. 1867.[130]

Marjān Kūrī, pte. 1863; sgt. 1867.

Muḥammad 'Alī, pte. 1863; sgt. 1867.

Muḥammad Baḥr, pte. 1863; cpl. 1866; w.o. 1867.

Muḥammad Issāra [?Assāra/?Ishāra]; pte. 1863; killed in action 21 July 1866.

Muḥammad Sulaymān, pte. 1863; on 14 May 1865, the same day on which he was promoted cpl., he was committed to prison at San Juan de Ulua; on his release on 1 July 1865 he returned to his unit. X

Mursāl 'Abbās, pte. 1863; pte. 1 cl. 1867; sm. 1867.

Mursāl 'Abdallāh Rāḍī, pte. 1863; pte. 1863; pte. 1 cl. 1863; on 4 September 1866 sentenced to two months' imprisonment at San Juan de Ulua, sentence quashed on appeal; cpl. 1867; w.o. 1867.

Mursāl 'Abd al-Rāsikh, pte. 1863; died in hsp., Veracruz, 3 March 1863.

Mursāl Abū Bakr, pte. 1863; died in hsp., Veracruz, 27 May 1864.

Mursāl Ḥāwī, pte. 1863; sgt. 1867.

Mursāl Khamīs, pte. 1863; pte. 1 cl. 1863; sm. 1867.

Mursāl Muḥammad al-Kūh, pte. 1863; cpl. later; w.o. 1867.[131]

Nasīm Muḥammad Fā'id, pte. 1863; pte. 1 cl. 1863; sm. 1867.

Nāṣir Sūdān, pte. 1863; sgt. 1867.

Nondī Kūmī, pte. 1863.[2] X [132]

Nūnū Biḥayr, pte. 1863; sm. 1867. X[133]

Raḥma Jum'a, pte. 1863; sgt. 1867.

Rīhān 'Abdallāh, pte. 1863; sgt. 1867.

Rīhān Aḥmad Zaytūn, pte. 1863; pte. 1 cl. 1863; M.M. 1867.

Rīhān Ḥasan Rikābī, pte. 1863; sentenced by a court martial at Veracruz on 30 September 1863 to five years' hard labor as an accessory to murder at Medellin.

Sa'īd 'Abdallāh, pte. 1863; sgt. 1867.

Sa'īd 'Abdallāh Ḥashīsh, pte. 1863.

Sa'īd 'Alī, pte. 1863; pte. 1 cl. 1863; M.M. (arrêté of 20 April 1867), citation; "energetic and most worthy"; sm. 1867.

Sa'īd Bakhīt, pte. 1863; sgt. 1867.
Sa'īd Guerildi; pte. 1863; died in hsp., Veracruz, 11 February 1866.[135]
Sa'īd Muḥammad, pte. 1863; 1867.[136]
Sa'īd Ṭib [?Ṭayyib] drummer, 1863; sgt. 1867.[137]
Ṣālih Bakhīt, pte. 1863; died in hsp., Veracruz, 2 March 1866.
al-Shaykh Farajallāh, pte. 1863; sgt. 1867.
Sulaymān Khamadān [?Ḥamḍān/?Ramaḍān] pte. 1863; died at sea on board *La Seine*, 30 January 1863.
Sulaymān Zā'id, pte. 1863; sgt. 1867.
Surūr Ibrāhīm Abū Quffa, pte. 1863; sgt. 1867.[138]
Surūr Rizqallāh Manṣūr, pte. 1863; sgt. 1867.
Tūtū Abū Qīr, pte. 1863; pte. 1 cl. 1867.[139]
Zā'id Muḥammad, pte. 1863; disappeared 25 November 1866, posted as a deserter 27 November 1866.
Zā'id Sa'īd, cpl. 1863; w.o. 1867.
Zūwayra Kūkū, pte. 1863; sgt. 1867.

No. 4 Company

Officers

Ṣāliḥ Ḥijāzī (later col. and bey), a Burnāwī from the region of Lake Chad who had enlisted in 1853 and at the date of embarkation for Mexico had attained the rank of sm.; commissioned 2 lt. on 11 March 1863; by arrêté of 20 April 1864, decorated with the Legion of Honour (chevalier), citation: "a brave officer abounding in military ardor"; on 12 August 1865 led a detachment of 20 men to reinforce the fortified post of Cotaxtla when they were set upon by about 200 Mexicans; they defended themselves with vigor until relieved.

On his return from Mexico he was in May 1867 gazetted adj.-maj. and posted to the Eastern Sudan command where, for a time, he commanded the post at Mitatayb (Mitateb on Sudan Surveys maps [75 km NNW of Kasala]) with rank of maj.; after a short turn of duty in Egypt he returned to Khartoum in A.H. 1290 [A.D. 1873]; in 1874 he took part in the occupation of Dār Fūr in the army of Isma'īl Pāshā Ayyūb and died at Dārā of which he was governor, about A.H. 1293, thus Ṭūsūn 120. Probably, from external evidence, about A.H. 1295= about A.D. 1878. (Plate 17).[140]

'Abdallāh Sālim al-Faqī, sm. 1863; M.M. 1864, citation; "a good leader, never ceases to set a good example" (arrêté of 20 April 1864); 1 lt. 1867; he served in Baker's mission to the Equatorial regions and in 1870 was appointed to command the Sudanese detachment with rank of adj.-maj.; he was later transferred to the Eastern Sudan when, during the opening stage of the Mahdist war, he was commanding garrisons at the frontier posts of al-Jīra and al-Qallābāt with rank of maj. and finished his active service in garrison posts at Muṣawwa' and Sawākin; retiring to Egypt he settled at al-Ma'ādī where he died; portrait in Ṭūsūn. (Plate 17).[141]

'Abd al-Raḥmān Mūsā, by tribe a Dinka, his sobriquet 'al-miṣrī' suggests domicile in Egypt, enlisted in 1852[142] and at the date of embarkation at Alexandria was a sgt.; promoted 2 lt. 11 March 1863 by arrêté of 3 January 1866 he was appointed to the Legion of Honour (chevalier), citation: "he has at all times succeeded in communicating the *élan* and courage of which he himself has given numerous examples, notably in the action at La Barranca de las Palmas on 8 October 1865." He had already trained and commanded a troop of mounted Sudanese, drawn mostly from No. 2 coy, for patrolling the line of communications; on his return to Egypt he as gazetted capt. Portrait Plate 14.[143]

Marjān 'Alī al-Danaṣūrī, Dinka, sgt. 1863; awarded M.M. for bravery in the assault of Conejo, 9 April 1864; and in the defence of Tlacotalpan, 14 July 1864; 2 lt. 1867. On his return to Egypt he was appointed an officer in Baker's picked force which, in January 1872, left Gondokoro, then the southern limit of Egyptian military penetration, to reconnoitre the country of the Acholi and Bunyoro. By the time of the extension of the Mahdist power to the Southern Sudan he had been promoted to adj.-maj. He was governor of Amādī in the Equatorial province west of the Nile in 1883 in command of a force of 1100 men, four guns and a rocket battery when the post was threatened by an advancing Mahdist army under the amīr, Muḥammad Karamallāh Kurqusāwī which, having overrun most of the Egyptian-occupied Bahr al-Ghazāl basin, was now closing in on Emin Pāshā's general governorate. The Mahdist vanguard besieged Amādī where, after several weeks of desperate fighting and some indecision within the Egyptian command during a time of great confusion, Maj. Marjān 'Alī was killed near Amādī and his head taken to the Mahdist commander Karamallāh in March 1885.[144]

Marjān Sulaymān Sharīf, pte. 1863; pte. 1 cl. 1863; sg. 1867; 2 lt. 1867.[145]

Salīm Sīd Aḥmad al-Ashqar, sgt. 1863; 2 lt. 1867.[146]

Mabrūk 'Abdallāh, pte. 1863; pte. 1 cl. 1863; qms. 1867; 2 lt. 1867.

Other ranks

'Abdallāh al-'Abd, pte. 1863; sgt. 1867. After his return from Mexico to the Sudan he served as a sm, in the defence of Kasala against the Mahdists in 1885 and, on the fall of the town, he, with other troops of the Egyptian army, escaped to Musawwa‘, sailed to Egypt and enlisted in the reorganized Egyptian army as a private.[148]

‘Abdallah ‘Abd al-Nabī, pte. 1863; sgt. 1867.[149]

‘Abdallah ‘Alī ‘Aṣr; cpl. 1863; w.o. 1867.[150]

‘Abdallāh Ḥamza, pte. 1863; died at sea on board *La Seine*, 6 February 1863.

‘Abdallāh Safti, pte. 1863. X

‘Abdallāh Sūdān, pte. 1863; died in hsp., Veracruz, 3 April 1864.

‘Abd al-Bā’in ‘Abd al-Bakhīt, pte. 1863. X[151]

‘Abd al-Khayr Baraka, pte. 1863; sgt. 1867.

‘Abd al-Raḥmān Adran [?Adnān] pte. 1863; sgt. 1867.

‘Abd al-Raḥmān Orneh, pte. 1863. X[152]

‘Abd al-Sīd Sulṭān, pte. 1863; died in hsp., Veracruz 6 March 1863.

Adam Aḥmad, pte. 1863; sgt. 1867.

Aḥmad Ibrāhīm, pte. 1863; sgt. 1867.

Aḥmad Khamīs, pte. 1863. X

‘Alī Ḥamad, pte. 1863; sgt. 1867.

‘Alī Ḥamad, pte. 1863; died in hsp., Veracruz, 24 August 1864.

‘Alī Ibrāhīm, pte. 1863; sgt. 1867.

Amān al-Nūr, pte. 1863; one wound, awarded M.M., 1867; cpl. 1867. X

Amīn Manḍūr/Manṣūr Shīsha/Shaysha, pte. 1863; posted as a deserter 14 November 1866. X[153]

Anjalū ‘Alī, pte., pte. 1 cl., 1863; wounded at Tlacotalpan (undated ?1864); M.M. 1867; sm. 1867.[154]

Bakhīt Abū’l-‘Innīn (the Submissive One or, in popular use, the Man with a small Penis) (‘Awn al-Sharīf, 797).

Bakhīt Abū’l-Qumsān (He of the Shirts, i.e. the long civilian outer garment), pte. 1863; sgt. 1867.

Bakhīt Aḥmad al-Miṣrī, pte. 1863; sgt. 1867.

Bakhīt Baḥr, pte. 1863; bugler or drummer, drafted to No. 4 coy, March 1863; sgt. 1867.

Bakhīt Ḥasan, pte. 1863; sgt. 1867.

Bakhīt Ibrāhīm, pte. 1863; sgt. 1867.

Bakhīt Kunjārī, pte. 1863; M.M. 1867; sgt. 1867.

Bakhīt Musallam, cpl. 1863; w.o. 1867.

Bakhīt al-Sāmi‘ Mūsā, pte. 1863; pte. 1 cl. 1863; sm. 1867.[155]

Baraka ‘Abd al-Rāziq, pte. 1863; sgt. 1867.

Bilāl Mūsā, pte. 1863; sgt. 1867.

Dāldūn Yan Aghā, pte. 1863. X[156]

Daysh Akhoumed [?Aḥmad], pte. 1863; posted as a deserter, 22 May 1865. X

Dekis Adam, Pte. 1863; pte. 1 cl. 1867. X

Faḍlallāh Muḥammad, pte. 1863; sgt. 1867; sm. 1867.

Faḍl Sulaymān Faḍlallāh, pte. 1863; sm. 1867.

Faraj 'Alī, bugler; died hsp., Veracruz, 24 February 1863.
Faraj 'Awn al-'Abd, pte. 1863; pte. 1 cl. 1863. X[157]
Faraj El Chaed [?al-Shāhid], pte. 1863; died hsp., Veracruz, 11 March 1863. X
Faraj Ibrāhīm Rabī', pte. 1863; pte. 1 cl. 1863; sm. 1867.
Faraj Muḥammad Abū Shanab, pte. 1863; pte. 1 cl. [?1863]; sm. 1867.
Faraj Ziyāda Ḥasan, pte. 1863; died hsp., Veracruz, 14 August 1863.
Ḥamad Muḥammad, pte. 1863; pte. 1 cl. 1867. X[158]
Ḥammād/Ḥammaḍ Adam, pte. 1863. X
Ḥammad Ḥasan, pte. 1863; sgt. 1867.[159]
Ḥasan Ḥammād, pte. 1863; sgt. 1867.[160]
Hillāl Jum'a, pte. 1863; sgt. 1867.
Ḥusām al-Nūh, cpl. ?1863; w.o. 1867.
Ḥusayn Sūdān, pte. 1863; drummer drafted to 4 coy, March 1863; sgt. 1867.
Ibrāhīm al-Ḍawa, pte. (bugler) 1863; sgt. 1867.
Idrīs 'Adlān, pte. 1863; sgt. 1867.
Idrīs 'Īsā, drummer, 1863. X
Īsāwī 'ḍrīs 'Adlān, pte. 1863. X (? Variant of Idrīs 'Adlān above)
Ismā'īl Adam, pte. 1863; sgt. 1867.[161]
Jamāl Muḥammad, pte. 1863; sgt. 1867.
Jum'a Ibrāhīm Shirbīnī,[2] pte. 1863; admitted to hsp. Veracruz, 21 August 1866; died 25 January 1867. X[162]
Jum'a Khamīs, pte. 1863; sgt. 1867.
Jum'a Muḥammad, pte. 1863; sgt. 1867.
Jum'a Nūr, pte. 1863; sgt. 1867; in hsp., Veracruz, 29 November 1866 - 29 January 1867.
Khamīs Aḥmad/Ḥamad, pte. 1863. X
Khayr Ḥamad, pte. 1863; pte. 1 cl. 1863. X
Khayr Nūr, pte. 1863; two wounds in action at Tlacotalpan, 1864; sgt. 1867.
Khayr Yūsuf al-Sīd, pte. 1863; sgt. 1867.
Kūkū Kūrnuk, pte. 1863; sgt. 1867.[163]
Laghīdā Sa'īd, pte. 1 cl., 1863; sm. 1867.[164]
Mabrūk 'Alī, pte. 1863; pte. 1 cl. 1863; sm. 1867.
Mabrūk Sūdān, pte. 1863; died in hsp., Veracruz, 1 July 1863.[165]
Marjān 'Abdallāh, bugler, drafted to no. 4 coy. March 1863; in hsp., Veracruz, 12 March -30 May 1866; re-admitted 1 July, died 7 July 1866.
Muḥammad 'Abdallāh, pte. 1863; promoted pte. 1 cl. for his part in defending an ambushed train, 2 October 1863; sm. 1867.
Muḥammad 'Īṣā, pte. 1863; sgt. 1867.
Muḥammad al-Ḥājj Khalīl, pte. 1863; later cpl.; w.o. 1867.
Mursāl Ibrāhīm, pte. 1863; sgt. 1867.
Mursāl Khayr [? Waqqād], pte. 1863; sgt. 1867. X[166]
Mursāl 'Uthmān, pte. 1863; sgt. 1867.[167]

Nasīb 'Abdallāh, pte. 1863 killed in action at Tlacotalpan, 5 July 1864.
Raḥma Muḥmmad, pte. 1863; pte. 1 cl. 1863; sm. 1867.
Rajab 'Afīfī, pte. 1863; sgt. 1867.
Ramaḍān Maḥmūd, pte. 1863; died in hsp., Veracruz, 3 October 1863.
Sa'd Ḥarāwī/Sarāwī; pte. 1863; pte. 1 cl. 1867; sm. 1867.[168]
Sādiq Adam, pte. 1863; sgt. 1867.
Sa'īd 'Abd al-Karīm, pte. (bugler or drummer) 1863; sgt. 1867.
Saīd Aḥmad 'Arīrī, pte. 1863; pte. 1 cl. 1863; sm. 1867.
Sa'īd Ḥasan al-Ḥājj, pte. 1863; died in hsp., Veracruz, 8 May 1866.
Sa'īd Khidr Yūsuf, pte. 1863; pte. 1 cl. 1863; sm. 1867.
Sa'īd Mu'awwad Sulaymān, cpl. 1863; w.o. 1867.
Sa'īd Muḥammad, pte. 1863; pte. 1 cl. 1863; sm. 1867.
Sa'īd Muḥammad 'Abd al-Halīm, pte. 1863 pte. 1 cl. 1863; sgt. 1867.
Sīd Aḥmad, pte. 1863; pte. 1 cl. 1863; sm. 1867.
Sīd Aḥmad Azha [?Adha], pte. 1863; died in hsp., Veracruz, 23 March 1963. X
Sīd Aḥmad Ghārib/Gharīb, pte. 1863; pte. 1 cl. 1863; killed in action at Tlacotalpan, 14 July 1864.[169] X
Sīd Aḥmad Ḥamza, pte. 1863; cpl. 1867; w.o. 1867.
Sīd Aḥmad al-Khūtī, pte. 1863; died in hsp., Veracruz, 14 March 1863.
Sayyid Muḥammad Sulaymān, pte. 1863; later cpl.; w.o. 1867.
Surūr Ḥasanayn/Ḥunayn, pte. 1863; sgt. 1867.[170]
al-Tāhir Muḥmammad, pte. 1863; sgt. 1867.
Tawakkul Muḥammad, pte. 1863; sgt. 1867.
'Umar Muḥammad, pte. 1863; promoted pte. 1 cl. for his part in defending an ambushed train on 2 October 1863; sm. 1867.
'Uthman Adam, pte. 1863; sgt. 1867.
Waldūn Bin'aja, pte. 1863; sgt. 1867.
Wanīs Adam, pte. 1863; pte. 1 cl. 1863; sm. 1867.[171]
Zakariyya al-Nūr, pte. 1863; pte. 1 cl. 1863; sm. 1867.

Notes

1. Archivio di Stato, Alessandria Piemonte (processo contro Michele Amatore ed altri. Tribunale di Novi Ligure, No. 113, 1848-9).
2. *Taqwīm* 705-706; Ṭūsūn, 71, 77, 85, 111.
3. *Le Moniteur Officiel*, 9 Mch 1867.
4. W.O. Mangin and W.O. Charpplain had both joined *La Seine* at Toulon before the outward voyage from Alexandria and during the voyage took the first steps to organize the bn. after the French system.
5. Tegalhusi on Sudan Surveys maps.

6. *Taqwīm* 706; Ṭūsūn 6, 44 53, 71, 78, 85-86, 112-117. As 'Alī Dinar's presence on the battlefield at Kararī on 2 September 1898 is disputed, it is not possible on present evidence to confirm that Faraj 'Azāzī was beyond doubt a combatant in the battle.
7. Thus cn.; Ṭūsūn 81 has 1853; both Gregorian dates would probably be approximate.
8. *Taqwīm*, 705; Ṭūsūn 53, 71, 78, 81.
9. *Taqwīm*, 706 has Ḥusayn Muḥammad; cn. and Ṭūsūn have Ḥusayn Aḥmad passim.
10. *Taqwīm*, 707; Ṭūsūn 50, 95, 103-11, 121-22; Ṭūsūn records two variant versions of his death: the first that he was killed in battle with the Shilluk, the second that he died a natural death in Kordofan during the Mahdist regime.
11. *Taqwīm*, 706; Ṭūsūn 45, 71, 81-82, 86-88; *Ta'rīkh* I; Baker under "Major Abdullah," *passim.*
12. *Taqwīm*, 706; Ṭūsūn 46, 73, 94; cn. and *Historique* have Oenni. Wani is a Bari name.
13. *Taqwīm*, 706; Ṭūsūn 13, 45, 94.
14. *Taqwīm*, 660; cn. Ṭūsūn 49 adds al Miṣri indicating domicile in Egypt.
15. *Taqwīm*, 706; Ṭūsūn 45.
16. *Taqwīm*, 707; Ṭūsūn 72 (ex. No. 4 coy).
17. *Taqwīm*, 706; Ṭūsūn 45.
18. Mas'ūd the Peacock. *Taqwīm*, 706; Ṭūsūn 45.
19. S.H.A.T., G7, 204 (bis), Registre d'écrou 220, under 'Abdallāh Sin [*sic*].
20. Dāyīm, name found in Kordofan.
21. Thus cn. =?Abyssinien, of doubtful ethnic significance.
22. Thus *Taqwīm* 660; Ṭūsūn 58 and cn. Not Abu Nazzāra.
23. Possibly the "Abd el Seed" of the mounted detachment (*'Alī Jifūn*, 329; *Historique*, 243.
24. It is remotely possible that he was later Maj. Aḥmad 'Alī, of the 1st bn. of the Egyptian force resisting the Mahdist advance into the Equatorial Province in 1885, and with Emin Pāshā on the eve of the Egyptian evacuation in 1888-1889. *Ta'rīkh* II, 279; III, 21, 313, 331-37.
25. Ḥabashi = Abyssinian = Ethiopian, giving no indication of ethnic origin.
26. *Taqwīm* 660; Ṭūsūn 56; cn. Anjalu, borne by six men in the bn. The version Ankallu in cn. suggests Angallo, a common name in the Nuba Mts. Unlikely on chronological grounds to be an adopted Christian name, Angelo, popularized by Catholic missionaries on the Upper Nile, e.g., Angelo Vinco, who lived among the Bari, 1852-3.
27. *Taqwīm* 706 Badr; cn. Badran; Ṭūsūn 74 Badr, 131, 136. Badram, doubtfully said to be a Nuba name.
28. Registre d'écrou du Fort Saint-Jean d'Ulloa (S.H.A.T., G7, 204 bis, No. 236). Barac is a Dinka name.
29. *Taqwīm* 660 has al-Nās; Ṭūsūn 57 al-Naqī; cn. el-Fehī.
30. Thus cn. battalion state, 1866 (S.H.A.T., G7, box 224); his existence appears to depend on a mistake of identity in the hsp. records.

31. cn. Chila; Ṭūsūn, 55; Shīha following *Taqwīm,* 660.
32. 'Alī Jifūn 329, undated. He was accompanied by a second ex-prisoner of war, Rizq Aḥmad, identity uncertain, possibly (Rast [?Rizq] Aḥmad below (Ṭūsūn 77). For Sandalūba see Note 37 below.
33. Cn. Ittoum - ? Arab. al-Tūm, or Shilluk Othwon.
34. A Koḍī Aghā (Capt. Koḍī Aḥmad) served under Emin Pāsha in the Equatorial province. *Ta'rīkh* II, 279; III, 3, 10, 50, 62-64, 95, 114-116, 118, 282. Koḍī is common among the Nuba and the Jur Belli sw. of Rumbek, and possibly the Moru who share a number of names with some Nuba tribes. Its use among Nilotics must be exceptional.
35. Kūkū (a first-born son), a widely used name among the Nuba.
36. *Taqwīm* 660, Sindāla, the other versions cn. Possibly an elision of Arab. *Sandal* (sandalwood) + Arab. *lubb* (essence) incorrectly spelt in the rolls.
37. Kabbāshī is said to be a popular Nuba name unconnected with the nomad Arab tribe, al-Kabābīsh.
38. *Taqwīm,* 706; Kurmuk; Ṭūsūn, 45; cn. Kurmukra.
39. *Taqwīm,* 660; Ṭūsūn, 56.
40. *Taqwīm,* 660; Ṭūsūn, 57.
41. Thus cn. *Historique,* 243; 'Alī Jifūn 329. Simbil, name common in Nuba Mts. 'Awn al-Sharīf, 66, used in Dār Hamar, Western Kordofan, for long-haired.
42. cn. Ragheb; *Taqwīm,* 706; Rajab.
43. Thus cn.
44. Thus *Taqwīm,* 661 and Ṭūsūn, 56; cn. Nondi Komi. Kuma/Komi used among the Nuba and among Shilluk, Dinka (as Akoma), Nuer and Anuak, as short for Arab. ḥukūma = government.
45. Probably Nuba.
46. See note 37 above.
47. Registre d'écrou, No. 287, 1 January 1865 (S.H.A.T., G7, box 204 bis).
48. Registre d'écrou, ibid., possibly an alternative name.
49. A Surūr Ḥasan, not necessarily the same man, served three months imprisonment at San Juan de Ulua; discharged 3 march 1866. Ṭūsūn, 58.
50. cn. Possible mis-hearing of Tibinī (Arab., straw-coloured) a common name in Western Sudan. The addition of "Adam" to the name strengthens the probability of a western origin.
51. *Taqwīm,* 660; Ṭūsūn, 56. cn. adds Camaroui, an inhabitant of the Bahr al-Qamr, the Upper White Nile, and elsewhere supplies an alternative version, Damasoui (?Damasūrī, after Damasūra, a village in the Nile Delta, an indication of domicile).
52. Kūnda, a name common among the Nuba.
53. Qazqaz, a Sudanese nickname meaning "very special" or, more likely here, "a glass! a glass!" suggesting a thirst for liquor. *Taqwīm,* 660; Ṭūsūn, 58; can.
54. For its composition, see *The Sudan Memoirs of...Giegler Pāsha, 1873-1883,* ed. R. Hill, (1984), 205-6.

55. *Taqwīm,* 706; Ṭūsūn 6, 46, 53, 71, 78, 82, 100-3; BD. 274 Muḥammad Bey Sulaymān, line 8: for Dār Fūr read Jabal Qadīr, Nuba Moutains.
56. *Taqwīm,* 706; Ṭūsūn, 41, 71, 82, 97; Nuṣḥī, 30, 35, 69, 76, 79; *Ta'rīkh* I, *passim*; III, 102.
57. *Taqwīm*, 706; Ṭūsūn, 48, 93.
58. S.H.A.T., G7, 125, Registre, 2249.
59. *Taqwīm*, 706; Ṭūsūn, 6, 33, 46, 53, 71, 80.
60. *Taqwīm,* 660; Ṭūsūn, 18, 91, 94.
61. A British war correspondent, W. B. Burleigh, in his *Khartoum campaign*, 1899, 309-11, was the first to publicize 'Ali Jifun's presence in Kitchener's expedition at Fashoda, 1898.
62. *Taqwīm*, 706 spells his name al-Fawd (al-Faw, p.705, is a misprint); Ṭūsūn, 6, 46, 71, 80 follows *Taqwīm*; the official version may have resulted from a misreading of al-Ḍaw as al-Fawd; cn., weak in Arabic spelling, heard him say "Eddaou" (1863) and possibly altered it by misunderstanding to "Eddaoud" (1867).
63. *Taqwīm*, 706; Ṭūsūn 47, 90; Baker, under "Lieutenant Ferritch," i, 298, 349; ii, 5, 461, 487.
64. *Taqwīm*, 662, but on 706 mistakenly has 'Abdallah Ḥasan; Ṭūsūn 13, 14, 47, and cn. have 'Abdallah Ḥusayn; "Basha" probably self-conferred or the title of a former master retained out of piety, or a son of the pasha by a concubine.
65. *Taqwīm*, 706; Ṭūsūn, 47.
66. *Taqwīm*, 706; Ṭūsūn 47, 72; cn. has Faraj Badawī Ḥusayn.
67. The Baka, from the Nile-Zaire watershed, though integrated with the Zande group, are ethnically Sudanic, akin to the Moru.
68. Possibly the company clerk's misspelling of al-Kabārī, a quarter of Alexandria, 'Abdallāh's supposed domicile.
69. Though the announcement of his award was made in the arrêté of 20 April, which contained the names of Sudanese for their gallantry in defending an ambushed train on 2 October 1863, his own award seems to have been in respect of some other action. His name is not mentioned in the dispatches concerning the ambush (S.H.A.T., G7, box 124 or in Ṭūsūn, 130-32). *Historique,* 104, 283, has Abd al-Kal, a misprint.
70. *Taqwīm,* 661 has 'Abd al-Nabāt; cn. has Abd al-Banat which, by the transposition of two Arabic letters, produced a more enticing name, Slave (dévoué) of the Girls.
71. An "officer," elsewhere a "sergeant" named 'Abd al-Rijāl serving in the Equatorial province in 1885 occurs in W. Junker, (*Ta'rīkh,* II, 314, 456; III, 7).
72. Ṭūsūn, 47 has Abū Anīn; *Taqwīm,* 706 has Abū Ghabra, cn. has Abohanze (?Abu 'Anja/Abu Hanisa).
73. Ṭūsūn, 62 has Subhī, cn. Sebki (? for Subqī).
74. *Taqwīm,* 661; Ṭūsūn, 60; cn., in the form Angallo Kūkū a typical combination in a Nuba name, especially in the Eastern Jabals.

75. The name suggests Dār Berta, the home of several peoples including the Burun, on the left side of the Blue Nile, on the present Sudan-Ethiopian border.
76. Baku said to be a Nuba name.
77. Probably the "Barak Aḥmad" recorded in 'Alī Jifūn, 329, as having been attacked at night by a Mexican with a knife while on sentry duty at Veracruz. 'Alī Jifūn added that, like himself, Baraka Aḥmad subsequently enlisted in the new Egyptian army created in 1883 and joined the 10th Sudanese bn. from which he was pensioned c. 1896.
78. Rukūmī in *Taqwīm* 661 and Ṭūsūn 7; Dekomi/Rekomi in cn.
79. Lt. Faraj Sīd Aḥmad served in the Equatorial province, 1885. *Ta'rīkh*, III, 282, 294, 297.
80. Ṭūsūn 47, 74. A Capt. Faraj Aghā Yūsuf was o.c. Labore post, Equatorial province, c. 1879. *Ta'rīkh*, II *passim.*
81. Jaddayn, or possibly Gaden, a Nuba name. *Taqwīm,* 661; Ṭūsūn, 59, both Jaddayn; cn. Gaden; *Ta'rikh* II, 278. See Jaddayn under Officers, No. 2 Company.
82. See 'Alī Jifūn, note 62.
83. Kāfī, a common Nuba name.
84. cn. Dogal.
85. cn. for both (1) and (2).
86. Every Kūkū here could be a Nuba name.
87. Aton, said, but doubtfully, to be a Nuba name.
88. Kūnda, a common Nuba name.
89. cn. versions unclear.
90. Malath, a Dinka name.
91. 1 lt. Mursāl Sūdānī appears among troops and their families evacuated from Equatoria via Mombassa, 1892, but the time-lag makes identification uncertain (SAD 253/8/46).
92. On 25 June 867 he landed at Alexandria from France after a period in hsp. in Paris (Ṭūsūn 76).
93. *Taqwīm,* 661 has Nīya Nafda; Ṭūsūn, 59, Nīya Nanda. A reader suggests Nīya may be a common Dinka name. Nhial = Heaven. ? or variant/mishearing of Nuba Tia Tanda below?
94. *Taqwīm* 661. Probably from Nyāla, Dār Fūr.
95. Both variants of his name from cn.
96. *Taqwīm,* 661; Five *jabals* in the western Nuba hills are named Katla.
97. cn., Tia a common Nuba name, a third-born son.
98. ?a variant of Nīya Nanda (note 94), a Nuba name.
99. cn. Karkar, a Nuba name, Also Arab., to laugh loudly, guffaw.
100. *Taqwīm,* 707; Ṭūsūn, 6, 13, 18, 48, 53, 71, 79, 86, 91-92, 96-97, 137; *Ta'rīkh* III, 102; Nuṣḥī, 24 passim; Gordon, *Journals*, British Library (Oriental Mss. 34, 474-34, 479), Douin, III, pt. 2, 560.
101. *Taqwīm,* 705, 707; Ṭūsūn, 6, 48, 53, 71, 81, 87-88, 126-29; Nuṣḥī, 6, 28-34; BD. 250.

102. *Taqwīm,* 707; Ṭūsūn, 49, 72, 83, 88. It seems that he was promoted lt.-col. by General Gordon during the siege and that his elevation to the grade of bey was subject to confirmation, like his promotion, by the Egyptian war office. For his service in the Equatorial province see *Ta'rīkh* I, 321, 323; Nuṣḥī 76, 78, 81.
103. Ṭūsūn, 88-89.
104. *Taqwīm,* 707; Ṭūsūn, 45, 49, 64, 72, 84, 90; Baker I, 327; II, 5; *Ta'rīkh* I, 50, 321.
105. *Taqwīm,* 707, has 'Abd Rādī; Ṭūsūn, 48, has 'Id Rāḍī, both apparent misprints. Ṭūsūn, 71, has 'Abd al-Rahmān Rādī al-Sūdānī; and 83, 'Abd al-Rādī al-Sūdānī.; cn. has Abderradi Soudan.
106. *Taqwīm,* 707; Ṭūsūn, 49, 72.
107. *Taqwīm,* 662. Pte. 'Abdallāh Ḥusayn is recorded as sentenced for intention to desert; entered prison 8 January 1866; discharged 12 May 1866 (S.H.A.T., G7, 204 (bis), Registre d'écrou, 251).
108. cn. Abu Kassem.
109. cn. Rasseiz (?Rasikh).
110. Possibly a duplication of preceding. *Taqwīm,* 662; Ṭūsūn, 63. Abū Ya's = Father of Hopelessness.
111. Abū Surriyya = Father of a Slave Girl, a concubine.
112. *Taqwīm,* 662; Ṭūsūn, 63. Probably Nuba.
113. cn. Abū Surayba, Father of a Little Lizard, probably Nuba.
114. Atem, Dinka name.
115. *Taqwīm,* 662; Ṭūsūn, 63; his name indicates a connection with Shirbīn, a small town in the Nile delta.
116. Taqwīm, 662; Ṭūsūn, 66; Nahā il, a Dinka and Shillūk name.
117. Thus cn., Dāldūm, a Nuba name.
118. 'Iffa = continence, effacement; uffa = dirt of the ears, etc.
119. *Taqwīm,* 662. Probably same as following.
120. Ṭūsūn, 117. Deserted to join the Mahdist cause at a date unknown; escaped with Faraj 'Azāzī Bey to Dār Fūr after battle of Kararī, 1898; subsequent fate unknown.
121. *Taqwīm,* 662; Ṭūsūn, 64; Kūrī, a Nuba name.
122. Thus *Taqwīm,* 661; Ṭūsūn, 64; cn. Lamin. (Arab. dialect, Kordofan = al-Amīn).
123. *Taqwīm,* 661 has al-Mahjar; Ṭūsūn, 63 al-Ḥajar, cn. Maghar (? al-Mahjar).
124. Of probably Bari descent (Jada Lado).
125. *Taqwīm,* 661; Ṭūsūn, 63, has Khabīr Jābir; cn. Ghabir Gaber.
126. *Taqwīm,* 662, has Shakūr, cn. and *Historique* have Mashkur.
127. *Taqwīm,* 707; Kabbāsha, cn. Kabbashi. A Nuba name, cf. Kūkū Sūdān al-Kabbāshī, 2 coy. All Kūkūs in cn. are probably Nuba.
128. *Taqwīm,* 661, has Faydūn, cn. Kaidu/Kaidun.
129. cn. Kūr Torr/Thor; Kir and Torr/Otor said to be common to Dinka, Nuer and Shilluk. Kir = any running water, notably the Nile.

130. A Nuba name.
131. If Kua, a Nuba name (sixth-born son).
132. Kūmī could be a Nuba name.
133. *Taqwīm,* 662; not in Ṭūsūn. Nūnū, onomatopoeic word for baby used widely in the Sudan; 'Awn al-Sharīf, 1164.
134. cn., possibly nickname for preceding name. The components Sa'īd 'Abdallāh are too common to identify him confidently with 1 lt. Sā'id 'Abdallāh, a member of the party of military evacuees from the Equatorial province via Mombasa, 1892 (F. R. Wingate, Rept., on the arrival in Cairo of 21 officers etc. Appendix 2, SAD 253/8/26).
135. cn. Could a former Turkish-speaking master or officer have nicknamed him from the past tense of gerilmek, "he resisted"?
136. Committed to prison at San Juan de Ulua, preventive detention, 10 February 1867; released 12 March on day of departure for Egypt. Registre d'écrou 287 (S.H.A.T., G7, 204 (bis).
137. Tibo is also a Shilluk name.
138. cn. has Abou Offa. See note 119 above.
139. His Muslim name unidentified. Tūtū (fourth-born son) a common Nuba name; Tut (= bull) common among the Nuer.
140. *Taqwīm,* 705, 707; Ṭūsūn, 6, 32-33, 50, 53, 71, 79-80, 91-92, 95, 113, 117-20; Kirk 124-25; BD 328, confusing two officers of the same name, wrongly attributed his Dār Fūr service to another Sālih Bey Hijāzi (d. c. 1897).
141. *Taqwīm,* 707; Ṭūsūn, 50, 83, 90-91, 94-95; *Historique,* 282.
142. Ṭūsūn, 80, has 1850.
143. *Taqwīm,* 705, 707; Ṭūsūn, 6, 35, 50, 53, 71, 80-81. Though 'Alī Jifūn, 187, calls him simply "Egyptian" the face in the portrait suggests mixed Sudanese of possibly Turco-Egyptian (*muwallad*) origin.
144. Ṭūsūn (*Ta'rīkh* I, 378n.) derives his name from his place of residence, Danasūr, a village in the district of Shibīn al-Qūm, in the Nile delta.
145. *Taqwīm*, 707; Ṭūsūn, 50.
146. *Taqwīm,* 707 (misprint); cn. Kashkar; Ṭūsūn, 50, 73, Ashqar, the least improbable variant, a color between red and yellow, his complexion.
147. Ṭūsūn, 72.
148. cn.; 'Alī Jifūn, 490; *Taqwīm,* 663; Ṭūsūn, 68.
149. *Taqwīm,* 606; Ṭūsūn, 60; possibly same as prec.
150. *Taqwīm,* 707; cn. Hasser.
151. cn. Bein.
152. Thus cn. Two suggestions; (1) a Turkish nickname Ornek, sample, pattern (2) a Hausa place name, Wurnu, in the Sudan Maiurno.
153. cn. has Cheicha.
154. *Taqwīm*, 663; Ṭūsūn, 67. Angallo 'Alī, a characteristic Nuba combination.
155. *Taqwīm,* 662; Tūsūn, 68.
156. cn. Dāldūn/Dāldūm, a Nuba name.? Yan is unidentified.
157. cn. Ouan, name in 1867 roll only.

158. A lt.-col. Ḥamid Bey Muḥammad commanded the 1st bn. of the Egyptian army based on Rajjāf in succession to Maj. Rīhān Ibrāhīm, c. 1885 (*Ta'rīkh* II, 278, 373, 374; III, *passim*).
159. *Taqwīm,* 663; Ṭūsūn, 68; cn.
160. cn.; Ṭūsūn, 69.
161. A Capt. Ismā'īl Adam served in 1st bn. Equatorial force, 1885. (*Ta'rīkh* II, 278).
162. Shirbin, a village in the Nile delta, Lower Egypt.
163. Sounds a typically Nuba name.
164. Thus *Taqwīm,* 663, Ṭūsūn, 68, has promotion to sgt.; cn. confirms Ṭūsūn. Origin of name Laghida unknown; suggested misprint for Arab. Lajlaja = to stutter.
165. His death from yellow fever at age 14 prompted Fuzier at the military hospital, Veracruz, to assure his readers that the patient was not Sudanese but "a native of Abyssinia," no guide to his ethnic origin.
166. cn. Ouagued.
167. cn. Eitman, colloquial rendering of 'Uthman.
168. *Taqwīm,* 612; Ṭūsūn, 67.
169. cn. Ghouarb.
170. *Taqwīm,* 663, has Surūr Hunayn; Ṭūsūn, 70, and cn. have Ḥasanayn. A Pte. Surūr Ḥusayn is recorded as having been sentenced for intention to desert and imprisoned 19 May 1865; in hsp., 23-27 May; discharged from prison 17 June 1865 (S.H.A.T., G7, 204 [bis], Registre d'écrou, 221).
171. *Taqwīm,* 773; Ṭūsūn, 69; cn. has Waldūn, a possible misprint for Dāldūn, probably not Wal Dut. Bin 'Ajja [?Benaiah] name found among descendants of Sudanese soldiers in Uganda.

Other Sources Used

The Historical Background to Slavery

Introduction

We offer a modest word of bibliographical advice to readers who seek a balanced understanding of events in the history of Islam such as this: to avoid the illusion that politics and religion can be usefully studied in isolation. In Islam they form a unity.

No discussion of slavery in Islam would be intelligible without some basic knowledge of the Koran (*al-Qur'ān*), the guide and stay of the Muslim way of life, and the early collected traditions of the Prophet Muhammad. For the English-speaking non-Muslim reader without Arabic, there is a moving rendering of the Koran by A. J. Arberry, *The Koran Interpreted*, (Oxford University Press) 1955- and a *Handbook of Early Mohammadan Tradition* by A. J. Wensinck, Leiden (Brill) 1927.

African Slavery

A comprehensive study of African slaves and their marketing in the nineteenth and twentieth centuries is a symposium entitled *Slaves and Slavery in Muslim Africa*, ed. J. R. Willis, 2 vol., London, 1985, and an earlier symposium, *The Ideology of Slavery in Africa*, ed. P. E. Lovejoy, Beverly Hills, Calif., 1980.

Slavery: Abolition in the United States

The ethos of the Abolition movement, which was finally decided by civil war, is concentrated in two books, both by Harriet Elizabeth Beecher Stowe:

1. *Uncle Tom's Cabin*, etc., a social novel, published serially, 1851; in book form, Boston, Mass., 1852 (many reprints and translations), a major example of the deep social appeal of the Romantic approach with its special emphasis on pity.
2. *A Key to Uncle Tom's Cabin, Presenting the Original Facts and Documents*, etc., Boston, Mass., 1853; turgid, a publishing failure. Its value to the resolute reader lies in its dogmatic exposition of the case for Abolition.

   The "missionary" influence of *Uncle Tom's Cabin* in Great Britain is well known. Less well known was its reception in Europe and its influence on European attitudes toward the United States. Barbara Karsky has recorded the book's appeal to the educated middle classes in France during the Second Empire. See under, Napoleon III below.

Military Slavery in Islam

The theme of our present work has the briefest bibliography of all. It was only the realization that the world had been mis-classifying military slavery, and with it the Egyptian Sudanese Battalion, that history could be rewritten. Among the first historians in this readjustment is Daniel Pipes, *Slave Soldiers in Islam: the Genesis of Military System*, (New Haven, Conn.:Yale University Press, 1981).

The French Intervention: Napoleon III

The French were among the first Europeans to develop a scholarly curiosity in the ancient civilizations of the Nile Valley. These intellectual influences are considered by H. Laurens in *Les origines intellectuelles de l'expédition d'Égypte: l'ouverture de l'orientalisme islamisant en France 1698-1798*. varia turcica V (Assoc. pour le développement des études turques), Paris 1987.

A concise description of the formation under French officers of the *nizam-i cedid* (Turk.), *nizām al-jadīd* (Arab.) is D. Farhi's "Nizam-i cedid, military reform in Egypt under Mehmed 'Ali', Jerusalem, *Asian and African Studies*

III, 2, 1972, 151-83. A continuing French interest in Egyptian nineteenth-century history is demonstrated in three general works on the theme of Muhammad 'Ali's new model army: Gen. M. Weygand, *Histoire militaire de Mohamed Aly et de ses Fils*, 2 vol., Paris, (Imprimerie Nationale) 1936; G. Guémard, *Une oeuvre française, les réformes en Égypte*, Le Caire (Paul Barbey) 1936, and G. Douin's unfinished *Histoire du Soudon Égyptien* (Le Caire: Société de Géographie, 1944) based, as were Weygand's and Guémard's works, on translations from Turkish and Arabic originals. For the contrast with the difficulties attending the imposition of the reforms by the Ottoman sultans to the central structures of the state, see B. Lewis, *The Emergence of Modern Turkey*, (London: Oxford University Press, 1961).

Napoleon III

A critical study of Napoleon's ideas and plans for French intervention in Mexico is Christian Schefer, *La Grande pensée de Napoléon III: les origines de la campagne du Mexique (1858-1862)*. Paris 1939.

The Second Empire, 1852-1870 was a dramatic period of French history which has attracted a voluminous literature most of which lies beyond the reader's basic requirement: to gauge the personality of the man whose dreams and policies for the Americas resulted in the creation of the Egyptian Sudanese battalion, whose name appears at intervals in the annals of their campaign in his service in Mexico and who, when their service to him ended, was their host for nine days in Paris. What kind of man was he?

The *Revue d'histoire moderne et contemporaine*, Paris, xxi (Jan.-Mar.) 1974, suggests a brief, lively appraisal of the historiography of the Second Empire. Those branches of particular background interest with bearing on the French intervention in Mexico are:

Fohlen, Claude, "Les Historiens devant la politique americaine du Second Empire," 127-34.

Meyer, Jean, "L'Expédition du Mexique après les documents et études mexicaines," 135-41.

Charles-Vallin, Thérèse, "Le Duc de Morny dans l'historiographie du Second Empire," 75-85.

Karsky, Barbara, "Les Libéraux français et l'émancipation des esclaves aux États-Unis," 575-90.

Bury, Patrick, "Quatre générations d'historiens anglo-saxons devant le Second Empire," 86-93.

Brunn, D., "Les Historiens anglais et américains et le Second Empire," 92-104.

Martinière, Guy, "L'Expédition mexicaine de Napoléon III dans l'historiographie française," 142-73.

Finally the reader, in search of Napoleon himself, the husband, the father, the family man, *Napoléon intime*, written in superb English by a bi-lingual scholar without flattery or denigration, will read H. W. C. Smith, *Napoleon III: The Pursuit of Prestige* (London: Collins and Brown, 1991).

The Sudanese Battalion in the Mexican Campaign

Maps, Military Engineering

For field operations: (1) Carta de Mexico topografica 1:250000, 1st ed. 1984, Mexican Government (I.N.E.G.I.), sheets E 14 3 Veracruz; E 14 6 Orizaba; E 15 1-4 Coatzacoalcos. (2) Carta de Mexico topografica 1:50000, 1st ed. 1987 Mexican Government (I.N.E.G.I.), sheets E 15 A 51 Alvarado; E 15 A 61 and E 15A 71 for detail of the Rio Papaloápan. For Sudanese participation in combined military-naval operations see Plate 8, Tierra Caliente.

For troop movements: sheets prepared by the French Service topographique 1:500000, difficult to interpret owing to subsequent landscape and demographic changes, but still usable guides.

Maps and plans for the defense of Veracruz in 1866 and maps of the railway from Veracruz to Paso del Macho and Medellin are preserved in boxes numbered S.H.A.T., Génie, 1-4. No Mexican or foreign historian to our knowledge has yet published a technically accurate description of the Mexican railway between Veracruz and the interior during the years 1863-67 when track and trains were guarded chiefly by the Sudanese. The superbly illustrated *Railroads in Mexico*, vol. I, by E. Garma Franco (Denver, Co., 1985) is factually insufficient for this early period. For the Sotavento de Veracruz see Plate 8.

Medical

The importance which the French military medical service attached to the health of the Sudanese is reflected in the archives of the Service de Santé des Armées (S.S.A.), Musée du Val de Grâce, Paris, Expédition du Mexique 1862-1867, boxes 53, 54, and 60. The acute problems of epidemiology presented by Sudanese patients and the difficulty of communicating with them are sympathetically described in the published report of J. B. F. F. Fuzier, médecin-major commanding the military hospital of San Juan de Ulua, Veracruz, "Extrait d'un rapport sur le service médical de la Vera-cruz pendant le mois de février 1863" (*Recueil de mém. . . milit., 1863* 3 sér., IX, 265-275. The same medical officer's studies on yellow fever during the campaign, *Résumé d'Études sur la fièvre jaune observée à la Vera-Cruz pendant les épidémies de 1862 à 1867*, were bound in one volume with J. C. Chenu, *Aperçu sur les expéditions. . . du Mexique. . . bataillon égyptien, 207-211*. The apparent contradiction between the total resistance to yellow fever of the Sudanese in Mexico and an epidemic of yellow fever in their African homelands is reported in T. F. Hewer, "Yellow fever in the Anglo-Egyptian Sudan," London (*The Lancet*, CCXXVIII) 1934, 497, and W. T. de Vogel, "Un bataillon soudanais en garnison dans un foyer de fièvre jaune," *Bull. de l'office d'hygiène publique*. Paris (World Health Organization XXVIII, 7), 1935.

Campaign Records

French

Location

The following Parisian archives, libraries and museums hold almost all the documentary evidence of the Sudanese Battalion in the Mexican campaign: the archives of the Ministry of Foreign Affairs, Quai d'Orsay; the Archives Nationales (C.A.R.A.N.) the Historical Services of the Armée de Terre (S.H.A.T.) and of the Marine (S.H.M.P.) both at the Château de Vincennes, the Service Historique de la Marine, Toulon (S.H.M.T.), the Service de Santé des Armées at the Val de Grâce Military Hospital. The Service archives have their attendant libraries of printed material. For military and naval illustration: the Musée de l'Armée (Hôtel des Invalides) and the Musée de la Marine (Palais Chaillot, Trocadero).

Bibliography

Guide bibliographique sommaire d'histoire militaire et coloniale française, S.H.A.T. (Paris: Imprimerie Nationale, 1969), 191-92.

Archives

E. de la Torre Villar, Las Fuentes Francesas para la Historia de la Guerra de Intervención. Publicaciones especiales del Primer Congreso Nacional de Historia para el Estudio de la Guerra de Intervención, No. 10 Mexico, D.F. (Soc. Mex. de Geogr. y Estadistica), 1962.

The boxes containing the principal military archive of the campaign area collected under catalogue reference G7 (Expédition du Mexique, 1862-1867) in S.H.A.T.

The records of the voyages out and home are deposited in the following collections:

Outward, Jan.-Feb. 1863

1. Archives Nationales (C.A.R.A.N.), Marine BB4, 806, fos 30-32 and 50-51; 819, fos. 28-29, 54, 91-92; 882, fos. 515-522; 5JJ, 255, dossier 2, sous-dossier *Seine*, 1st report by Commandant C.L.J.B. Jaurès, 25 Jan. 1863.
2. S.H.A.T., G7, box 224, 2nd report by Commandant Jaurès, 25 Feb. 1863.

Homeward, Mch.-May 1867

1. S.H.M.T. rôle d'équipage de *La Seine* (lc 5166/), escales de navire et liste des passagers. Service record of Commandant L.A.A. Pagel (1M3/2, fos. 37, 38). For the navigational record: Lt. Vcte de la Tour du Pin, *Traversées de France au Mexique* (etc.), Paris, 1868.
2. Return to Egypt: two press reports: (1) *L'Égypte*, Le Caire, 6 June 1867, p.l., "Le Bataillon envoyé au Mexique"; (2) *Le Nil*, Alexandrie, 9 June 1867, p. 2, "Bataillon nègre égyptien."

Austrian

Reports by Lts. Codelli and Mickl of two actions shared with the Sudanese under overall French command: on the Rio Blanco 28 February 1865 and near Tlalixcoyan (Collejon de la Laja) 2 March 1865 (Österreichisches Staatsarchiv/Kriegsarchiv, Vienna, Mexikanisches Freiwilligen Corps, fasc. 11 fo. 525, 20 November 1864.

Egyptian Sudanese

Among the Egyptian State Papers is a box, transferred from the library of the Qaṣr al-'Abidīn (Palais Abdine) Cairo formerly No. 58 and labelled *al-Ḥamla al-miṣriyya bi'l Maksīk* (The Egyptian campaign in Mexico).

Mexican

The documents filed in the historical section of the Ministry of National Defense, Mexico, D.F., covering military operations against the French and their allies, 1863-7, were not available. Based on these documents is *Historia documental militar de la intervención francesa*, compiled by Gen. Jésus de León Toral (Mexico, DF, Secretaria de la Defensa Nacional, Comision de Historia Militar) This contains rare references to small enemy units, but is an indispensable record of the course of the campaign.

Campaign Memoirs

French

The Egyptian Sudanese attracted the attention, amounting to affection, of two French authors of campaign memoirs: Gén. François Charles du Barail in *Mes Souvenirs*, 3 vols., Paris (Plon-Nourrit, 17 rpr.) 1894-1913, and Col. [Auguste] Charles Philippe Blanchot, in *Mémoires, l'Intervention française au Mexique*, 3 vol., Paris, 1911.

Egyptian Sudanese

The only memoir known to us, by a member of the Sudanese Battalion is the autobiography of Adjutant-Major (later Bimbashi) 'Ali Jifūn dictated by him in Arabic to his British c.o. Kaimakam P. W. Machell Bey who translated and published it in *The Cornhill Magazine*, n.s., 1, London, 1896, an entertaining, but in places suspect, narrative of a long military career.

Mexican

The broad, even-handed memoirs of "Comandante" Sebastian I. Campos, *Recuerdos historicos*, Mexico, D. F., 1895; rpr. in 2 vol., Veracruz (Instituto de Cultura), 1962-63. In his *Diario de las operaciones militares del sitio de Puebla* (Mexico, D.F., 1909) Col. F. de Paula Troncoso, a Republican prisoner of war, writes of his Sudanese guard with whom he shares the food which the guard had brought him from the out-of-bounds canteen.

The Mexican Polemic

Under military occupation it is the ordinary citizen and his family who are likely to suffer most from military excesses. A simply-worded denunciation of alleged French outrages against unarmed citizens was a crude, ironical polemic entitled *Apuntes para la historia de la civilización francesa, dedicados a la Brigada de Sotavento del Estado de Veracruz*, por R. (Oaxaca, impreso por Manuel Rincon, Calle del Estanco num. 1, 1864 (Notes on the history of French "civilization" dedicated to the Sotavento Brigade of Veracruz State, by R., etc.).

The polemic is the most ancient weapon in the warrior's literary arsenal. It can express absolute hatred for any enemy and admit no failure on its own side. Historical accuracy is not expected in war propaganda and the truth can be bent to advance the writer's cause. Even so, there is a compelling sincerity in the simple polemic from Oaxaca whose author had the moral advantage of being able to cite living witnesses by name who could testify to their sufferings. The Sudanese were the particular objects of his condemnation, for the *Egipcios* had already drawn unwelcome attention to themselves in the year before when they had killed eight civilians at Medellín in retaliation for the shooting of one of their sentries by night.

Historique

The French military *Historique* is a conventional, unofficial document of widely varying quality which records the exploits of a single military unit usually in a given operation. It tends to be self-congratulatory. It lacks the immediate appeal of war propaganda. The *Historique du Bataillon Nègre Égyptien au Mexique (1863-1867) par MM. Raveret et Dellard, attachés au Cabinet du Ministre de la Guerre en France*, Le Caire, "Revue d'Egypte" I, 1894, 43-53; 104-23; 176-85; 230-45; 272-85, was published 30 years after the Mexican Republicans had launched their heart-rending *Apuntes*. It was published serially in a French journal during a period of intense Anglo-French rivalry, four years before the Fashoda incident. Though a useful supplement to the French military correspondence in S.H.A.T. (G7), its editorial carelessness in recording Arabic names severely reduces its value as biographical evidence.

Historians

The first historian to publish systematically the record of the battalion from the Egyptian army nominal rolls was Prince 'Umar Ṭūsūn whose *Buṭūlat al-orṭa [āwrṭa] al-sūdāniyya al-miṣriyya fī harb al-Maksik* [The exploits of the Sudanese Egyptian battalion in the Mexican war] (Alexandria, 1933) is made particularly valuable by the author's inclusion of biographical notes supplied by correspondents on the subsequent careers of personnel of the battalion of whom all memory might otherwise have been lost. G. Douin, *Histoire du règne du Khédive Ismaïl*, 1 ch. 1, "Le bataillon nègre au Mexique," (Le Caire: Société de Géographie, 1933), relies excessively on Raveret and Dellard. In contrast, the author's narrative of the mutiny at Kasala of the relief battalion intended for Mexico, in vol. 3 pt. 1 of the same work (Le Caire, 1936) is firmly based on translations from the official documents, as is his final vol. 3, fasc. 1 and 2 (1944-46).

Interest in the English-speaking world came late. In 1941 P. Hogg made an English translation (unpublished) of 'Umar Ṭūsūn's *Buṭūlat al-orṭa al-sūdāniyya*. Using Hogg's translation, R. Kirk of the Sudan Medical Service published a brief account of the battalion, "The Sudanese in Mexico," (SNR XXIV, 1941, 113-30), a pioneer English introduction to the episode. A second short study on the same them, "An Egyptian battalion in Mexico (1863-

1867)" in *Der Islam* (Strasburg, 53, 1, 1976, 70-86) by C. and A. Crecelius, has a wider bibliographical basis than Kirk.

Three capital introductory works are recommended:

1. Gén. G. Niox, *Expédition du Mexique, 1861-1867* (Paris: J. Dumaine, 1874), by an officer who had served in the Mexican campaign.
2. J. A. Dabbs, *The French Army in Mexico. . . a Study in military Government*, (Mouton: The Hague, 1963), based on the Bazaine and allied archives in the University of Texas, Austin. Encyclopaedic and scrupulously objective.
3. Col. F. Willing, *L'Éxpédition du Mexique (1861-1867) et la guerre Franco-Allemande (1870-1871)*, a rich collection of portraits and other illustrations of the French forces in Mexico and their armament, (Paris: Arcueil, 1984).

The Sudanese Veterans in African History

There is no general bibliographical record of the Sudanese covering this revolutionary period of 30 years after their return from Mexico, a period which saw Africa transformed. The printed sources in Arabic and English are scanty on the veterans from Mexico: 'Abd al-Raḥmān Zakī's *I'lām al-jaysh wa'l-baḥriyya fī Miṣr, Cairo*, 1947 [Notable soldiers and sailors in XIXth century Egypt], excludes them all; BD. contains a mere seven, five needing revision.

The Equatorial Province

'Umar Ṭūsūw's *Ta'rīkh mudīriyyat Khaṭṭ al-Istiwā' al-Miṣriyya*, [History of the Egyptian Equatorial Province], 3 vol., Alexandria, 1937, a comprehensive history from its creation in 1869 to its abandonment in 1888. Baker Pasha's record of his rule, *Ismailia* (1874), contains several names of officers from the Sudanese battalion in Mexico, whom he praised. His successor, Col. (afterwards Gen.) C. G. Gordon, was impressed by the officers and men whom he inherited from Baker; they gave him lifelong respect for them. Emin Pasha, the last general governor, left a record of six officers from Mexico.

Two recent studies, while adding no hitherto unidentified names of veterans from Mexico, bear directly on the fate of Emin Pāshā's Nizam garrisons which had received several, still unnamed, veterans. Ibrahim El-Zein Soghayaroun, *The Sudanese Muslim Factor in Uganda*, Khartoum, 1981, investigates the dark period of Egyptian military decay and the political chaos and sectarian acrimony which resulted. D. H. Johnson's paper, "The Structure of a Legacy: Military Slavery in Northeast Africa" *Ethnohistory* (Durham:

Duke University Press, 1989), vol. 1, no. 1, extends the possibility of research to the "Nubi" Nizam diaspora from the White Nile basin over a wide area of Central Africa where fading family memories of an ancestor fighting in Mexico may yet survive.

Dār Fūr

Lt. Col. Ṣāliḥ Hijāzī (No. 4 Coy), himself a Westerner from Bornu, and Lt. Col. Abū Bakr Bey al-Ḥājj Muḥammad (No. 1 Coy) are the only veterans from the Mexican campaign whom we have identified as having served in the Egyptian army in Dar Fur before the Mahdist occupation. The two Sudanese field officers who deserted to their former Mahdist opponents, Col. Faraj 'Azāzi Bey (No. 1 Coy) and the above Lt. Col. Abū Bakr Bey were both given responsible posts in the Mahdist armies.

The Ethiopian Fiasco, 1875-1876

The Egyptian-Ethiopian war merited a less uninformed bibliography than it received. There seem to be no primary sources by participants on the Egyptian side not weakened either by the ignorance of the writer or his conscious efforts to salve his reputation. Two books of reminiscences by American officers of the Egyptian General Staff, are W. Mc E. Dye Bey, *Moslem Egypt and Christian Abyssinia; or military service under the Khedive. . . as experienced by the American staff*, New York, 1880, and W. W. Loring Pāshā, *A Confederate soldier in Egypt*, New York, 1884. Both give an impression of good but baffled men floundering in a strange new world which neither understood. The circumstances which caused Col. Arendrup to accept command of the first Egyptian expedition to invade Ethiopia where he and half his army were destroyed, remain unexplained.

Egyptian Nationalism, 1881-1882

Faraj al-Zayni, now colonel, fell foul of Egyptian Nationalists eager to harm him as a potential enemy. No other veterans from Mexico were found. The satirical journal *Abou Naddara (Abu Naẓẓāra)* pitched into him in its issue of 24 June 1881, p. 158, and the future head of the Nationalist ruling triumvirate, Aḥmad 'Urābī Pāshā, accused him in more laboured terms in his memoirs, *Kashf al-sitār 'an sirr al-'aṣrār* Cairo, nd. A. Schölsch makes a strong defense of the Egyptian Nationalists against the Turco-Egyptian ruling body in *Ägypten den Ägyptern!*, Freiburg, i.B., 1973; Eng. tr., *Egypt for the Egyptians!*, Oxford, 1981.

The Mahdist Revolt

We do not know whether veterans from Mexico deserted to the Mahdist armies other than the two field officers, Col. Faraj ‘Azāzi Bey and Lt.-Col. Abū Bakr al-Ḥājj Muḥammad (both No. 1 coy) recorded above. Nor do we know if any veteran other ranks enlisted with the Mahdist Jihādiyya riflemen.

The Siege of Khartoum, 1884-1885

Kitchener’s report on the fall of Khartoum, completed 18 August 1885, appears as Appendix 47 to H. E. Colville, *History of the Sudan campaign*, 2 vol, 1889.

Gordon’s journals in the British Library, London (Oriental section) Mss. 34474-34479, contain much on Faraj al-Zayni, General Gordon’s chief of staff. G. Elton, ed., *General Gordon’s Khartoum Journal*, 1961, is unsafe as the editor repeats Gordon’s mis-spellings of Arabic names and omits parts of the original journals. For the fate of some of those Sudanese officers who were with Gordon at Khartoum during the siege of 1884-1885 there is (1) a report in Arabic by a committee of Egyptian officers under the presidency of Muḥammad Nuṣḥī Pāshā, Engl. tr. in SNR XIII, 1, 1930, 1-82. (2) Evidence taken at a general court-martial held in Cairo in June 1887 for the trial of Col. Ḥasan Bey Bahnassawi, acquitted of the charge of having treacherously delivered up his post to the enemy, rpr. in F. R. Wingate, *Mahdiism and the Egyptian Sudan*, (London: Macmillan, 1891), 556-90.

The New Egyptian Army, 1883-

The names of a few aged officers who had begun their careers in the Sudanese Battalion in Mexico may be traced in the half-yearly issues of the bi-lingual *Egyptian Army List/Kashf al-jaysh*, Cairo (War Office), 1883-. Unofficial records preserved by the piety of Egyptian and British officers contain biographical material of interest such as ‘Umar Ṭūsūn’s collection in *Būṭūlat al-orta*, and *Historical records of the Tenth Sudanese*, compiled by Col. N. H. Hunter, o.c. Xth bn., (Royal Army Museum, London), describing ‘Alī Jifūn in battle on the Red Sea coast.

Index

A

al-'Abd, 'Abdallāh, 12, 142, 176-77
al-'Abd (meaning of), 11
'Abdallāh, Mabrūk, 176
'Abdallāh, Muḥammad, 42, 178
'Abdallāh, Nasīb, 59, 179
'Abdallahi, Khalifa, 143, 144
"Abd el Seed," 180n.23
'Abduh, Sa'id al-Ḥajj, 48, 162
Abou Naddara (journal), 135, 196
Abu Ḥarāz (Egypt), 138, 142, 171
Abū'l-'Innīn, Bakhīt, 177
Abu'l-Qumsan, Bakhit, 177
Abyssinians, Sudanese known as, 44, 53n.34
Africa: Central, 125; Sub-Saharan, 35. *See also* Alexandria; Egypt; Equatorial Province; Ethiopia; name and ethnic origins; slavery; Sudan; Sudanese Battalion
agha (Turkish), xxi
Aḥmad, Barak, 100, 105n.11, 183n.77
Aḥmad, Faḍlāllah, 71, 160
Aḥmad, Ḥasan, 158
Aḥmad, Ḥusayn, 21, 25, 57, 101, 157, 180n.9
Aḥmad, Jaddayn, 67, 167
Aḥmad, Khayrallah, 71
Aḥmad, Kuku, 174
Aḥmad, Mahmud wad, 150n.56
Aḥmad, Rizq (Rast), 120n.8, 162
Aḥmad, Sīd, 59, 179
Aḥmad, al-Zubayr, 48, 163
Aḥmadī, Muḥammad b., 115, 156
alcohol, abuse of, 10. *See also* food; food types
Alexandria, (Egypt), 21, 22; Sudanese evacuation stop, 116, 117-19
Algeria, 34
Algerian troops, 97, 115
'Alī, 'Abdāllah, 158
'Alī, Aḥmad, 159, 180n.24
'Alī, Baraka Ahmad, 142, 167
'Alī Dīnār (Sultan), 144, 157, 180n.6
'Alī, Mehemet. *See* 'Alī Muḥammad
'Alī, Muḥammad, 25, 90, 92n.2; 161
'Alī, Muḥammad (Ottoman). *See* Muḥammad Alī Pāshā
'Alī, Sa'id, 174
Almās (meaning of), 11
Alto Liman (Mexico), 57
Alvarado (Mexico), 30, 39, 56, 57, 58, 59
American Civil War, surplus supplies and Egypt, 38. *See also* slavery
American views of the Sudanese, 45

B

C

D

G

H

I

J

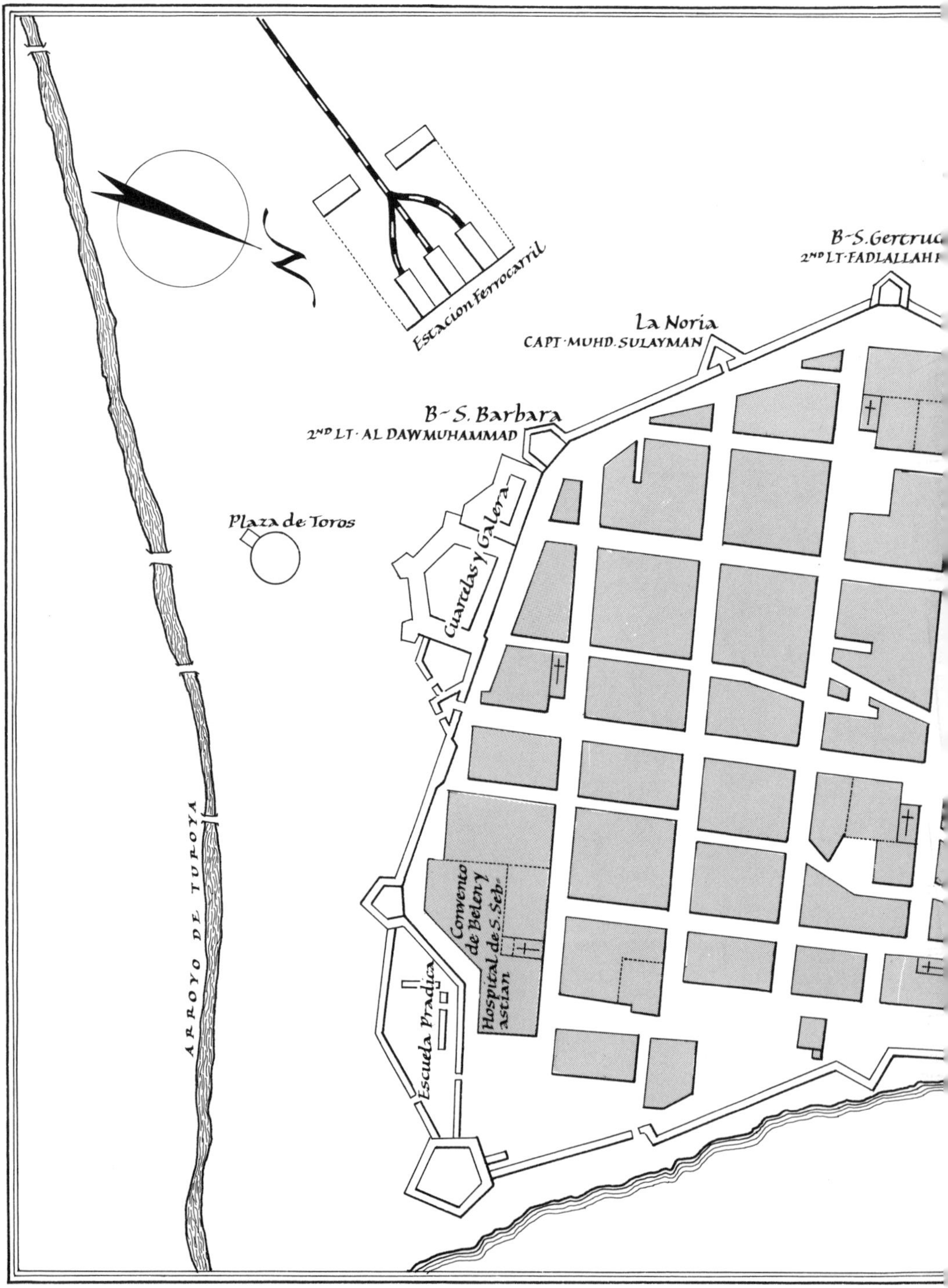
Estacion Ferrocarril
B~S. Gertruc
2ND LT·FADLALLAH
La Noria
CAPT·MUHD. SULAYMAN
B~S. Barbara
2ND LT· AL DAWMUHAMMAD
Plaza de Toros
Cuartelas y Galera
ARROYO DE TUROYA
Convento de Belen y Hospital de S. Seb-astian
Escuela Pradica